MARY DURACK was b...
1913. She spent her earli...
the East Kimberley district of the far north of W...
Australia. Educated at Loreto Convent, Perth, she returned
North in 1929 and wrote sketches of station life illustrated
by her sister Elizabeth. These were published serially and later
in book form by the Sydney *Bulletin*. After a year abroad
from 1936 to 1937 she joined the staff of West Australian
Newspapers. She was married in 1938 to Captain Horrie
Miller, co-founder of MacRobertson Miller Airlines and
reared a family of four daughters and two sons. She has
written books, articles and stories for newspapers and
magazines, book reviews, talks and radio plays for the
Australian Broadcasting Commission as well as stage plays
and sketches and an operatic libretto.
Her mono-drama, 'Swan River Saga', the story of Eliza
Shaw, written for Australian actress Nita Pannell, was
produced for the Perth Festival of 1972. It was taken over
by the Elizabethan Theatre Trust and toured all capitals of
Australia and Tasmania. The interest aroused by this
production led to the writing of *To Be Heirs Forever*,
a completed documentary of the Shaw family.
The author has maintained close ties with the Aboriginal
people in both outback and urban areas. She served
from 1971–1975 on the executive of the Aboriginal
Cultural Foundation.
She was a foundation and executive member and sometime
President of the Fellowship of Australian Writers (West
Australian branch), a member of the Australian Society
of Authors, the Royal Western Australian Historical Society,
P.E.N., The National Trust and Kuljak Playwrights.
She has lectured widely on Australian literature and
Aboriginal problems.
In 1973 she was awarded a Fellowship by the Australian
Council for the Arts for the furtherance of her
literary projects.

To be Heirs Forever

Mary Durack

CORGI BOOKS
A DIVISION OF TRANSWORLD PUBLISHERS LTD

TO BE HEIRS FOREVER
A CORGI BOOK 0 73380 000 9
First published in Great Britain by Constable and Company Ltd.

PRINTING HISTORY
Constable edition published 1976
Corgi edition published 1979
Reprinted 1985
Reprinted 1989
Reprinted 1992, 1994, 1995

Bantam books are published by

Transworld Publishers (Aust) Pty Limited
15–25 Helles Avenue, Moorebank, NSW 2170

Transworld Publishers (NZ) Limited
3 William Pickering Drive, Albany, Auckland

Transworld Publishers (UK) Limited
61–63 Uxbridge Road, Ealing, London W5 5SA

Bantam Doubleday Dell Publishing Group Inc
20th Floor, 1540 Broadway, New York, New York 10036

Printed in Australia by McPherson's Printing Group

This book is set in Linotype Plantin.

10 9 8 7 6

Contents

7

Acknowledgements

Throughout my research for this book I have had the warmest co-operation from descendants of the Shaw family and from historically-minded friends and fellow writers in the Swan, Geraldton and Toodyay areas. Among these I would especially like to thank that dedicated naturalist and historian, Mrs Rica Erickson, our former chief archivist Miss Mollie Lukis, her successor Miss Margaret Medcalf and assistants at the Battye Archives and Library, Mrs Judy Hamersley (neé Harper), whose roots go deep into the soil of the Swan district, Sister Albertus Bain, OP, who has so generously kept my project in mind during the wide range of her own research, and Mr W de Burgh of Baramba, Gingin for information concerning that area.

My thanks are also due to Mr Robert Nicholson for advice on legal aspects of this history, to Professor G C Bolton who has so warmly encouraged my historical journeys over many years, to my niece Perpetua Clancy for time spent on research, and to my daughter Marie Rose Megaw for the preparation of family tree and regional maps. Acknowledgements for illustrations is made to the Battye Library, Perth, Western Australia, and to the Rex Nan Kivell Collection in the Western Australian Art Gallery.

I also owe a special debt of gratitude to the Australian Literature Board whose fellowship grant has enabled me to secure the services of that loyal friend and most efficient of secretaries, Miss Constance Hooker.

To others who have helped in divers ways I offer my warmest thanks.

MARY DURACK
April 1976

'... Settlers will have no purchase money to pay for their lands ... Their grants will be conveyed to them in fee simple and will descend to their assignees or heirs for ever ...'

Advertisement for the
Swan River Settlement, London,
December, 1828

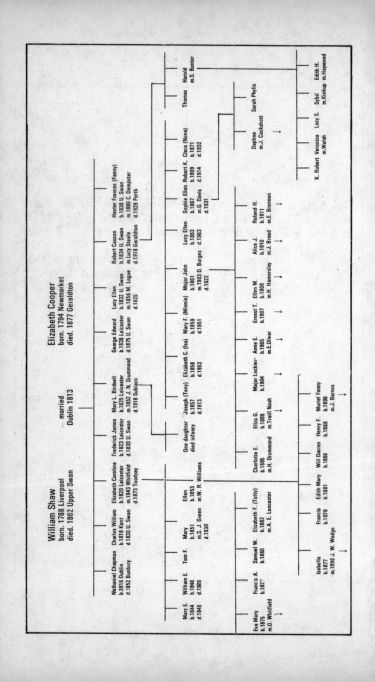

William Shaw
born. 1788 Liverpool
died. 1862 Upper Swan

— married
Dublin 1813

Elizabeth Cooper
born. 1794 Newmarket
died. 1877 Geraldton

Nathaniel Chapman
b.1816 Dublin
d. 1852 Bunbury

Charles William
b.1818 Kent
d.1830 U. Swan

Elizabeth Caroline
b.1820 Leicester
m.1843 Whitfield
d.1873 Toodyay

Frederick James
b.1823 Leicester
d.1830 U. Swan

Mary L. Birdsell
b.1825 Leicester
m.1852 J. N. Drummond
d.1918 Subiaco

George Edward
b.1828 Leicester
d.1875 U. Swan

Lucy Ellen
b.1832 U. Swan
m.1856 M. Logue
d.1925

Robert Casson
b.1834 U. Swan
m.Lucy Steele
d.1919 Geraldton

Hester Frances (Fenny)
b.1838 U. Swan
m.1880 C. Dempster
d.1929 Perth

Thomas

Harold
m.S. Bunter

Mary E.
b.1844
d.1848

William E.
b.1846
d.1926

Tom F.
b.1851

Mary
b.1851

Ellen
b.1853
m.W. R. Williams
d.1930

One daughter
died infancy

Joseph (Tony)
b.1857
d.1913

Elizabeth C. (Isa)
b.1858
d.1953

Mary F. (Minnie)
b.1859
d.1951

Major John
b.1861
m.1903 D. Burges
d.1922

Lucy Ellen
b.1863
d.1963

Sophie Ellen
b.1867
m.G. Davis
d.1931

Robert K.
b.1869
d.1914

Clara (Nona)
b.1871
d.1932

Daphne
m.J Cockshott

Sarah Phylis

Francis A.
b.187?

Samuel W.
b.1880

Elizabeth F. (Totty)
b.1882
m.A. E. Lancaster

Charlotte E.
b.1885
m.H. Drummond

Eliza G.
b.1888
m.Traill Nash

Major Lockier
b.1904

Anne E.
b.1905
m.E.Oliver

Ernest T.
b.1907

Ellen M.
b.1908
m.H. Hamersley

Alice J.
b.1910
m.J. Broad

Roland H.
b.1911
m.E. Brennen

Eva Mary
b.1875
m.O. Whitfield

Isobella
b.1877
m.1896 J. W. Wedge

Francis
b.1879

Edith Mary
b.1881

Will Dacres
b.1886

Henry F.
b.1888

Muriel Fanny
b.1899
m.J. Barnes

K. Robert

Veronica
m.Walsh

Lucy S.

Sybil
m.Kinkup

Edith H.
m.Haywood

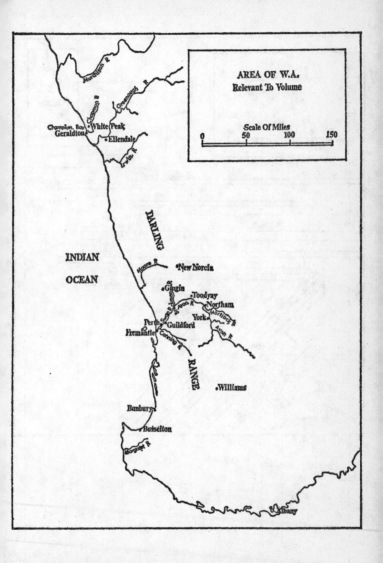

AREA OF W.A.
Relevant To Volume

Scale Of Miles

0   50   100   150

Muchison R

Chapman R

Greenough R

Champion Bay
Geraldton   White Peak

Ellendale

Irwin R

DARLING

INDIAN

OCEAN

Moore R   New Norcia

Gingin   Toodyay
                Northam
Swan R   Avon R
Perth   Moore R
Guildford   York
Fremantle   Avon R
        Canning R

RANGE

        Williams

Bunbury

Busselton

Margaret R

Albany

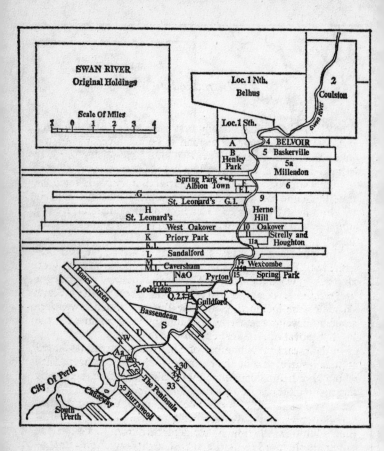

Introduction

The story of the Shaw family first came to my notice when I was looking for a pioneer woman to be portrayed by Australian actress Nita Pannell. This was for a fund-raising soirée to be held at the Western Australian Art Gallery in 1971. A series of letters written by Eliza Shaw to friends in England from the time of her departure with her ex-military husband and six children in 1829 appealed to us both as ideal material for our purpose, and we soon produced three episodes in mono-drama form.

The performance aroused more interest than we had bargained on. There were many requests for repeat runs and soon afterwards, when the late Sir Tyrone Guthrie was producing a programme at the University Octagon Theatre, these Shaw sketches were included. Following this performance we were asked to develop the theme to a full-time programme for the Perth Festival of Arts in February 1972.

In the meantime a number of Shaw descendants, delighted at this resurrection of their almost-forgotten forebears with whom Nita had so convincingly peopled her stage, had come forward with more information, letters and documents. With these, and the result of further delving in the Western Australian Battye archives, we were able to give an impression of Eliza's life from the time of her departure from Leicestershire to her death in 1877 at the age of eighty-two. This mono-drama was presented under the title of 'Swan River Saga'.

Having played to big audiences in Perth during the festival season it toured other Australian capitals under the auspices of the Elizabethan Theatre Trust. By this time it was generally assumed that there must be a book available about the Shaw family, but although they had been referred to in other pioneer histories there was no detailed account of their activities and vicissitudes in the new land. I therefore decided to set down what information on the family we had come upon and whatever else could be unearthed by further research.

It is true that many other families, some never properly documented, have made a greater mark, at least in the male line of descent, on the history of Western Australia, and that Eliza Shaw herself, though a woman of great fortitude, intelligence and initiative, was no more worthy of immortality than numerous other unsung pioneer women of her generation. There are few, however, who left their footprints so firmly on the sands of their time and few who, if they produced the like of her written record, had friends and relatives wise enough to preserve it for posterity.

Descendants of the Waghornes of Leicestershire, to whose forebears she wrote so fully during her early years in the settlement, sent her letters to the Mitchell Library in Sydney from whence copies were made available to the Battye archives in Perth. These letters ceased after a few years so there is less intimate detail of the family available between that time and when she began writing to her daughters as they married and moved from home. Enough of these letters have been preserved to give a more or less continuous, if sometimes sketchy, picture of the family's subsequent activities, but unfortunately only the last year of Eliza's meticulous and revealing daily journal has so far been located. Official records and newspapers of the time help fill a number of gaps but there are stages in the chronicle where detailed information is limited.

Eliza Shaw was among the longest lived of the early settlers. She survived her husband, five of her nine children and most of her contemporaries, and saw out the régimes of no less than eight successive governors. Her story therefore encompasses almost the first half-century of Swan River settlement. It is to a great extent the story of her times and of the policies of local government, especially on issues relating to labour and land tenure, that were of such vital importance to the early colonists. It is the story of people who, while so earnestly striving to shape a colony to their own ends, were being as surely shaped by their new environment.

The process of settlement was one of constant adaption to a locality and an ecology in which patterns were reversed and where the soil, so deceptively generous to its native vegetation, was reluctant to bestow its favours on imported plant life—with the exception of certain noxious weeds. It was also a process in which the landed gentry was forced into the hardworking mould identified elsewhere with 'the lower orders'.

Faced with the harsh reality of what had seemed an enticing chance of escaping the problems and evils of the Old World and of building a Utopia on a nice selection of worthy principles, those first comers whose options had remained open for the most part returned home or sailed on in search of brighter prospects elsewhere. Those who remained faced, with varying degrees of fortitude, the bleak fact of their unique isolation and what was to prove for many years a lonely and more or less friendless battle for survival.

Within two decades of their arrival the western settlers, originally so proud of their status as members of a free colony, were generally agreed that only the introduction of convict labour could free them from the doldrums in which they were trapped. Eighteen years of transportation served them well, providing roads, bridges and public buildings, farm labour and increased population. It is indeed surprising that it did not more drastically alter the social pattern of settlement established in earlier years.

The inhabitants of this State have long since developed an almost Aboriginal sense of identification with their environment and have come to affectionate terms with what was once dubbed 'the land of sand, sin, sorrow and sore eyes', cheerfully accepting the once derisive soubriquet of 'sandgropers'. The fact remains, however, that for all the subtle changes wrought by local conditions, and despite the extent and variety of subsequent immigration, Western Australia still carries the inescapable stamp of her English provincial pioneers. Under the easy-going exterior of the typical native-born, there burns a fervent devotion to the past and the standards of their pioneer forebears. While anxious to achieve personal security and collective independence, and though delighted at their State's deliverance from the position of 'Cinderella' of the Australian Commonwealth, they have tended to look askance at ostentatious wealth and the purely money-based values of blatant 'go-getters'. They also have an inborn reverence for culture, as witnessed by the support given to their annual six-week-long summer festival.

Many of the descendants of the old 'first-families' who appear in this book still figure prominently in local public and business life, their origins never forgotten even though their original properties have for the most part changed hands many times. The idea of hereditary land-holdings died hard, if it died at all, but continued ownership was subject not only to the exigencies of drought and depression but to the lure of new pastures and more lucrative prospects in conditions of developing settlement. In fact Australian families who have retained their original estates beyond the second or third generation are few and far between.

None of the nine children of Will and Eliza Shaw inherited the coveted Swan or Avon river acres that, according to the alluring notice issued by the Colonial Office in 1828, were to have descended to their heirs forever. The four girls married and moved to other areas and only one of the five sons outlived his mother. This was the youngest, Robert Casson, whose intemperate and restless disposition did nothing to save the estate from bankruptcy. The name of Shaw is not, therefore, generally remembered among the first families although, as will be seen, it was passed down to children of part Aboriginal blood whose existence, though not unrecognized, remained inevitably obscure.

The inheritance of the Shaw descendants, like that of many other pioneers, was of another kind. Theirs was a legacy of new horizons and new fields of endeavour, an inheritance of untapped potential of which even the first born generation was vaguely aware. At that time this was seen to lie in the extension of the wool and cattle industries, and the breeding of horses over ever-expanding areas, and also after the discovery of gold in other colonies, of a similar stroke of luck befalling 'the west'. In the following generations fortunes were made from all these avenues but the most dramatic development was to come only in the 1950s with the discovery of untold wealth in the north-west of the State.

Eliza Shaw lies buried in an unmarked grave on White Peak Station, near Geraldton, far removed from her old home at Belvoir, Upper Swan and from the last resting places of her husband and children. However, Lord Cadogan, the present owner of Belvoir, after seeing a performance of 'Swan River Saga', set up to her a memorial inscription at the entrance to the property.

Of the original homestead, extended in Eliza's lifetime from the humble cottage seen in her early sketch, nothing now remains but part of an outbuilding to the comfortable home built by the Loton family, who subsequently owned the property. The original estate has been whittled away over the years to a comparatively small property given over to the agistment of horses and the growing of fodder crops. Much of the land that comprised the Shaw's holding continues, however, to produce some of the finest wines in Australia.

Somewhere under the flourishing vines above the river lie the remains of the two Shaw boys who were drowned in 1830, the tombstone that marked their grave having come to serve as a doorstep to the old farm house at Baskerville.

Chapter 1

1829

'Swan River Mania'

Free land for posterity! Background of Captain Will
and Eliza Shaw, married Dublin, 1813. First son born
Dublin, 1816. Move to Kent and Leicestershire. The
Shaws' social circle. The Waghornes of Frisby. Post-
war problems and industrial revolution. Shaw retired
on full pay, 1826. Captain James Stirling returned
from New Holland. New settlement mooted. Captain
Fremantle sent to claim west coast of New Holland,
1828. Stirling and party sail in *Parmelia*, 1829. Shaw's
pension cut by half. He decides to emigrate with family.
Preparations for the great venture. Departure from
Gravesend in the *Egyptian*, September, 1829.

Even Captain Stirling at the height of his infectious optimism
had not foreseen the heady effect of that advertisement for his
proposed new settlement on the west coast of New Holland:

> ... Settlers will have no purchase money to pay for their
> lands, nor will they be chargeable *for any rent whatever*.
> Their grants will be conveyed to them in fee simple and
> will descend to their assignees or heirs for ever ... thereby
> affording them the satisfaction of knowing that their labour
> will be wholly expended on their own property, and that the
> results of their patient endeavours will be enjoyed by their
> children, and their names transmitted with such estates to
> distant posterity.[1]

This tempting statement—and much besides—appeared as
though in answer to prayer at the end of 1828, soon after
Captain Will Shaw received advice that his military pension
was henceforth to be cut by half.

21

Born of a military family in Liverpool, young Shaw had joined the Leicestershire Militia in November 1806, at the age of eighteen,[2] and two years later stood in Britain's 'thin red line' of infantry against Napoleon's troops on the Peninsula. When and where he met Eliza Cooper is not known, but their marriage is recorded as having taken place in the Round Church of the Anglican parish of St Andrew's, Dublin, on 8 April, 1813.[3]

Eliza, the daughter of a British soldier, Captain Nathan Cooper of Leicestershire, was born in Newmarket in 1794 and some time during her childhood moved to Dublin with her parents, two younger sisters and only brother. Of her Irish–English upbringing there is no record, though her letters and journals of later years bear testimony to a sound and fairly liberal education. She was familiar with the classics, was well abreast of the affairs of the day, showed some knowledge of history, and had a firm grasp of the Scriptures. She was an excellent needlewoman, having learned her craft from earliest years by the painstaking sewing of samplers, one of which, dated 1803, has come down to posterity. It is obvious that a number of the household skills she displayed in her colonial life were acquired of sheer necessity, but they show her to have been both practical and resourceful. It is clear too that she was a fluent and often witty conversationalist with a sharp edge to her tongue for any who appeared wanting in a matter of manners or moral obligation, evaded the path of duty or presumed beyond his station in life.

According to an oral tradition of her descendants, the Coopers were related to the Duke of Rutland[4] though no confirmation of this has been discovered. The idea may have derived from the marriage of a Duff Cooper into the Manners family at a later date and from the fact that the Shaws named their Swan River property after the historic Belvoir Castle (pronounced 'Beaver'), close to which they were stationed for some years before leaving England. Eliza herself, in her effusive correspondence, makes no reference to any such aristocratic connection. It was actually her husband who chose the name of their new home, 'out of sentiment' as he explained it, 'for that area in England'. Be that as it may, the Coopers were undoubtedly of 'the quality', and both Eliza and her husband were accustomed to moving in elevated circles.

Will Shaw was a personable young man of good education but no financial substance apart from his military pay. A keen huntsman, he had an eye for a good horse, a leaning towards the gambling table, a liking for good wine and convivial company. These characteristics Eliza viewed with a fondly tolerant eye though her parents do not seem to have done likewise as her correspondence suggests an estrangement from her family dating from the time of her marriage. Nor does the situation appear to have improved when, two years later, Will emerged with the rank of Captain from the battle of Waterloo.

The Shaws' first child was born in Dublin in June 1816 and christened Nathaniel Chapman after Eliza's father and Will's mother's family. In the following year they moved to Shorncliffe military camp in Kent and here a second boy, Charles William, was born in 1818. Two years later they were posted to Leicestershire where, during the ensuing eight years, their family had increased by two daughters and two further sons.

Will Shaw had been so far more fortunate than many veterans of the Napoleonic wars who were eating the bitter fruits of victory in retirement on half-pay. Living in the charming village of Thrussington, about six miles from the county capital of Leicester, he and his family, though by no means wealthy, had all the ordinary comforts of life and Eliza, with the help of a devoted Nanny, a cook, housemaid, laundress and groom, had time enough for the social activities she enjoyed. Will continued meanwhile to cut a handsome figure on the parade ground or riding to hounds with the Duke of Rutland's famous Belvoir pack.

Inside a wider range of acquaintances the couple enjoyed the close friendship of a select little group centred around their beloved Waghornes, at whose comfortable home, Frisby, also in Thrussington, they spent a great deal of time. Mrs Waghorne, *née* Casson, was the daughter of the revered vicar of Thrussington, and sister of Robert Casson, the Shaw family's solicitor. Miss Anne Dibben, a sister-in-law of Mrs Waghorne's previous marriage, another cherished friend of Eliza, was also a member of the *ménage*, while Ellen Waghorne, the only daughter of the house, was a gentle girl with a keen amateur interest in the natural sciences shared by so many cultivated young ladies of that era. It was to her that Eliza was to address long letters on the curious flora and fauna, geological structure and indigenous inhabitants of her new home in the antipodes.

Many people, so clear in the writer's eyes, in ours mere shades of a time past, are evoked in her correspondence. There is the forthright Mr Woodthorpe Clarke, the prudent Mr Gamble whose son Johnnie was young Nat Shaw's closest friend, and 'dear old Dr Birdsall', who so wisely foresaw that Will should learn how to suture a wound, to apply a splint or a poultice, to treat a snake bite and to administer a basic range of medical preparations. Then there were Sir Frederick and Lady Fowke, members of the landed gentry who had a wide acquaintanceship of interesting and influential people and often conveyed items of news well in advance of the press.

How often Eliza was to recall the cheerful room in which they most frequently assembled, the elegant furniture with its green velvet upholstering, firelight playing on the rich colours of the Persian carpet, glinting on the cabinets filled with precious china, silver and glass. There, on the settee to the left of the fire-place, forever in memory, sat Mrs Waghorne at her tapestry, Will Shaw beside her, permitted to snip the threads as she worked, Anne Dibben and Ellen otherwise usefully employed, sewing, knitting, pouring tea, as conversation—an art form long since declined—flowed on through the many channels of cultivated minds.

Comfortably situated though they were, talk at the Waghornes was not noted for its complacency. The company that gathered there found much to be deplored in contemporary England and indeed the world at large. Mr Waghorne and Sir Frederick lamented the too sudden shifting of power from the upper classes, with their hereditary sense of responsibility, into the hands of an increasingly wealthy and self-seeking middle-class. In the rapid increase and growing discontent of the working people they heard ominous rumbles of revolution and doubted the Government's ability to exert suitable disciplines. By this they did not mean that the rising voices of social reform should be ignored, for they thought it certainly desirable that the working time of children under nine years of age should be restricted to no more than twelve and a half hours a day. But why, they asked, as unemployment rose, must the government introduce a system of Poor Laws that, instead of encouraging workers back to the land, engendered nothing

24

but idleness and its attendant vices? Transportation to New South Wales was no longer a sufficient outlet for the grossly overcrowded prisons and poor-houses. Besides, how long could it last in the face of increasing public outrage?

Then there was the vexed question of Protections, that not only throttled foreign trade and raised the price of bread but encouraged a lawless breed of smugglers with unscrupulous confederates infiltrating all walks of life.

The Reverend Casson, his priorities differing to some extent, was also much concerned by the soulless and callous march of industrial capitalism—the arrival of an era innocently ushered in with the advent of steam power and flying shuttle, hurried on by the coming of the spinning-jenny and power loom. How, he asked, had what seemed to promise the dawn of a new age of opportunity for the poor working man degenerated into such a state of affairs as prevailed in the rapidly spreading factory towns, the sweated labour of women and children, miserably crowded into nauseous slums? He saw in the situation a vicious circle in which poverty was generating crime, crime perpetuating the hopeless misery of the poor, and he blamed the complacency of the Established Church for the stronghold being gained by dissenting religious movements in the northern industrial areas. Eliza apparently agreed with him wholeheartedly and also with Mrs Waghorne and Lady Fowke who deplored the depravity of the court and the shocking example it set for young people who naturally looked for example to those in high places.

But although, in the words of the good Vicar, the times were 'awful and portentous', the Shaws then saw little reason to fear for their own livelihood. Even when Will was retired unexpectedly at the age of thirty-eight it had been allowed that, as a veteran of the Peninsula and Waterloo and the father of a large family, his salary might remain intact. Retirement was probably of little hardship to him since it gave him more time with his family, freedom to follow the hounds, to play at chess and baccarat and indulge in other pursuits open to the gentleman of leisure. It seemed reasonable to suppose that with good budgeting the boys could be educated for suitable careers and the girls for successful marriages. Nat, then ten years old, was already horse crazy and it was thought he might join a cavalry regiment. Young Will who, at eight years old, showed a more scholarly bent had been sized up by Robert Casson as a promising recruit for a legal career. It was impossible as yet to predict a future for the three-year-old Frederick, but being a thoughtful child with the looks of a Botticelli angel, it had been fondly suggested by the Rev Casson that he might some day take the cloth. Six-year-old Elizabeth and the baby Mary would not, of course, do anything so vulgar as to marry for money, but moving in the upper strata of society they could hardly do otherwise than to wed appropriately.

When a fourth son, George Edward, was born in July 1828 the Shaws still saw no threat to their future though they were keenly interested in news brought them around that time by Sir Frederick Fowke who had been on a visit to Surrey. While visiting friends in that county he had met a Scottish seaman named James Stirling, Captain of HMS *Success*, recently returned from a tour of duty in Australian waters during which he had visited the west coast of New Holland. In his opinion a situation known as Swan River was eminently suitable for settlement, the landscape park-like, the soil rich, the climate salubrious and the inhabitants, although primitive savages, harmless and tractable. In fact Stirling had waxed quite rapturous about the place. He considered that of all parts of the world he had encountered it possessed the greatest natural attractions, being not inferior in any basic quality to the plain of Lombardy. A spot so eligible for settlement could not, he thought, remain long unoccupied. There was, to be sure, a small military garrison at King Sound in the south-western corner but no permanent settlement in the area and nothing to prevent a foreign power annexing land on this side of the large island continent. French vessels were known to have been recently in the vicinity and Stirling feared that if Britain did not act quickly she might well lose her claim to what was possibly the richest part of New Holland yet discovered.

The subject reminded Mr Waghorne of having heard from his friend and fellow Sussexman, Mr Thomas Henty, that he had been much inclined to emigrate with his family to New South Wales, but thought that if Stirling were to win his case with the government for a settlement on the west coast of the continent, that area might offer the better opportunity.

Stirling's proposal, at first turned down on the grounds of

26

expense to the government, was then modified to a request for a formal colonizing charter to be granted to private enterprises. This proposal, however, was looked upon with some suspicion and on 5 December, 1828, the Colonial Office published a statement announcing its decision to establish a crown colony on the western coast of New Holland. The enterprise was to be initiated under the administration of Captain Stirling and was open to such persons as were prepared to proceed at their own cost before the end of 1829 in parties of not less than five females and six males. They would receive grants of land in fee simple in proportion to their capital investment. It was made clear, however, that His Majesty's Government did not 'intend to incur any Expense in conveying Settlers or in supplying them with Necessities after their Arrival'.

Despite this uncompromising statement the Colonial Office was immediately inundated by enquiries. On the one hand came members of the old landed gentry, hopeful of perpetuating a way of life now rapidly declining at home, and on the other small struggling farmers anxious to become landed gentry of a new country. Also, eagerly clamouring for information, were naval men and military officers skimping on half-pay and restless for the action and excitement of which they had been deprived by peace; professional men and tradesmen of all kinds eager to escape the bleak prospects of advancement at home. The press dubbed this excited interest 'Swan River Mania', and such indeed it was, especially when it became known that Thomas Peel, a cousin of the Prime Minister, was planning a syndicate to bring out 10,000 settlers to occupy a 500,000 acre grant. Meanwhile, Captain Fremantle had been dispatched in the ship *Challenger* to the Swan River to take possession of all such Australian territory as was not already within the boundaries of New South Wales. This meant in fact one-third of the Australian continent, otherwise one million square miles with 4,300 miles of coastline, an area in which the British Isles could be swallowed up ten times over.

It is hardly to be wondered that people reading in blank amazement of such a vast potential heritage should have conceived of it in European images. How different might have been its history had some seer given warning of those unimaginable desert wastes that had pared down their spindly inhabitants in numbers and in enterprise to meet the cruel limitations of the environment!

If the Shaws had toyed with the idea of emigrating before the dread news of Will's reduced pension, they were indeed vitally interested when, on 17 January, 1829, *The Times* announced the imminent departure of Captain Stirling and his company for the new settlement. The Lieutenant-Governor, as he had been designated, was to set out with his wife and infant son in the hired vessel *Parmelia* taking with him a number of intending settlers with their families, stores and equipment. They were to be escorted by the naval vessel *Sulphur* with a detachment of the 63rd Regiment, a number of soldiers to remain, some with their wives and families, for the protection of the settlers.

For those intending to follow there was no time to dally for it had been clearly stipulated that free grants of land, in proportion to investment, were available only to those who arrived in the colony before the end of 1829. With this in mind a number of private emigrants were fitting out ships, securing equipment and engaging servants as quickly as possible. Among these people were the Hentys who were preparing to set sail in a hired ship named the *Caroline*. This was a matter of keen interest to Mr Waghorne who was confident that any venture to which Thomas Henty, stalwart farmer and banker, lent his support stood every chance of success. With people of this quality, members of fine old country gentry and yeoman families, Western Australia had a distinct advantage over New South Wales, which even though now attracting free emigrants —mostly of the 'bounty' class—was, alas, indelibly stamped with the broad arrow of her convict origins. Captain Stirling was himself confident that, with the help of trusty free servants, life at Swan River settlement would soon be firmly established according to the best traditions of English provincial society. He had already conjured up in the minds of his followers a picture of the vanishing idyll of English village life regenerated in a new land, each township with its church and parsonage, its squire, tenants and farm labourers forming a colony soon to grow rich at a trading centre for eastern merchants.

Every day word came of others, old friends or friends of friends, who had left with Captain Stirling on the *Parmelia*, or with the military contingent on HMS *Sulphur* or were preparing to leave on other vessels. Eliza, while living with Will's regiment in Kent, had become friendly with an officer's wife whose sister, Frances Hamersley, now the bride of Mr William Locke Brockman, was soon to sail with her husband on the ship *Minstrel*. It was William Brockman's father, the Rev Julius Brockman, who had baptized the Shaws' second son William, so there were links in many directions.

By this time the Shaws were seriously considering the state of their finances with a view to joining the eager throng of emigrants. As a means of encouraging 'a desirable type' of settler it was laid down that military and naval officers could commute their half-pay to the government in return for a specific sum. Shaw found that his commission was worth £550 which could be counted as part of his investment in the colony. His other assets were to include the number of people and the amount of stock and equipment they brought out, their land entitlement to be reckoned at forty acres for every £3 invested. Apart from the commission money the Shaws, who lived well up to their income, had little with which to equip themselves for such an adventure. Eliza's father, who died about this time, had left his widow, two other daughters Caroline and Sophie and son Nathaniel well provided for but Eliza's share, probably owing to the mysterious estrangement, was no more than a bequest of £200 left her in a codicil to the will, but which had not been paid her up to this time. There must also have been some provisio that certain money would go to her were she to survive other members of the family. Eliza's need, however, was not in the speculative future but here and now, and it was after all the Waghornes who came forward with the necessary assistance. This the Shaws accepted joyfully, little doubting that it could soon be repaid with interest from their colonial estate. As Will Shaw reckoned it, his total investment counting his commissions, family and hired servants, stock, farming and building equipment and passage money amounted to £1,385 which should entitle him to no less than 18,466¾ acres.

Apart from this monetary assistance, the Waghorne and Casson families and Sir Frederick Fowke donated a selection of stud animals from their own properties. These included a white Leicester sow and boar, a fine Leicester ram and six ewes, a good milking cow and a selection of poultry, including some bantams that were a present to Nat from Sir Frederick. One of the Shaws' retainers, by the name of Boswell, who but for his age would gladly have accompanied them, insisted on their taking his dog which was to become their faithful friend of many years.

Their decision made, they wrote at once to a Captain Friend of the ship *Wanstead*, due to sail in July, asking for details concerning fares and accommodation. The reply, however, seemed to them lacking in suitable courtesy and despite their anxiety to arrive in the colony within the stipulated time, Will, providentially as it so happened, made similar enquiries of Captain Lilburn of the *Egyptian*. How different was the response of this courteous man who was to become their helpful and trusted friend! They were informed that the vessel (359 tons) was a fast-sailing and elegant conveyance, fitted up as a regular Indiaman, with separate children's dining-room below. It was well armed and carried a surgeon. The Captain moreover expressed himself happy to be of service to people of such distinction and enterprise.

Passages were promptly booked on the *Egyptian* for eight members of the Shaw family and two servants—a farm labourer named Markram and a fifteen-year-old girl named Anne Haggs engaged, with glowing references, from a local workhouse.

Then began the anxious process of making lists of equipment required for starting life from scratch in a place where there was nothing to be had beyond a few raw materials such as timber, stone, sand and clay. In this task the Shaws' farming friends were of the greatest help, for many items considered as basic necessities neither Eliza nor her husband had ever heard of, let alone knew how to use. On the other hand some things they considered essential were ruled out on practical advice. What, for instance, was the use of a carriage where there were no roads? There would be room only for the most basic furniture. Such items as books and a piano could come later when there was time for the refinements of life. First they must consider such things as building and agricultural tools. They must take crop and garden seeds, stores, strong clothing and cooking utensils. They must have a wagon, a good plough, a harrow and a winnower. They must take spades, shovels, saws, pickaxes, matchets, hammers, an anvil, a forge, horse-shoes and nails.

During this time there was optimistic talk of the family making occasional trips home and of the children returning for at least part of their education. A number of their friends, including Robert Casson, also expressed the intention of joining them in the colony, but when the time came for the final leave-taking it was impossible not to fear that they were looking their last on most of their dear ones and their native land. It was good-bye, perhaps for ever, to the beautiful Leicestershire countryside, to the fair vale of Belvoir overlooked by the great castle haunted by the ghosts of its antiquity, good-bye to all that was hallowed by age and steeped in history. In the place for which they were bound there would be no history other than what the colonists might initiate, no traditions, at least of a civilized nature, but what they themselves might implant.

When the ship sailed at last from Gravesend on 15 September, 1829 the Waghornes and Cassons, Sir Frederick, 'dear old Birdsall', and Will's sister who had come down from Liverpool to help them pack, were all assembled to see them off. There too, with his father, was Nat's friend Johnnie Gamble, bravely fighting back the tears while vowing soon to follow the family to Western Australia, Nat meanwhile promising to write him every detail of the voyage and life in the colony. We find, however, no reference to any of Eliza's family being there, though they were apparently residing at that time in Leicestershire. Where were her widowed mother, her sisters Sophie and Caroline, her brother Nathaniel? By innuendo we gather their disapproval of what they may have considered just another error of judgement on Eliza's part. As if her marriage to the impecunious and improvident Will Shaw had not been enough without this ill-advised exodus, with six helpless children, to a savage land at the nether end of the earth!

Chapter 2

September 1829–February 1830

Five Months at Sea

Passengers on the *Egyptian*. Mishaps at sea. At the Cape of Good Hope. Generosity of Captain Lilburn. Arrival at Fremantle. Disappointment and delay.

Of the five months' journey Eliza wrote in considerable detail to her beloved friends. The travellers had been fortunate in encountering summer weather all the way, and except for the children going down with whooping-cough at the outset of the voyage, maintained good health throughout. They were fortunate too in their fellow passengers, their being for the most part people 'of quality' migrating from various backgrounds for the single purpose of establishing firm feet in a new land. Some were to hold out against all odds to become big names in the colony, others soon to fade from the local scene to seek their fortunes elsewhere. They included Mr and Mrs J Purkis with their four children and three servants, and the brothers Lionel and George Lukin and their several farm labourers. Lionel Lukin had already had a colourful career as a Hussar Lieutenant in the service of the Czar of Russia, from which post he resigned in 1825. Finding it hard to settle down to the humdrum life of an English country gentleman, he had decided to take up this new challenge. Then there were Captain Boyd, late of the Horse Guards, and his gentle wife Eliza who was a friend of Mrs James Stirling; the DuBois Agetts with their six young sons and four farm helpers; the Alexander Andersons with their large family; and a grandiose clergyman named Bambrick who had brought out the makings of a considerable mansion, complete with furniture and (evidently in anticipation of made roads and smooth travelling) an elegant carriage. All in all they were good company, Eliza

32

finding much in common with Mrs Agett whose children were of an age with her own.

The voyage, however, was not without its problems and alarms. Markram took to the bottle, neglected to tend the stock and 'gave much impertinence', while the girl Anne Haggs soon proved herself to be both obstinate and unruly and displayed much more interest in the sailors than in her young charges. Eliza conceded, however, that 'so many men on board a ship would corrupt the morals of a saint'. The most alarming incident of the voyage occurred just before reaching the equator when a line was cast to hook a shark.

When the cry was given 'he has taken the bait . . .' there was a general rush into a boat which is hung at the stern to lower in case of danger. The number and weight was so great as to break a piece of wood to which the boat is attached. It gave way with a tremendous crash and 11 persons were precipitated into the sea . . . In a few seconds every piece of wood and other floating thing that could be lain hands on were thrown over. Every mother's cry was 'where are all the children?' 'All safe' was echoed from voice to voice for the purpose of quieting maternal fears, but picture my agony on looking out our good Captain's window, to see poor Nat's pale face further out than we could distinguish his features. Providence had prompted me before we came on board to tell all the young ones if they should fall over to keep treading water as if they were going upstairs. Nat, in his peril, remembered this and acted upon it for ten minutes, when miraculously a mat and oars floated to him on which he rolled until a boat was lowered . . . Nat was the first taken up. He was very nearly exhausted, but much better than we could have hoped. Unfortunately, two of our passengers were lost, a Mr Williams and a servant boy of one of the passengers. To describe the agonizing scene would be in vain . . . Our Captain was so hurt at the melancholy catastrophe that he immediately ordered every shark hook to be given to him and he threw them overboard.[1]

Soon after this, young Frederick narrowly escaped having his head taken off between the ship and the boat as he was peering over the rail. Later in the voyage little Mary somehow contrived to fall fifteen feet into the hold, landing on some barrels of porter. 'She was taken up for dead, with her mouth and eyes fixed but, thank God! No bones broken. We had six leeches to her temples and she was soon perfectly sensible. Our Surgeon apprehends not the slightest danger from the fall ... How merciful is Providence to children and drunken men!'[2]

King Neptune with his sea nymphs boarded the vessel at the line, and attendants supervised the initiation of the 'Johnny new overs'. The occasion 'passed off with the utmost hilarity and good humour and in the evening all on board had as much rum punch as they could drink, danced and enjoyed themselves in every way.'

They touched land only once—at the Cape of Good Hope —where they remained for several days, taking on water, provisions, livestock and a variety of seeds and cuttings including grape vines to try out in the new colony. (It might be here noted that most of these specimens transplanted successfully—some, tenderly nurtured, to proliferate in their new environment with such vigour as to become noxious and incorrigible weeds.) The Shaws' good milch cow, one ewe, a precious sow, and all the poultry died on the voyage, but they were able to secure at the Cape a sow in farrow, some further fowls and two milking goats. Eliza strongly advised all newcomers to bring no livestock from England as it was readily procurable at this port and was thereby saved the hazards of a longer journey.

Captain Lilburn more than lived up to the impression made by his introductory letter. He proved a charming and a generous man—in striking contrast to Captain Friend of the *Wanstead* whose discourteous reply had so fortuitously aroused their suspicions. Although the *Wanstead* had left London a month before the *Egyptian*, the two ships arrived at Cape Town at much the same time, the passengers of the former expressing the greatest dissatisfaction with their martinet Captain, who, Eliza tells us, had 'actually ordered cabin passengers from the dinner table in disgrace and in some instances put them in irons! ... Several of them came on board our ship and offered to exchange their *Wanstead* cabins with our steerage passengers, but would you believe it could meet with not one who would do it.'

34

The Shaws dined out with their Captain at a Cape Town Hotel—a memorable meal often to be relished in retrospect, 'soup and beef steak pie removed, then boiled turkey, tongue, spring cabbage, french beans, peas and potatoes, these removed, jellies, a jolly plum pudding, green gage tart, apple pie, cheese, cucumbers, dessert plums, oranges, almonds, green gages ... Port, Cape and Claret wines ... the liberality of Captain Lilburn is very great ... After dinner we strolled and enjoyed ourselves and bought curiosities ...'

It was a happy, carefree time, hardly even disturbed by ominous accounts of the Swan River settlement which they were inclined to dismiss. Eliza reports thus:

> The Cape people are jealous of Government patronizing this new Colony. Besides they took out a cargo of rif-raf cattle for the settlers to purchase which were so indifferent that they were obliged to ship them home again. Consequently nothing they can say is bad enough for the new settlement. Two officers of the *Chanticleer* Brig of War lying here ... told us to believe no Cape reports as they had seen letters from the settlers wherein they say that although obliged to pitch their tents close to the landing place in sandy soil they had already a constant succession of beautiful cabbages, peas and potatoes etc, and that the land up the river was most excellent and rich.
>
> It is true every ship has received more or less damage from not knowing the coast properly and one ship, the *Marquis of Anglesea*, is wrecked, but not a soul lost or any cargo except a little livestock and that not above one or two head.[3]

Of her family she wrote that 'Shaw grows fat as a porpoise' and they were all the colour of 'new mahogany'. Nat was 'grown nearly a young man' and had taken over many of the tasks neglected by the intemperate Markram. He spent much time writing to his friend Johnny Gamble, permitting no one to see his letters, which were obviously 'the outpourings of his heart'. What, one wonders did this boy, already old beyond his years, report of that long journey to the devoted friend he was never to see again? Nine-year-old Elizabeth was inclined to 'run wild' on board but her mother was confident she would be the greatest comfort to her in their new life. The child was missing her friends at Frisby, and spoke much of dear Ellen and the garden they had tended together. Little Fred too, often betrayed some homesickness. 'Mama,' he had said one day, 'I wish I were a bird, for then I would fly home again to the White Hart.' Four-year-old Mary was as pretty as a picture, despite her bruised face. The baby George had taken his first steps, to the tremendous pride of his eleven-year-old brother Will who had constituted himself his guardian-in-chief.

The letter, posted that day, ended with messages to her various friends. 'We shall think of you all on Christmas day; the last time we have dined with you, and now how many thousands of miles separate our bodies? May that Power who looks on our earthly vale but as an atom among His wondrous works, guard, shield, bless and preserve our best and dearest of friends and all their household ... Should you have any friends coming out tell them to ferret us out and if we have but one biscuit they shall share it ...'

Disillusionment with 'the land of promise' began for Eliza within sight of land on 14 February, 1830. That curling summer surf, that dazzle of white sand, one day to blossom forth in a perennial display of gay beach umbrellas and brightly minimal swimsuits held no charm for the newcomers. Here was no familiar pebbled strand, no cliffs that for some reason they had expected—only a monotony of beach backed by scrubby dunes with the faint blue smudge of a low range far beyond. Scattered along this dreary shore and clustered around a flagstaff atop a small rise were makeshift huts and tents, dismal-looking encampments from which rose the smokes of cooking-fires. The inhabitants, faintly discernible, looked more like people shipwrecked on a desert island than settlers come to establish themselves forthrightly in a new land. 'What are they waiting for?' Nat asked. Captain Lilburn pointed out that the flagstaff denoted the new port of Fremantle, and suggested that the people round about were either port officials awaiting the arrival of stores and mail or shiftless types to be found in any circumstances—though certainly not among the enterprising passengers on the *Egyptian*.

It was at once decided that the women and children should remain on board while the men-folk went ashore in a small boat to interview the Governor concerning their grants of land. Naturally they had been expected back later in the day. What was the general consternation therefore when two days passed without a sign of their return. On the third day as the boat was sighted at last everyone crowded to the ship's side in eager anticipation of good news. But alas, Eliza wrote: 'They returned with countenances blank and disappointment on all their brows.'

They had expected to interview the Governor in Fremantle but soon learned that he was then established at a site he had named Perth about twelve miles up the Swan River. Fortunately they had encountered in Fremantle young James Henty, one of the sons of Mr Thomas Henty, Mr Waghorne's countryman, who had arrived in October 1829. The Hentys had a Swan River grant which was being carried on by two younger brothers, but they were sadly disappointed with the quality of the land and were awaiting a chance of exploring further afield. James Henty, who had meanwhile set up a little trading-post at Fremantle, had kindly arranged for a boat to take the newcomers up the river—which was in fact the only thoroughfare in the colony. They were thus able to interview the Governor, who received them in his dressing-gown and with bare feet, no less, 'walking in his garden, for so they call it, though there was not a green leaf in it'.

We could glean but little from them, [Eliza continues] but that the Governor told them there was no land to be given away on the Swan River, and he would advise all who could to go to the southward where the land was reported to be much better than here. By the bye, it would cost as much or nearly as much to go there as to come from England. The fact is simply this—all the land that is good for anything, and that is but a small patch here and there, is kept as Government reserves and what land is given is to Jews, Stockbrokers, Men of Wars etc, etc, and out of 1,800 souls now come to this Colony in hopes of living, or at least of not being starved to death, there are not a dozen who know what to do or where they are to go. The people here look actually horror-struck one at another in absolute despair ... There are some who have been here nine months and have sown different seeds at different times, but they have all invariably died away and there is not one who has been able to raise either potatoes, cabbage or any other vegetable. That man[4] who reported this land to be good deserves hanging nine times over ... Each side of the river is nothing more or less than sand—white sand—incapable of being made to produce anything for the sustenance of man![5]

Reflecting bitterly on the sanguine reports of flourishing vegetable gardens, the Shaws and their fellow passengers gathered up their goods and few head of stock and struck out for the uninviting shore.

Chapter 3

February 1830

Facing Reality

Battle for survival on Fremantle beach. Eliza Shaw describes tent life. The Lieutenant-Governor's problems. Thomas Peel's misfortunes. Land allocations criticized. Captain Stirling sails south. Homesick letters dispatched. Will Shaw finds river site for temporary hut. A garden planted. Servant problems.

Faced at last with the stark reality of their undertaking, the would-be settlers began to realize just what they had so innocently embarked upon. The idea of coming out, not as members of a colonial company such as was originally intended, but as individual investors, had appealed to most of them as a challenge to their initiative and enterprise and a unique opportunity of acquiring vast private estates. What it meant in fact was a battle for survival that few of them were equipped to face. It meant that gentlemen must become labourers and not even in the accepted sense of European rustic tradition, for here when one was lucky enough to secure a grant, there was no soil ready for the plough, but virgin scrub and forest to be cleared with the axe, and sand to be somehow coaxed to fertility. It meant that gentlemen's wives who had never soiled their hands must turn to menial tasks and use initiative in place of equipment that their servants at home had taken for granted. It was to be every man for himself in this outlandish place. There was no representative body in England with a financial interest in their venture; none to whom they could explain their difficulties and appeal for assistance. Pity help the people of no finance and faint heart! Fortunately the Shaws, though they might have numbered in the former category, were certainly not of the latter.

From the shade of a tent on the Fremantle beach, Eliza wrote again to her friends:

It seems a complete burlesque altogether, not a farce, for *they* are generally laughable, but all here is really and truly cryable ... You will think I am giving you a woeful description but you, in England, can have no idea of what is going on here. Still, we live in hopes that something may yet turn out better.

Here we are under our tents, set down close to the sea beach, higgledy-piggledy up to our ankles in sand. Our eyes suffer dreadfully, as the winds are so high at times they raise the sand and cover everything. Our sofa serves Shaw, myself and George, and sometimes Mary, for a bedstead. The boys and Markram lie on beds on the ground and more complete gypsies you never beheld. But we all bear it much better than you could expect. You would smile to see ladies, gents, children and working people, many without shoes or stockings, some carrying wood to make fires, others cooking, washing and nursing their babies ...

Captain Stirling with Mrs S, another lady, Mr (James) Henty and some others went off last week to explore the land to the Southward. This ought to have been done before people arrived. They are all at their wits' end.[1]

It was natural enough in the circumstances that the disappointed—indeed sadly apprehensive—settlers should have looked for someone to blame. The logical scapegoat was of course the Lieutenant-Governor, as the harassed man was himself well aware. In his eagerness to launch the Swan River Settlement project he had agreed to terms that made his position almost impossible. He had been given a total grant of £2,000 to meet all contingencies but with it no official commission, no power to make laws or punish offenders. To issue an order he had, officially at least, to obtain the consent of the Home Government, and if it was at last granted he had no means of enforcing it. Little wonder it was said of him that 'he was at once a dictator and a man of straw'.

Stirling was not to have foreseen the tremendous rush of would-be settlers who set off for Swan River in the immediate wake of the *Parmelia* and its hand-picked band of pioneers.

Within six months of their arrival, long before enough land for the first comers could be properly surveyed, twenty-five ships had arrived at the mouth of Swan River. By the end of January 1830, instead of an anticipated 200 to 300 settlers there were 850 souls classed as 'permanent residents' and 440 'non-residents' for all of whom the Lieutenant-Governor was held in some way responsible. Even the failure of Thomas Peel's enterprise by which he was to introduce to the settlement 450 immigrants to be dispersed over a grant of 500,000 acres, was laid by many at the Governor's door. According to the stipulated terms, Peel could claim his Swan River grant only if he arrived by 1 November, 1829. His departure was delayed and his first ship arrived six weeks later, by which time Stirling had been forced to distribute his priority grant to previous arrivals. This meant that Peel was obliged to accept inferior land, of half the area originally agreed upon, along the coast south of Fremantle. Meanwhile many of his people, miserably camped on the site of the town that was to have been the centre of his grand settlement scheme, died of sickness, exposure and malnutrition, which added to the general depression hanging over the settlement at the time of the Shaws' arrival.

In a minor way the Shaws had suffered the same disadvantage in having been delayed by adverse winds and an untoward hold-up at the Cape. It had not occurred to them that by reason of their arriving a few weeks later than the stipulated time, others with considerably less investment should be ahead of them in obtaining grants of land and that Stirling, although hoping to satisfy the expectations of all, was not actually obligated to fulfil the generous terms of land allotment to any but those who arrived before the end of 1829.

Eliza's statement that all the land that was good for anything had been given away to 'Jews, stockbrokers and Men of War' was at least partly true. Within the first weeks of settlement Stirling, anxious to deal fairly with all, had offered the first land surveyed to Captain Fremantle and officers of the *Challenger*. This was seen as just reward for their services in having, by the simple symbolic act of hoisting the Union Jack at the mouth of the Swan, formally taken possession of the west coast, and also for having held the fort until the arrival of the *Parmelia* and the *Sulphur* three months later and rendered willing assistance to the settlers over the first difficult weeks. Few of these men of the sea, however, were prepared to remain in the colony and it was not long before their grants were either sold or had reverted to the crown.

Certain officers of the *Sulphur*, also in return for services of one kind or other, had been awarded grants; as had some of the Governer's own officials including Peter Brown, his Colonial Secretary, John Septimus Roe, his Surveyor-General, Captain Mark Currie, the Harbour Master, James Drummond, Government Naturalist and the Rev John Burdett Wittenoom, Colonial Chaplain. Stirling himself, who had in lieu of salary been promised 100,000 acres by the Colonial Office, had taken up a small grant on the Swan, while making up his mind where the best prospects lay. The 'Jews' referred to probably included Lionel and William Samson who had arrived in the *Calista* in August 1829, admirable settlers who had immediately embarked on a mercantile business that was not only to enrich themselves but to serve the ends of the settlement at large. She may also have been alluding to Charles Pratt and James Solomon but these men although then pressing their claims had so far received no satisfaction.

Among the stockbrokers and speculators would have figured George Leake, another *Calista* passenger, who was given a sizeable grant on the Swan and set himself up at the same time in a merchant business at Fremantle—a venture from which he and his family would never look back and which would also greatly profit the colony. Into this category also, no doubt, came Colonel Peter Lautour, an absentee speculator who had shipped out his agent with settlers and stock on the same vessel and was granted a considerable area on the Upper Swan.

It can well be seen how, although Stirling could hardly be blamed for trying to do his best for all comers, some of the land allocations thus hastily made and tied up by men with no intention of developing them were so bitterly resented by later arrivals, uncomfortably and impatiently camped on the open beach.

Early in March, when most of the Swan River grants had been allocated, Stirling, as mentioned by Eliza Shaw, set off in the schooner *Eagle* to examine the prospects of further settlement to the south. His party included the Surveyor-General

J S Roe, Dr Collie Surgeon of the *Sulphur*, Lieutenant Preston of the same ship, James Henty and Stirling's wife Ellen (*née* Mangles), who at twenty-three years old had already taken upon her shoulders the onerous role of mother of the infant colony. Western Australia was to owe a great debt to this charming and courageous girl, who gave it her support and confidence through the perilous days of doubt and penury, of failing crops and fading hopes.

All those gathered on the beach awaiting grants looked forward eagerly to Stirling's report on the prospects for out-settlements in the south-west, but the Shaws knew that for themselves there could be no such outlet in that direction. Their small resources were almost at an end. The fine Leicestershire ram continued to thrive and fend for itself but otherwise their stock was dwindling from eating poison weeds or being attacked by hungry dogs. Their only hope seemed to lie in securing a grant close at hand. However pleasure-loving and impractical Will Shaw may have been in other circumstances, he now set to work courageously and with fanatical dedication to establish his family in the colony.

Captain Lilburn agreed to delay the departure of the *Egyptian* until Stirling's return from the south. This gave the Shaws time to write more fully to their friends, their letters at last entrusted, for his personal delivery, to the Captain himself. Will's letter to Mr Waghorne was considerably more restrained than Eliza's general account to their circle. Having no ready cash himself he was forced, with obvious embarrassment, to call on Waghorne to advance the sum of £20 to defray his debt to Captain Lilburn for freight on goods and stock purchased at the Cape. This he asked, with his wife's approval, to be deducted from Eliza's £200 bequest, which their solicitor friend Robert Casson was still trying to secure for them. He gave a little news of Mr Waghorne's friends the Hentys and observed with careful understatement that Peel and his party were 'doing but very so-so'. There was indeed some talk of their returning to England with a number of other would-be colonists who would be no loss to the settlement since they were totally unfit for such an enterprise. Many had come expecting to find that all was prepared for them and that life on standards enjoyed at home would be resumed at once. They had no intention whatever of roughing it. Shaw was careful to qualify the gloomier side of the situation, for it is obvious that he in no way wished to discourage his friend Robert Casson from joining him as soon as possible. He seems to have been more homesick than Eliza ('to dwell on what is past and the many hours we have spent together reduces me below childhood'), but he genuinely believed that he and Casson were of the type with every prospect of making good in the settlement in the fullness of time.

In the first trying weeks, chafing at the enforced inactivity, he learned some hard lessons about the nature of the Australian bush. If land could not be found for him, he would, he declared, go out and find some for himself! With this end in view he asked for a chart indicating which areas had been taken up, and on being informed that there was nothing of the kind available, set off on foot with Markram, who since his arrival at Swan River had been more co-operative, resolved to find a spot somewhere on the river where they could at least set up a temporary abode, plant some vegetables and put their stock to graze in safety. They returned the following day, 'black as chimney sweeps' from close contact with the charred stems of the blackboys—'large stumpy trees of actual natural charcoal'—hands and faces scratched and clothes torn by the prickly undergrowth of the summer bush. They had, however, found a spot about a mile and a half up the river where Shaw thought the soil looked reasonably good. He made immediate application for a small plot in the area but was refused on the grounds that the land thereabouts was in reserve for a future town site. Since there was, however, no objection to their making a temporary camp in this locality, they set about building a hut for shelter against the winter rains that they had been warned were likely to set in at any time. So far, 'salubrious' though the climate might be with four walls and a roof above one's head, it had, under the circumstances, proved rigorous in the extreme. For days they would swelter in intolerable heat, plagued by flies and mosquitoes, beset by ravenous ants and fleas that proliferated in the hot ground; then would come a cold wind from the sea, driving before it a whip-lash of stinging sand that forced them to what poor shelter they could find, carried off clothing spread to dry on the stunted scrub, frantically agitated the canvas tents, and scattered their cooking-fires.

The hut, set further upriver from the open beach, was soon

ready for occupation. It was formed from woven boughs and thatched with rushes, while Markram had found some planks from the wreck of a ship with which he constructed a door. The inside was divided by boxes and sheets into three compartments, one serving as a living- and dining-room, another as a bedroom for Eliza, Will and baby George and a third for Elizabeth, Mary and the servant Anne Haggs. Markram and the boys slept in the marquee which also served to cover the stores and heavy baggage. A friend in need supplied two horses to convey their goods to the new site, the heavier stuff being floated up the river on a raft, their few articles of precious furniture suffering considerable damage from salt water in the process.

From the time they were established in their new abode Eliza's letters take on a more cheerful tone:

We had scarcely got into the hut before a garden was formed, seeds in and all was bustle and stir. Shaw also put in some wheat and rye and other grain experimentally, which promised well, but whether from too much salt or what, at a certain stage the shoots fell off and went to decay and we never gathered one vegetable, though our garden and little wheat beds were visited by almost everybody and admired by all. I believe several who saw them in their flourishing condition became reconciled and stayed in the Colony who would otherwise have left. Indeed, I know it for a fact.

Poor Shaw fags worse than a slave. The greatest comfort we now have is in the mutual support and consolation we can give one another and our greatest happiness is talking of your dear circle—doubly dear now we are 18,000 miles off. Markram does well enough since we arrived, but Anne has turned out very sadly. She is without exception the idlest, dirty, saucy slut that ever got into anyone's family! Nat and William are capital fags and also Elizabeth. Frederick is an angel as always—Mary and baby George are sadly off with the sand and the flies which are intolerable.

I hope in a few months to have more favourable accounts to send. Depend upon it I will never let an opportunity pass for writing you the history and adventures of old Will Shaw and his hopeful family—now what do you think of that for the title of a book?[2]

Chapter 4

February–September 1830

Turn of Fortune

Shaw permitted to select 8,106-acre grant. With Agett and Lukin he explores north of Fremantle. Their application refused by Surveyor-General. Methodists lend their premises to Rev Wittenoom for Anglican services. The man with his head in a bag. Eliza writes of Aborigines. Perth town-site proclaimed. Aborigines placed under the protection of British Law. Shaw granted ten acres at Fremantle. Shaw meets Robert Menli Lyon who offers him grant at Upper Swan.

In March 1830 Shaw was granted written permission to select 8,106 acres of free land to which his investment entitled him. There is no mention in the brief Government Notice[1] of any official commitment to the further 10,376¾ acres which he ever afterwards believed due to him, but since the 264 people eligible for free grants received an average of only 4,380 acres each he could not reasonably claim prejudicial treatment. It was made clear to the selectors that as Swan River grants were the most sought-after, those lucky enough to obtain one of the ninety-four Swan blocks available must be content with a limited acreage in that area and take out the rest of their entitlement elsewhere. For this reason, Shaw, hoping to secure his allotment within a single grant decided not to wait about for a coveted Swan selection but to look around elsewhere. With this in view he joined forces with his ship-mates DuBois Agett and Lionel Lukin who were camped nearby also awaiting grants.

The three men set out on horseback and, penetrating inland about fourteen miles north of Fremantle, came upon a series of swamps or lakes surrounded by what looked to be very promising country. They took a compass bearing and hastened

46

back to apply for a grant in the vicinity.[2] Roe, the Surveyor-General, urgently employed in many directions, declared that he could not recognize the position from their given bearings and had then no time to assess the area personally. The matter was set aside to be forgotten by the department, and probably more or less by the Shaws in the excitement of other developments, though to become a heated issue at a later date. Shaw seems never to have approached the Surveyor-General on his own business when that gentleman was not harassed about something else. At the time Shaw was sympathetic with the overworked official and was impressed by his adventurous naval career during which, between 1817 and 1823, he had accompanied Captain Philip King in the ships *Mermaid* and *Bathurst* on surveys of the Australian coast. Roe had also seen service in the hydrographical department at the Admiralty and had been a natural choice for the post of Chief Surveyor. Although he and Shaw were to clash so bitterly in later years, they met at this time, however unsatisfactory the immediate transaction, with a feeling of mutual respect.

During this time the Shaws became friendly with the Colonial Chaplain, a cultured apostle of joy named John Burdett Wittenoom, Nottingham-born and a graduate of Brasenose College, Oxford. A High Churchman of wide reading and liberal outlook, Wittenoom had emigrated with his mother, sister and five motherless sons on the ship *Wanstead*, and it is possible that the Shaws had first encountered them in Cape Town along with other disgruntled victims of the misnamed Captain Friend. Much in the conversation of those times, and for many years to come, were the settlers' ship-board experiences and associates. 'What ship did you come out on?' was almost the first question asked of everyone, the answer usually conveying its own story. Every voyage had a character or flavour of its own, often determined, for good or ill, by the nature of the captain and affected of course by the company, the sailing conditions and amenities and the element of luck. Absurdly slow and small by present standards, the biggest vessel to come out in the first year was the *Gilmore*, of 500 tons with 170 passengers, and the smallest the *Eagle*,[3] a mere 108 tons and carrying only 18 people. In many cases fellow travellers established an almost family relationship that was maintained throughout the years, while those who, like the Shaws, had formed a special regard for their ship and its captain would make every effort to renew contact on its subsequent visits.

This was especially so with passengers of the ship *Tranby*, a group of Wesleyan Methodists of farming background—'dissenters' in escape from the industrial problems of northern England, who had arrived at about the same time as the Shaws. These people had come well-equipped for a community-type project based on firm religious principles, and while awaiting a suitable grant, erected near Fremantle a prefabricated timber dwelling of which the largest section was used for meetings and church services. This building was the envy of the Anglican community who had nothing better for their religious gatherings than an indifferent tent. The Rev Wittenoom, himself of broadly tolerant religious outlook, feared that a request for a loan of the premises for his Sunday service might meet with a rebuff from these robust fundamentalists. It was his sister Miss Eliza who at last plucked up courage to make the bold suggestion. The response typified the spirit of co-operation of those early days, to which many settlers would look back nostalgically in less generous times. Permission was not only happily granted but the entire *Tranby* contingent turned up to the 10 am Anglican service. Since Mr Wittenoom was that Sunday conducting a service in Perth, the officiating clergyman was a fellow *Wanstead* passenger, the Rev R Davis.[4] At the conclusion, their spokesman, Mr Joseph Hardey, assured Mr Davis and his flock of a warm welcome to the Wesleyan service at 6 pm. This invitation, delivered in a broad 'black country' dialect, could hardly be refused and marked the beginnings of a happy relationship that was to extend, to the benefit of all, into many walks of life.

Gentle little Miss Eliza, forever busy with the Christian duties that fell to her lot as sister of a widowed clergyman, kept the Shaws abreast of the often curious happenings around the port. There was, for instance, the singular affair of the man whom Miss Wittenoom found lying on the beach in the full blast of the sun with his head in a canvas bag. Having ascertained that he was alive, she had spoken to him only to be told that he wanted to be left alone to die. Her efforts to reason with him being of no avail she returned daily leaving food and drink to hand. This was found each time to have been demolished but the man remained obstinately faceless and incognito. He soon became quite a *cause célèbre* in the settlement, and many people tried their persuasive powers with him in vain. The Governor's advice was at last sought and he was ordered to be brought to Perth in a cart. Here it was discovered that he was one of three young men—two medicos and an attorney—who had come to seek their fortunes in the new colony. Having little money and nothing to barter since they had brought only clothing and books, they soon found themselves unable to carry on and took to drink, presumably charged up to local hostelries. Finally one of the three died, another shot himself, and the third tried the rather impractical solution frustrated by the good Miss Wittenoom. The rest of his story is unknown, interest in it apparently having given place to one of greater excitement.

A five-year-old boy was at this time reported missing from the property of his parents, Mr and Mrs John Dutton, a few miles from Fremantle. Mounted members of the 63rd Regiment and a number of private settlers combed the bush for many days in vain, but during this time an Aboriginal was encountered with a piece of cloth said to have been identical with the child's clothing. From this it was deduced that he had been abducted by the natives and little hope was held for his recovery. The search was at last abandoned and, after figuring prominently in the letters and journals of a number of settlers, including Eliza Shaw's, was referred to no more. However, Miss Jane Roberts, who had been in Fremantle at the time, records in her book *Two Years at Sea* that after her subsequent arrival in Van Dieman's Land she learned that the child had been returned to his parents unharmed. It was said that a party of natives found him wandering in the bush and took him to display to their womenfolk who, kept well out of reach of the settlers, had been eager to see a white child. According to this source they were so fascinated and delighted by the fair-haired little stranger that they had been reluctant to surrender him, but he was restored at last in good health and none the worse for his adventure. So satisfactory an ending to the episode is not however conclusive, for two months later than Miss Roberts' report, Mrs John Whatley of Swan River implies in her diary that the child was still missing. 'How uncomfortable they [the natives] must be in this weather without any clothes,' she writes in July 1830, 'and poor Bonny, what can he do!'[5]

Eliza, knowing the keen interest of her friends in all the details of their new life, reported a good deal about the Aborigines—much of it, in the earlier months at least, founded on current misinformation.

The natives [she reports] have paid two or three visits to our encampment. They are black as ink and perfectly naked. It is not safe for white women to be seen by them as they are perfectly savage and would take them off by force if they could lay hands on them. Even female children are unsafe to be alone. They are very swift of foot as they run like deer. They throw their spears, which are their only weapons, most dexterously both at fish and animals. They are like parrots, repeating every word that is said to them. They are to all appearances harmless unless ill-used. They are frightened at a gun or a dog or horse. They appear very numerous and live in caves underground. They are, particularly the women I am told, hideously ugly, but I have never seen them near enough to judge. They appeared on our first arrival to be most astonished at the strength of Europeans' stout arms and legs and would laugh and feel them with wonder, their own full grown men being far slighter than our females. They seem delighted with a fat white baby or piccaninny as they call them. They have their Chiefs who always lead them in their warfare and are the last of the tribe to either eat, drink or sleep. They are chiefly wanderers and the women carry their children over their shoulders.

Some Europeans have been clever enough to show them the use of flour, bread, sugar, rice etc, the consequences being they have broken open stores and stolen them whenever they could.[6]

It seems never to have occurred to the settlers that the Aborigines should show them anything but gratitude for their annexation of the tribal hunting grounds. In fact it was blandly assumed from the beginning that, since they established no villages, sowed no crops of any kind and built no permanent dwellings, they had no sense of land ownership or any allegiance to or preference for one part of the country above another. Nor did the people themselves, lacking all understanding of what was afoot, show any resentment of the white intruders, some of whom, including Stirling, they claimed to have recognized as the white-skinned reincarnations of their departed relatives. It would be many years, and then too late, before the intricate social and territorial structure of tribal life would begin to be studied and understood. Stirling, on proclaiming the site of Perth, had behaved in what he saw as a most liberal and enlightened manner when he declared the Aboriginal people subjects of His Majesty King William III, and placed them under the protection of British law.

The Aborigines, however, were at that time the least of Eliza's worries. Her main concern was how the family was to carry on until they received a grant of suitable land. They had hardly expected in the balmy days of late summer that winter would be upon them without the warning of an autumn leaf, that fierce storms blown in from the north-west would bring driving sheets of rain, reducing the sand to mud and sending them shivering to the shelter of their hut. Such cooking as was then possible at all was done by holding an umbrella over the open fire, the cook being soaked to the skin in the process. Little wonder that Eliza, to her exasperation, went down with what she describes as 'a sort of rheumatics' and was for two weeks almost unable to move.

They had still enough flour and dried yeast brought from England to make bread in a camp oven bought at the Cape. They had also a small supply of salt meat but fresh meat was scarce, and with vegetables unattainable scurvy was soon added to their litany of trials.

But apart from her first outburst of disillusionment Eliza's letters invariably reflected her buoyant and optimistic temperament. Her critical remarks about the Lieutenant-Governor were never to be repeated from the day he called on them in their humble hut. Observing their efforts to establish a garden, he praised them for their enterprise and told them that they might regard the surrounding ten acres as their own. This gesture 'gave Shaw great satisfaction', for although it was but a small area and the soil poor he realized that a site so conveniently situated to Fremantle would one day be of considerable value. Moreover it was a foot in at last and a heartening indication of the Governor's concern.

It was at this stage that there began for the Shaw family the unfolding of a series of simple incidents that were to have a profound bearing on their future. Eliza relates it from the beginning, craving the patience of her friends at what might seem to them a prosy account of inconsequentials 'since every circumstance bears reference to something which turns out of importance to us'.

During our stay at the hut there were some wild pigs straying about belonging to the Government, which Shaw bought at so much a head for all he could catch. Tell Boswell he could never have done this without the aid of his dear old dog. He is so faithful and in capital condition ... Well we used to eat some part of the pigs so caught. The rest Markram used to carry down and sell among the settlers who were ready enough to buy being like ourselves with the scurvy from living on salt meat and no vegetables. It happened one day Markram had taken some pork down to the landing place for sale when a poor man, evidently suffering from some illness came up to him and said he had not tasted fresh meat since he came to the colony and would be so happy if he could have a bit of the pork. He had no money but would give Mr Shaw what he thought proper in return. As luck would have it Shaw came up at that very moment and seeing directly that the man was sick ordered Markram to give him what was left of the meat. 'Much good may it do you' he said, 'I shall not take your salt meat for I have plenty to go with and am happy to have it in my power to give you a taste of fresh pork.' This was all that passed and to this hour I believe Shaw has not seen the person since and would perhaps never have remembered the circumstance had it not been afterwards recalled to his memory.[7]

Soon after this they received a visit from Mr William Locke Brockman, whose father, the Rev Julius Brockman, Rector of Cheriton, near Kent, had as may be remembered, christened young Will Shaw when his parents were at the Shorncliffe Camp in 1818. William Brockman's young wife who had been Miss Frances Hamersley, was known to the Shaws through her sister whom they had met in Kent. The Brockmans with their infant son had come out in the *Minstrel* that arrived in January 1830, and had received one of the first grants made on the Upper Swan. They had named this property Herne Hill after a family estate in England and had already erected a timber house brought out from home in numbered sections which, like the Tranby building, foreshadowed the prefabricated structures of a future day. They were most anxious that the Shaws should secure a grant close to their own, for they believed the area to be of great potential and were confident that the two families would find much in common. While the two men were together in Fremantle that same day Brockman introduced Shaw to a Mr Robert Menli Lyon, whose greeting Eliza reports as follows:

'Mr Shaw, I have frequently heard of you. You, I believe, have a large family and have been in the Colony a long time, but have not yet got a grant.'

Shaw agreed that such was the case, at which Lyon continued: 'I have had the pleasure, though unknown to yourself, of seeing you before. Do you remember giving a person some fresh pork and would take nothing in return? I stood near enough to hear all that passed and am now delighted, in my turn, to be able to render a service to so kindly a gentleman. I have a grant of land which I cannot make use of. I have had money offered for it but you and your family shall have half of it. I will come over tomorrow and give you a letter to the Governor to that effect.'

All this seems fictitious but can be authenticated by Mr Brockman as well as by Mr Lyon's letters which shall be copied and sent to you. But this is not the only romantic circumstance connected with the wonderful history of Old Shaw, his wife and hopeful family, founded on facts.[8]

Chapter 5

October–December *1830*

The Move to Upper Swan

Robert Menli Lyon transfers his entire Upper Swan
grant to Shaw. Shaws leave Fremantle for Upper Swan.
Eliza calls on Government House. Colonel Lautour's
bailiff offers them hut near grant. Eliza nervous of
natives in area. Accepts Brockmans' hospitality. Tragic
death of the two younger sons.

Robert Menli Lyon was one of the most intriguing characters
to have set foot in the new colony. Born in Inverness in 1789,
he had come out on the *Marquis of Anglesea* in August 1829
with two servants and their four children. He described himself as 'an agriculturalist', but implied that he had been a
clergyman and had also at some time followed a military
career. There was much about him, too, as the colony was
soon to learn, of the frustrated business promoter, the would-
be missionary and the expatriate don. Greek and Latin pro-
verbs, idiom and classical allusions came readily to his lips and
his pen, and his knowledge of the Scriptures was formidable.
But somehow the reports he gave of his background and his
intentions seldom tallied, and he signed his name at different
times as both 'Lyon' and 'Lion'. He was later thought to have
been more probably Robert Milne, under which name he
operated after leaving the colony.

In the meantime he had been as good as his word in writing
to the Governor, and official notification of his Upper Swan
land having been transferred to Shaw was soon to follow. This
grant, sharing a northern boundary with the land of one James
Kenton and a southern with that assigned to Captain Fremantle, was fortuitously little over three miles from the Brockmans' property, about twenty-four miles up the river from

Perth, and Shaw with the help of William Brockman lost no time in inspecting it. He soon found that although there was much good alluvial soil on the property, the section he had been given, in all good faith he believed, consisted for the most part of stony ground and unpromising sand, ending up in the rocky foothills of the Darling escarpment. It was Stirling's policy, in order to arrive at the fairest possible distribution of land, to limit individual titles to river frontage on the Swan to half an acre on one bank only. In a few instances, owing to the curves of the river the stipulated area was exceeded to some extent, and one or two settlers somehow contrived to obtain land on *both* banks, but by and large the policy was maintained. This accounted for the long narrow aspect of most of the Swan blocks and since Lyon had proposed keeping the area of alluvial river flat it is no wonder that Shaw was chary of the offer. Backed by the advice of William Brockman he decided that to accept it he would be 'jumping out of the frying-pan into the fire'. It was a difficult situation which he appears to have handled with considerable tact. On his return he called on Lyon and thanked him in the warmest terms for his kindly intention. He explained, however, that the area in question was not suitable for cultivation and that since its being cut off would detract from the value of the block as a whole he thought it only fair and sensible that his would-be benefactor should keep the property intact.

Some days later Lyon called to inform Shaw that having been granted another twelve months to select land elsewhere, he would be delighted to give away his entire Upper Swan block which he believed to comprise about 3,813 acres. Having formally made over this land to the Shaws Lyon applied for a ten-acre grant adjoining the 'garden ground' near Fremantle where the Shaws had built their temporary hut. This was refused on the grounds that several allotments in both town and country had been assigned the applicant but he had made no effort whatever to improve them. Soon after this his interest in land seems to have been overshadowed by his absorption in the cause of the Aboriginals—his 'sable sons of Derbal'—of which more anon.

I cannot describe, though you may conceive, [Eliza wrote] our delight at this piece of good fortune, or rather of Providential care. And so, though all at sea again, as it were, we have yet a haven in view and an anchor of Hope to rest upon. Shaw ever makes all things subservient to the welfare and happiness of his family. A better man, father, husband, friend, cannot exist, though he is an old sinner as you, my dear friends, have many times heard me call him. Need I say he is generally respected, if not beloved, by all the worthy and good friends we have made in the Colony.[1]

And so, on 13 October—eight months after their arrival in the colony—'Will Shaw and his hopeful family' turned their backs on the little hut that had sheltered them through the winter months and set out on the next stage of their adventure. They had hired a big flat-bottomed boat to convey themselves and their belongings on the thirty-six mile journey up the river.

> You cannot think how comfortably everything was arranged [Eliza wrote cheerfully]. In the middle of the boat we placed our cart with my bedding in it and a long pole or beam overhead running the whole length of it, and over which at night was thrown a sail which, falling on each side of the boat, formed a room as comfortable and private as a tent. On one side of the cart was the boys' bedding and on the other that of the little girls and servant Anne. At the end of the cart stood a little table I brought from England on which we dined. We had several tremendous thunder storms with heavy rain but we were completely sheltered.[2]

By this time their stock was reduced to the two milking goats, two cocks, seven hens, a crate of chickens and the virile Leicestershire ram. The pigs they brought out had all died, but Elizabeth had adopted a tiny wild sow from which she was inseparable, and this and the faithful dog went on board with the family.

Eliza and the children had not before had the chance of venturing far afield and had seen little of the river estuary beyond the narrow section near Fremantle. Now, it opened out ahead of them in the full beauty of its broad reaches and curving bays, mirroring the primeval forest on its banks, its flocks of black swans, pelicans, shags and wild duck. They could now appreciate for the first time Captain Stirling's enchantment with the scene on his exploratory voyage—the wonder he expressed at the floral abundance of this antipodean spring, colourful blossoms clustering to the water's edge, creepers flung like bright shawls over shrubs and trees. So far reticent about the landscape, Eliza now groped for words to express her new-found delight in the countryside. The wild flowers, though few had more than the faint scent of honey, were amazingly varied in colour and form. The wild creatures were curious and interesting and, with the exception of a few snakes, scorpions and spiders, quite harmless to mankind, while the birds though not possessed of the musical range of thrush and nightingale were not songless by any means. Magpies and butcher birds lifted their beaks to heaven in full-throated joy of life, and a local variety of cuckoo sounded the familiar English note with a slightly foreign intonation.

Here and there along the banks were the wattle-and-daub and timber houses of a few first-footers in tentative clearings hard-hacked from the virgin scrub. Some of these settlers, sighting the cumbersome craft approaching, came to the water's edge with offers of hospitality but the family, anxious to complete their journey, pressed on. It was only briefly, at the invitation of Harbour Master Captain Currie, RN, and his young wife, that they came ashore at a 'sweet spot'[3] on Matilda Bay where this couple had established their headquarters about a year before. They had applied for a 'villa grant' of thirty-two acres in this area[4] in anticipation of which they had put up a quaint rush house, outbuildings and stockyards and had begun to cultivate a vegetable and flower garden. Shaws and Curries chatted optimistically of their prospects while the children, with excited cries, discovered a fascinating menagerie including piglets, guinea chicks, milking-cows and goats.

And here at last was the capital of Perth—the seat of government—named by Stirling in honour of Sir George Murray, Secretary of State for Colonies, who hailed from that part of Scotland. Shaw was able to point out where new quarters were being built to replace the tents that the Governor and his entourage had originally occupied. Everywhere were signs of brisk activity, of farm blocks being cleared, fenced and cultivated on either side of the wagon tracks that were some day to become the thoroughfares of a thriving city.

Later in the day the boat put in at what Eliza calls 'Fisherman's Isle' (Heirisson Island) close to the causeway that now spans those once-treacherous river flats. Here they were obliged to camp for a couple of days while the boat was somehow negotiated over the muddy shallows into the deeper waters that gave ready access to the upper reaches of the Swan. During this time Eliza dressed herself in her Sunday best and paid a call on the Governor and his Lady, who received her 'with the most polite attention'. Here she met for the first time the wife of Colonial Secretary Peter Brown who offered to accommodate the family until they were able to proceed. Eliza, however, convinced that a family of the size and inquisitive enterprise of her own would strain the hospitality of the most forebearing host, politely declined. She protested that she found it not at all unpleasant on the island, where they occupied their time fishing, picnicking and paddling in the river shallows. Unfortunately none of the children could yet swim and Eliza had to keep a careful eye on them. She was confident, however, that they would soon enough master the art when established on their river property and she need then have no further apprehensions for their safety on this count.

They were scarcely over the river flats and on their way again than they rounded the river peninsula where their Fremantle friends 'the *Tranby* people' had begun their experiment in group agricultural settlement about six months before. In a brief conversation with Mr Joseph Hardey they heard how he had hardly finished building his first wattle-and-daub house when the river came down in flood and almost covered it. Given to interpreting all happenings in the light of the Good Lord's providence, he had taken this event as a timely warning that the river, though seemingly so benign, was a power to be reckoned with. He had at once built again, on higher ground, and had by that time almost finished thatching the roof. He hoped to see the Shaws before long at the townsite named Guildford some miles upstream, where he planned to preach from time to time as he was already doing on occasions in the main street of Perth. The last sermon he had delivered there—its theme being 'the barren fig tree'—had claimed the brief but respectful attention of important residents including the Governor's Lady herself.

Close to the *Tranby* people's holding was one referred to as 'the Government Farm' where James Drummond, the Colonial Botanist, had already established a home for his family. The Shaws and Drummonds, who were to be so closely associated in the years to come, probably met for the first time on this occasion. Nat struck up an immediate friendship with young John Nicol, the Drummonds' third son who was the same age as himself; but who, having been in the colony all of eight months longer, already talked like an old timer of his bush adventures, of collecting wild-life specimens for his father and hunting kangaroo with the Aborigines. The young Shaws were immensely impressed to learn that the four Drummond boys could already speak a little of the tribal language of that area. They also referred casually by name to a number of warriors, then shadowy figures, but soon to loom large in the colonial scene.

As the boat resumed its journey the country on either side assumed the 'new and park-like appearance' that Stirling had reported. Here at last was the river proper, its fresh waters running out into the broad salt water estuary below. At the little township of Guildford where the Governor had already established his farm, Woodbridge, they were welcomed by Captain and Mrs Boyd who had travelled with them on the *Egyptian*, and who were already fairly comfortably settled. A few miles further on they passed the block taken up by their friends the DuBois Agetts. They were also able to pick out from the sketch map provided by the Boyds, the holding of John Septimus Roe that he called Sandalford, the Barrett Lennards' block immediately opposite Herne Hill and the 10,000-acre property of Mr and Mrs Will Brockman. This kindly young couple invited Eliza to remain there with her children until a shelter of some kind had been established on their own block about three and a half miles upstream. Always sensitive, however, of overstraining her welcome, she again declined ('for fish and friends' as she was wont to say, 'seldom keep longer than three days'). Besides they had met a man named Cleaver who had come out as bailiff for the absentee speculator, Colonel Lautour, and he had suggested they might take over one of the so far uninhabited huts on a river grant not far from their own block. This, until they had a house of their own, however humble, seemed a sensible solution and it was there they landed their goods and chattels and made a temporary base.

From here Shaw went off each day with Markram and Nat

to work on their property, while Eliza remained at Lautour's hut with her little ones. It was not many days before she realized that the offer of this shelter had not been entirely disinterested, for the livestock grazing around Lautour's huts was being constantly preyed upon by the natives and obviously Cleaver had hoped that the Shaws' occupation would discourage them. It does not seem to have done so. Eliza felt obliged to keep a firearm to hand, and dress in Will's clothes, convinced as she was that the tribesmen must surely be plotting to kill Shaw 'for the sake of possessing a white *womana* as they call us and which they have many times attempted, I hear'. As if this anxiety were not enough, before long Eliza was so afflicted with dysentery, a prevalent sickness of those early years, that she finally yielded to the Brockmans' invitation. She took with her to Herne Hill only Elizabeth, Mary and baby George, Will meanwhile having pitched a tent on their block where he left the two boys William and Frederick and the servant girl, while he worked on the house with the help of Markram and Nat. Eliza found the Brockmans' home both soothing and reassuring, for in so short a time they had set themselves up with most of the essential comforts of home. They had brought out with them their fine crockery, cutlery, linen and basic furniture, one particular chair bearing the Hamersley crest having been, as Mrs Brockman laughingly recalled, one of the first articles to be put ashore from the *Minstrel* on the Fremantle beach. In this she had sat with her baby in her arms watching the unloading of so many necessary and unnecessary belongings, including carriages and grand pianos—mostly to be ruined by wind-blown sand and salty sea-spray.

In no time the two women had exchanged their respective life stories, some details to become confused over the years in the chancy process known as 'oral tradition'. Some of Eliza's grandchildren came firmly to believe that she and Will had run away when Eliza was seventeen years old to be wed by the blacksmith at Gretna Green—hence the disapproval of the Cooper family. In truth this was the Brockmans' story, for the Hamersleys having refused permission for their seventeen-year-old daughter to marry her Will and migrate to Swan River, the young couple had dared this romantic solution to their problem. The Hamersleys had thereafter relented and the couple were formally married from the bride's ancestral home of Pyrton, near Oxford, 1828. It was after this family seat that Edward Hamersley, Fanny Brockman's brother, who was to come out in 1837, named his property on the other side of the river.

But, alas, Eliza's happy reassurance at finding herself in comfortable surroundings and with people of like mind, was soon to be rudely shattered. Although she wrote at length meanwhile of other matters it was over a year before she could bring herself to recount the tragic details of that sorrowful day, 8 December, 1830. It had been left to good Captain Lilburn, whose ship was once more in Fremantle at that time, to break the news to the Waghornes, in person, on his return.

Until this day, [Eliza wrote] I have been unable to write of this terrible happening. Shaw has several times sat down to write to Mr Waghorne but each time he has burst into tears and walked away to his fields or into the woods to compose himself. Even now I do not believe he can write to you. You would scarcely know him, for from the fine, hearty, vigorous young man you knew he is reduced by sorrow, anxiety and hard work almost to a shadow. I was from home you see at the dear Brockmans being very ill at the time. It appears that Shaw and Nat left the riverside where our goods were landed and a temporary tent pitched, for the purpose of felling trees to make a road to the top of the hill where we had fixed to place our house. They left the two boys to put to rights any little packages that lay about and on the return of Shaw and Nat about two hours at the outside, that great girl appeared as if just awake from her sleep, the breakfast things all unwashed, the fire out and the two boys missing.

It is supposed they were either fishing or drawing water when Frederick was frightened into the water by the Leicester ram whose tracks were later found upon the bank. Poor William must have jumped in to save him and both were lost, but God only knows.

The natives were very troublesome at that time and it was at first thought they must have taken them. This I did not myself credit, though, had they been girls I might have thought differently. When it was broken to me by Mrs

Brockman that they had disappeared I immediately said 'the river!'

By that time the military were out and when I reached the bank I overheard them say 'one is found—the other not.' But it was not long before with my own eyes I saw them both—just one fleeting glance before I was led away. The same soldiers of the 63rd Regiment carried them to their grave and had they known us for years they could not have expressed a greater grief. They showed the deepest sympathy for poor Shaw and only with the greatest difficulty prevented him from throwing himself into the river. The moment little Frederick was taken out he fell senseless for some time ...

The grave of our dear boys is in a most romantic and beautiful spot, commanding a noble and extensive view, overshadowed by native cypress, black wattle and other weeping shrubs. Thank God it is past and I am become resigned to the Divine Will ... If ever an angel was on earth Frederick was one and William snatched from us before the taint of this world had made him unfit for another and better one. Surely, surely they are gone to Heaven![5]

Chapter 6

December 1830–August 1831

Settling In

Shaw parents' grief. No letters from home. Markram deserts. Pioneers' ingenuity. Upper Swan friendships and social life. Adoption of Mary Shaw vetoed by her father. Beginning of boundary dispute between Brown and Shaw. Settlement expands—Beverley, Northam and York townsites named. Shaw applies for Avon River grant. Is allotted 5,000 acres relinquished by the Rev Wittenoom. The end of free grants. Steady stream of settlers dries up. Appointment of Executive and Legislative Council. Agricultural Society formed.

The loss of the two Shaw boys affected their parents in rather different ways. Eliza, always a more resilient, perhaps less sensitive character than Shaw, became if anything more outgoing, more determined to look forward rather than back. Unlike Will she had no illusion of ever returning to England. She admitted to missing her friends but not to homesickness.

> Were all we regard and love with us, [she wrote] I do not think, apostate as I am for saying so, I should cast many longing, lingering looks back to England.[1]

But Will Shaw, according to all who knew him, was from the day of the tragedy a changed man. Never again was he the same gregarious, jovial fellow, ready in the midst of his most absorbing labours to play and joke with his family. He had worked hard enough before but he now toiled with a kind of desperation as though seeking forgetfulness in utter exhaustion. Unlike his wife who often spoke of her lost sons, remembering their little ways and incidents in which they had been involved, Shaw, apart from stating in his will that he would like if possible to be buried beside them, could never bring himself to mention their names again—nor, for the effect it had on him, did anyone dare name them in his hearing. As time went on he was again able to enjoy company, but with his own children, especially it seems with Nat, he was more withdrawn, fearing perhaps to indulge a love that could result in such suffering. The tragedy may even have had some bearing on the subsequent rather irrational behaviour that was to make him enemies and to embarrass his friends.

To make matters worse for both, they had not, in all this time, received a single letter from home. Their friends had written faithfully, but their letters had evidently been consigned to ships of which the passengers, on hearing bad reports of Swan River at the Cape, had decided to sail instead for New South Wales or Van Diemen's Land. In fact it was not until two years after their arrival that they received their first personal mail, though they themselves had continued meantime to write home as often as possible.

Compared to Eliza's effusive and detailed outpourings, Will's letters were terse and to the point, but even so, his longing for England and news of his friends was obvious and he was more anxious than ever that no one should be put off by bad reports. In April 1831 he wrote to Mr Waghorne daring to interpret their having had no mail as meaning that Robert Casson and perhaps other friends were on their way out. He was able to report that they were 'now fairly housed' on their location which they had named Belvoir 'from the magnificent views and park-like scenery it presents'.[2] They had in two acres of wheat and a great variety of vegetables. Eliza, having promised her friends to write them 'every particular' devoted pages (with paper, when available at all, selling at 7d a sheet!) to a description of their little 'plaster and dab' home. It had been built with the help of a good Sussex labourer they had been fortunate enough to secure when Markram deserted them. They had counted the latter no loss for 'the rascal had behaved so ill' that they were glad to get rid of him and had managed to extract half the passage money they had paid for him from his new master.

The little house, thirty-nine feet long by twelve wide, was partitioned with canvas into three parts, the main room featuring a big fireplace to make up for the previous winter at

Fremantle when they had had only 'a pudding tin of charcoal' to warm themselves. This room was also fitted with two small gothic windows they had purchased in Leicestershire. They had brought out only a minimum of furniture but had made shift very well with cretonne-covered packing-cases, timber forms, trestles and abundant shelves. Eliza reports that at table she sat on a camp stool at one end and Will at the other on a two-gallon water keg. 'Is not that grand?' Before the 1831 winter set in Will had added a small kitchen 'with a capital stone oven and a Colonial bedstead where the girl sleeps'. This oven soon won quite a reputation in the district, with the result that their neighbours also made use of it for cooking large joints and whole kangaroos.

Lack of money, though a matter of constant anxiety, was less vital once their garden began to bear fruit. Potatoes and onions did not flourish anywhere in the settlement in the early years, but Eliza lists any amount of other vegetables, including cabbages, peas, beans, mangel-wurzels, beet, lettuce, turnips, radishes, celery, pumpkin, cucumbers and melons of all sorts, that were in regular supply after July 1831. There was some apprehension of famine in the colony since so few ships were now calling at Fremantle, and Stirling had seen fit to introduce a system of rationing. However, with their home-grown produce including a small yield of wheat which they ground for bread-making in a steel corn mill, and with some of their own poultry and other meat supplied by neighbours, they themselves did well enough. Of this period Eliza writes:

I have not the slightest doubt but that I shall, if I live, yet see the day of plenteousness if not of affluence. I do thank the Great Giver of all good that I am the richest being in the world in possessing the best of friends in dear old England, and certainly the most respectable, kind and worthy ones in Western Australia ...

We are all *traders* here now and then. Ours is the most friendly neighbourhood you can imagine. Our own stock is little or nothing but whenever the Tanners kill either sheep, lamb, pig or other fresh meat there is sure to be a joint sent up here, besides sending for us to dine upon all extraordinary occasions, as well as whenever they have anything nice or out of the common routine of salt pork and beef.

The Browns also, on the other side of us, are quite as friendly, but they have lived in Perth until a few weeks since when Mr Brown gave Mr Henty £500 for a very indifferent grant near Perth where the Browns are now living.[3] Mr B used frequently to come up here to see his grant before he purchased the one I have just named as he had a large estate and stock here, generally 19 men, 200 to 300 sheep, 10 cows or cattle, 5 or 6 horses, I do not know how many pigs and poultry, besides geese and rabbits etc. The last time he came up he ordered half a fine, fat lamb to be sent to us.[4]

Peter Brown, a son of Sir William Broun, sixth baronet,[5] was born in the Channel Islands and had grown up in Scotland. Nominated as Colonial Secretary by Captain Stirling, with whom he and his wife had come out on the *Parmelia*, he now had an office and temporary quarters in Perth and was building himself a home not far from Government House. Apart from his £400 a year position he was entitled to 9,626 acres, part of which he had already taken up in a block adjoining the Shaws' northern boundary. He visited this property whenever possible and co-operated, as we see, in the local system of barter.

The Shaws for their part were careful to maintain a nice balance of reciprocity. Not only had they quantities of vegetables for exchange, but they had been given by Mr Cleaver an excellent hunting dog—a long involved story again illustrating the practical community system of give and take. With the help of this swift and virile animal they secured a plentiful supply of kangaroo.

Kangaroos, when we can get them, are delicious meat [Eliza writes]. You could scarcely tell them from beef though they have a somewhat wild flavour. We have had them weighing from forty to one hundred pounds and that is not to be sneezed at with fresh mutton selling at 1/6 to 1/10 lb ... The kangaroo is so formidable an animal that few dogs are able to kill them singly. Nat goes hunting with the three Mr Burgeses, who live about half a mile from us and are most excellent neighbours, so their dogs and ours run together and we divide the spoil.[6]

66

This 'spoil' being a popular item of barter in the settlement, the swift-footed Mr Rex more than earned his keep.

The Shaws were also able to lend items of farming equipment including a plough and harrows, 'superior to any we have seen in the colony', and, on request of the Governor, to exchange an excellent cart for its equivalent value in government stores—this vehicle to serve a party about to explore country over the Darling Range.

Many commodities, when available in the settlement, were expensive even by modern standards. Irish butter (10d a pound in England) was 4s 6d in the colony, and local, if to be had, was even dearer. Sugar was 3s 2d, tea up to 4s 6d lb, and vinegar 4s 6d a gallon. Starch (considered an absolute essential) was 5s lb, rum (also indispensable) up to 10s a gallon, and brandy so scarce as to be priced out of the general market. Clothing and material was always in short supply. 'There is not,' Eliza says, 'a yard of calico for sale and I am the only one in the colony with any flannel.' Will Shaw must soon have recovered from his shock at finding the Governor in his bare feet, for everyone had perforce to consider the wear and tear on boots and shoes. From the time of their arrival at the Upper Swan all the Shaw children went barefoot and their parents, except for social occasions, wore cloth shoes of Eliza's making. Eliza recounts how Mr Leake, who had land on the other side of the river and a merchant business in Fremantle, had received 300 pairs of shoes by the *Egyptian*, and sold every pair in one day!

But despite shortages, high prices and hard work there was already a surprising amount of social life in the colony. The Shaws were by this time close friends with the Brockmans and there was a constant interchange of hospitality between them in their modest but comfortable homes. Across the river immediately opposite were the Burges brothers, William, Lockier and Sam, to whom Eliza had referred. Of Scottish origin they had been, like many other Swan River settlers, resident in Ireland, and they had emigrated from Tipperary in 1830. Then there were the Tanners of Baskerville, with whom the Shaws shared their southern border. Eliza describes them as 'people of large fortune who left England merely because they were fond of seeing the world'. 'Mrs Tanner and myself' she adds 'are upon the most friendly—nay, almost sisterly—

terms. They have a very large, handsome wooden house ...
and are a most worthy and charming family ... They live in
good style, having brought 31 servants into the colony with
them.'[7]

The Tanners' considerable investment in the colony had
entitled them to select 35,000 acres. In 1832 they had been
granted the 5,000-acre Baskerville property originally taken up
and relinquished by Captain Fremantle and although they had
by that time secured other Swan River grants, probably by
purchase from needy settlers, had decided to build a residence
on this site. They were probably the wealthiest family in the
colony at that time and were undoubtedly generous and hospitable to their less affluent neighbours. It is also clear, however, that William Tanner was a shrewd businessman with an
eager eye for the acquisition of choice blocks and one who
contrived to live prudently on the interest of his invested
capital.

The couple had arrived in the *Drummore* in February 1831
with relatives named Viveash, Mrs Viveash being Mr Tanner's
sister, and Mrs Tanner sister to Mr Viveash. Discouraged by
the prevailing shortages and pessimistic forecasts regarding
Swan River, the Viveashs decided to continue on with their
twenty servants to Van Diemen's Land. While awaiting their
ship's departure, however, they had stayed with their Tanner
relatives and while there had formed a strong attachment to
the six-year-old Mary Shaw. Being themselves childless they
had earnestly sought to 'adopt, educate and bring her up as
their own in every way'. Eliza was by no means unmindful of
the disadvantages of life for growing girls in the raw young
colony where there were, as yet, no schools and few refinements. She realized, moreover, that the Shaws were unlikely
ever to have means enough to send their children home to be
educated or even for a taste of the life and standards of an
established society. She feared, however, that being an only
girl in a rich household could have more adverse effects than
otherwise apart from which the child's father refused even to
discuss the proposition. 'The two poor boys having been lost
but two months,' Eliza writes, 'it seemed to harrow his soul to
talk of losing another.' So Mary remained in the settlement
to become known, in time, as 'the belle of the Swan'—though
one wonders whether, had her parents foreseen the hard life

in store for her, they might have regretted their decision.

Sometimes, notwithstanding the good relations that existed between these pioneer neighbours, differences inevitably arose, mostly as a result of borders having been hastily defined or grants becoming confused in the constant process of reshuffling that went on in these early years. Often grants were exchanged, sold and sometimes forfeited as a result of their owners having for some reason failed to fulfil the conditions of tenure. The Shaws had realized from the beginning that much of their grant, probably then extending east to the foothills of the Darling Range, was of poor quality. It therefore came as a rude shock to them when Peter Brown announced his intention of building a stone house on a site that Shaw believed to be within the best part of his own block. Eliza tells us that it was only with the greatest difficulty that Brown was persuaded to have their boundary run by government surveyors. This was carried out on Christmas Eve 1830.

It was found that Shaw was right and the spot ours [Eliza reports triumphantly]. But this was not all, for it was also found ... that a most extensive, and one of the richest flats in the colony, was also ours. This Shaw told Mr Brown the first opportunity but for months—nay a year—he would not be persuaded, and it was not until a very short time since it has been ascertained past all doubt. The boundary is run and all is finally settled and we are now in possession of the finest grant of land on the Swan River.[8]

But despite this optimistic account the matter was by no means settled and since the argument was to prove a recurrent and finally a bitter one, the 1831 adjustment of the contended boundary is worth considering. Brown, evidently sure of his rights, insisted that the area in question—a matter of some 270 acres of river flat—be re-surveyed by three arbitrators, these being their mutual friends and neighbours, William Tanner, Henry Bull and George Fletcher Moore. Bull was an ex-naval lieutenant who had taken up land on the other side of the river to the north of Belvoir. He was a robust, practical farmer who had arrived with a herd of cattle purchased from the Duke of Bedford's stud farm at Woburn. Moore, a young law graduate from Dublin had taken a grant, which he had named

Millendon, close to Belvoir. Determined that the present transaction be legal Brown had had Moore draw up a form of agreement, signed by himself and Shaw and witnessed by neighbours William Burges and Edward Barrett Lennard of St Leonard's, that the boundary between Belvoir and Coulston (the Brown estate) be marked out by the arbitrators.

There was some altercation about compasses, Shaw suggesting that they obtained a proper azimuth instrument from the Survey Department, but Brown contending that there was no correct azimuth in the colony and that a pocket compass would be as fair for one as for the other. From this, as Shaw was later to testify on innumerable occasions, he gathered that 'each party was to abide the risk of any inaccuracy and to be bound by the result and that the arrangement was in the nature of a gambling speculation',[9] its object being to determine the proprietorship of the disputed land for good and all. They chose the best of three compasses and employed by way of a theodolite a long board with several lines of string attached. Then with Nat Shaw clearing the way through scrubby undergrowth, a line was run east half south from a marked tree on the river bank to a creek at the foot of the Darling Range. The process, with careful checking and re-checking and some altercation, took the better part of two days, the result, to Brown's considerable surprise and disappointment being again in favour of Shaw—and, as Eliza relates, with the addition of yet another good area of alluvial flat.

A statement of 22 August, 1831, to the effect that the boundary had been properly marked was signed by Moore, Tanner and Bull,[10] whereupon Tanner invited all parties to dinner at his house. There, in an atmosphere of some conviviality, Brown shook his opponent's hand and with the remark, 'Well Shaw, the land is yours', conceded him the victory. For the time being at least the matter was laid to rest and the social relations of all concerned continued as before.

During this time thin shafts of settlement had penetrated in other directions. Following a cross-country expedition to the military settlement at King George Sound that area was officially transferred to the new colony. It was named the Plantagenet District and its port Albany. Small detachments of the 63rd Regiment were then sent to protect isolated settlers in the recently opened south western centres of Leschenault, Augusta and Vasse.

In 1830 the energetic young Ensign Dale of the 63rd crossed the Darling Ranges and returned with news of good, well watered pasture land which he named for his native Yorkshire. In September of the same year Dale led Governor Stirling and a party including the Rev Wittenoom, Dr Collie (Colonial Surgeon), and George Moore on a further expedition during which they named the three townsites of Northam, York and Beverley at distances respectively of sixty-six, seventy-eight and ninety-eight miles from Perth. The river on which these centres were marked out and declared open for settlement was actually, as was discovered somewhat later, a continuation of the Swan, but having named it the Avon, as such it remained.

Settlers who had previously clamoured for larger holdings on the Swan and Canning rivers now began to look to this newly discovered country over the range. One can only conclude that Shaw decided, at this stage, to forgo all but his ten-acre block at Fremantle and the best 1,000 acres of his original 3,813-acre Swan block, taking out a grazing right or lease to the remaining 2,813 acres. In this way he gained legal entitlement to a further 7,096 acres in the recently opened area for which he at once applied to the Surveyor-General. Some time later, having had no reply to his letter, he went to Perth to interview Roe in person and was astonished to hear from him that his letter had not been received and that, in any case, all available land on the Avon had been allocated. Eliza records that Shaw 'did not take this very easily ... and spoke to the Governor upon it'.[11] Stirling had greeted him with characteristic courtesy, and advised him that James Henty had under option an Avon block about midway between the proposed townsites of York and Beverley, and that if he refused it the land should go to Shaw.

On hearing this Shaw was confident that the land was his, for he knew that the Hentys had fallen out with the Governor over the scattered nature of their land allocations and had become in any case sceptical of the settlement's ever succeeding as an agricultural proposition. They had therefore made up their minds to transfer their interests to Van Diemen's Land. This was generally acceded a loss to the colony as the Hentys were fine solid people and would, had they chosen to stay, have given added confidence and stability to the settlement. Shaw had heard of their decision with regret, but he saw now that it was to redound in his favour. He returned to

Belvoir bearing an official document entitling him to 7,096 acres with a considerable river frontage.

As it happened the Rev Wittenoom, who had a prior claim, decided at this juncture that he preferred 5,000 acres of the original Henty block to an adjoining area of the same size that he had been previously granted. Before so doing the reverend gentleman had expressed at least a token scruple that a man of the cloth should aspire to be a landholder. He had, however, allowed himself to be persuaded that it was his duty to provide for the future of his sons in a situation where they had little hope of entering the professions as they would have done at home. It was evidently with this principle in mind that he also allowed himself to take from his friend of the Fremantle beach what he considered the superior grant. The property came to be known as Gwambygine.

Shaw was accordingly given the 5,000 acres vacated by Wittenoom, keeping only 2,096 acres of the Henty selection.[12] The deal had been transacted in the nick of time for soon afterwards a new regulation was brought out by which no further land was to be given away in the colony and none sold by the crown under 5s an acre.

> Some think it a good regulation, [Eliza writes] others a bad one ... but I should say it should heighten the value of all our grants. They are asking immense prices for those on the Swan.[13]

From this account it might be supposed that the Shaws and other settlers lucky enough to have arrived in time to receive free allocations had their feet firmly planted on the ladder of fortune. Assuredly many were already finding compensations in their new lives, but the fact remained that the existence of the colony was extremely precarious. The British Government, apart from wishing it secure from foreign claims, apparently cared little for the present predicament or for the future welfare of its settlers. Stirling was still in the invidious position of a non-commissioned officer, and the land he and the botanist, Charles Fraser, had judged generally fertile from its abundant and attractive vegetation had so far proved to be of patchy quality, the natural shrubs and grasses almost useless for fodder, and although as yet unsuspected by the settlers, in some areas even poisonous. For the most part, as the Hentys had shrewdly deduced, the country was not generally suited to agriculture, and although a limited number of settlers might make out, few would make money—except from merchandise.

E W Landor who arrived in the colony some years later summed it up this way:

> My own opinion has ever been that colonists, with few exceptions, must always be poor men. They may possess large estates and numerous herds; but the more numerous these herds the less is their marketable value: for population and demand can never increase in equal ratio with the supply. A man therefore who possesses the element of wealth may still be poor in the article of money.
>
> Nor will his estates produce him more income than his herds; for in most cases the only rent which his tenants can afford to pay him is in kind. The only real wealth to a colonist is the incessant influx of immigration, combining capital and labour.[14]

But this necessary influx, too great to be coped with in the first tumultuous year, could no longer be counted on. Many settlers were leaving the colony and rumours, rife at home or at the Cape, that the enterprise had failed, dissuaded others from coming out or from continuing further.

In the meantime Stirling had appointed an Executive and Legislative Council. An Agricultural Society had been organized in the capital and Their Excellencies had issued invitations to the first ball to be held in the infant colony.

Chapter 7

August–September 1831

The Governor's Ball

Governor Stirling and wife visit Upper Swan. Invitations issued to ball at Government House. Preparations
for the great event. Journey to Perth. Assembly at home
of Colonial Secretary. The ball a brilliant gathering.
G F Moore composes song for the occasion.

However worried Stirling may have been, he presented, as he
moved briskly around the settlement, a front of unassailable
optimism and good cheer. Accompanied as often as possible
by his popular young wife, he visited all the scattered settlements by turn, cleverly managing to convey to each family that
it had merited his special interest and personal advice. He
praised each for its industry and commended the potential of
its land—not only in the hearing of those concerned but to
others who might be depended upon to repeat his remarks.
The Shaws, prejudiced at the time of their arrival, were by
this time full of praise and admiration for their first family.
'No persons,' declared Eliza, 'not even King William and
Queen Adelaide, are more popular in England than our Governor and his Lady are here.'[1]

In August, after the visit of Their Excellencies to the Upper
Swan, Eliza reported that they were most 'polite and affable',
while members of his party told her that he had many times
expressed the opinion that Shaw 'for his strength and means,
has exerted himself more than almost any other person in the
Colony'. To her considerable gratification Stirling had praised
their little homestead and expressed the opinion that their
block was second to none in the settlement, while his wife had
shown marked attention to the eleven-year-old Elizabeth. In
fact she even asked whether the child might spend a little

74

while with them in Perth. Eliza was pleased and flattered, but since no time had been specified she dismissed the suggestion as a kindly intention. It proved, however, to have been quite sincere. Despite her busy life with young children of her own, a complicated household to manage and many obligations, the Governor's Lady took the human aspects of her position very seriously. There seems to have been something about this bare-footed little girl, making her curtseys to the company, competently helping to serve the tea, that genuinely touched her heart. The child, although she could make bread, bake cakes, cook meals and mind the little ones, had been embarrassed to confess that she had hardly read any books and that her poor handwriting and spelling inhibited her in the matter of letter-writing. Eliza had had little time to attend to her children's education. Up at dawn, she worked inside and out until after dark. At night, by the poor light of an oil lamp, there was the bread to set, sewing to be done, letter-writing and book-keeping. Many outback mothers of later generations would have just as much to do, but they would be guided in educating their children by competent correspondence teachers, backed up by schools of the air. In those times there were no such aids and school books, in any case, do not seem to have figured in the Shaws' list of essentials.

> I am grieved that we have so little time to devote to the improvement of their minds, [Eliza writes] but, thank God, they appear to be naturally as good as the generality of young people and occasionally emit flashes of wit and good sense that would not disgrace the best educated.[2]

The Vice-regal visit was soon followed by an official invitation to Captain and Mrs Shaw, their son Nathaniel and their daughter Elizabeth to a ball to be held at Government House on 2 September. To this Mrs Stirling added a personal letter saying that although Elizabeth was so young, it would be a helpful step towards her debut if she could look on at this great occasion and be allowed to stay for a while at Government House after the ball.

Out of their moth balls came Will's regimentals and the finery in which Eliza had been presented at the Court of Their Majesties King William and Queen Adelaide. The gown required considerable letting out at seams and gussets for although the news had as yet been discreetly veiled in her correspondence, Eliza was at that time six months pregnant with her seventh child.

Elizabeth's wardrobe presented an even greater problem, especially in view of her extended invitation, for she had outgrown all the clothes she had brought from England. But Eliza was not one to be daunted on this account. Good frocks for which she had grown too stout herself, or for which she found little use in the colony, she cut down and refashioned, while Mrs Tanner came to light with a cherished length of book-muslin and a blue satin sash for a frock to be worn to the ball.

There was no need for concern about what poor Nat should wear, for it had at once been obvious that the attendance of other members of the family was entirely dependent on his staying to hold the fort. It says much for the character of this fifteen-year-old lad that he could be trusted not only with the care of the farm but, with the doubtful assistance of Anne Haggs, of the younger children as well. His schooling, like that of the others, had been completely neglected since leaving England and his chances of acquiring social graces since arriving in the colony had been almost nil. Little wonder that despite his dutiful compliance and dependability there was already a hint of bitterness in his attitude. Chided by his father for some lapse of etiquette unbefitting a young gentleman of quality, Nat had replied that he was in fact nothing but a labourer, to which exchange Eliza had added the pious rejoinder: 'But are we not all labourers in His vineyard?'

In the meantime Eliza records:

Our Colonial Secretary, next to the Governor the first man of consequence in the Colony, and his lady, Mrs Brown, who have ever shown us the most marked and friendly attention had written to say they would fully expect us at their house where beds etc, were prepared for us during the festivities.[3]

The Tanners invited the Shaws and Brockmans to travel down river in their boat. Eliza writes brightly of the expedition but was evidently not well enough to enjoy it and was besides haunted by memories that the river held of her still-recent loss. They broke their journey at Guildford, stayed overnight at the home of the Boyds and next day arrived at the home of the hospitable Browns on the corner of what were already known as Hay and Irwin Streets.

It seems to have been generally realized that there was more to this ball than a mere social occasion, for prospects in the colony had never been lower. It was obviously a valiant attempt on the part of the Governor and his Lady to raise the morale of the settlers by showing that, isolated though they were, something of the tradition and elegance of the Old World was still possible here. However far away, they were still a part of the glorious Empire that ruled the waves and whose people, hard though they might have to work, never, never, never would be slaves.

No one appears to have asked who was paying for this grand party. The Colonial Exchequer certainly did not provide for such things as entertainment. It would therefore appear that the expense was borne by the Stirlings themselves and since they were not at all well off it must have been a considerable strain on their resources.

As so many settlers had come to town for the ball the day was chosen for the first annual dinner of the Agricultural Society that had been formed during that year.

All Perth was alive [writes the Shaws' good neighbour George Fletcher Moore]. Upwards of fifty sat down to the Agricultural dinner at which we had (as Honourable Members) Lord F Beauclerk, Col Hanson and Captain Parker, RN.[4]

These three gentlemen, recently arrived from India on HMS *Cruiser*, said that they had heard the most gloomy reports of the colony, while the invalid Colonel Hanson confessed that when coming ashore he had considered the expediency of sending some provisions from the ship. He was amazed therefore at seeing ample supplies of butter, eggs, vegetables, poultry and butcher's meat. One gathers that the best of everything in the colony had been kept and produced for this festive occasion, as shortages were elsewhere recorded as being very real.

Eliza tells how after dinner at the Browns a number of people assembled in their drawing-room before proceeding to Government House, among them Colonel Hanson, Quartermaster-General of the Army in Madras, and the young naval lieutenant, Lord Frederick Beauclerk, adding lustre to the occasion. Mr Thomas Peel was in the party and so was Captain Bannister, a Sussexman who had arrived on the *Atwick* in October 1829, and had been overland to King George Sound, the prospects of which area he had not since ceased to extol. Also present with his daughter was Mr George Leake, one of the rich investors Eliza had not long since deplored but whom she now found to be a man of culture and charm. Then, too, there was Captain Dance of the *Sulphur* and his wife, who in August 1829 had had the honour of striking the first blow to a tree cut down to mark the foundation of the town of Perth. Colonel Hanson once more expressed his astonishment at the standard of living and the culture and elegance of the company he had so far encountered. In these sentiments he was apparently quite genuine, as on his return to India he was to write at length extolling the charms and advantages of Swan River Settlement as a health resort.

The stirring strains of the military band could be heard striking up from Government House, a few hundred yards away, as they proceeded merrily, the gentlemen carrying lanterns to light the ladies over wheel ruts in the unmade road and steer them around prickly shrubs that encroached on to the thoroughfare.

Eliza reports ecstatically on the brilliantly lit scene and tasteful decorations. She was charmed also to have had the honour of Mr Brown's arm—Mr Brown let it be repeated being second in status only to the Governor—as the 180 guests were ushered in to pay their devoirs to Their Excellencies. Stirling in his full-dress uniform cut a handsome and commanding figure, beside him his lovely lady, her gown low-cut over her perfect shoulders, jewels sparkling at her throat, her dark eyes aglow with friendly greeting.

According to Eliza the splendid and fashionable dressing 'would not have disgraced a first rate assembly at home' and the visitors were amazed that so many of the guests could dance the latest quadrilles, Spanish dances, waltzes and gallopades in such fine style.

Occasionally, however, [she tells us] in the course of the evening, two sets of old-fashioned country dances were called for, for those who did not dance quadrilles etc—so anxious were the Governor and his Lady to make all happy and enjoy themselves.[5]

George Fletcher Moore records that he:

never before witnessed such gaiety at a ball nor ever danced so much in one night; four rooms and an arcade were all filled, and connected with the verandah; a superb tent was filled up, decorated and festooned with naval flags, and in this we had supper—an elegant and abundant one.[6]

The banqueting rooms, thrown open at midnight, were, in Eliza's words:

so tastefully arranged that all seemed the effect of magic. Three large tables groaned with delicacies that would not have disgraced our Mother Country. In fact, for that evening at least you might have fancied yourself in reality at Home. The champagne sparkled and so did the eyes and jewels of many of our Australian dames.[7]

After the company had drunk the health of Their Majesties, the Governor called a gallant toast to the 'Ladies of the Colony who had so nobly and cheerfully borne fatigues and hardships with their husbands, among whom none had roughed it more than Mrs Stirling herself.'

Then came what many later recalled as the highlight of the occasion—a song composed by George Fletcher Moore, who had already won himself the reputation of being the first Bard of the settlement. It was sung to the tune of the rollicking Irish ballad 'Ballinamona Oro'.

From the old Western World we have come to explore,
The wilds of this Western Australian shore,
In search of a country we've ventured to roam,
And now that we've found it, let's make it our home.

And what though the colony's new, Sirs,
And inhabitants yet may be few, Sirs,
They'll soon be increasing here too, Sirs,
So Western Australia for me.

With care and experience I'm sure 'twill be found
Two crops in the year we may get from the ground,
Good wood and good water, good flesh and good fish
Good soil and good clime, and what more could you wish.

Then let everyone earnestly strive, Sirs,
Do his best, be alert and alive, Sirs,
We'll soon see our Colony thrive, Sirs,
So Western Australia for me.

No furious South-Easterns—no burning simoom
Our harvests to blight, and our fruits to consume,
No terrible plague, nor no pestilent air
Our 'livers' to waste, though our lives they may spare.

Our skies are all cloudless and bright, Sirs,
And sweet is our lovely moonlight, Sirs,
Oh this is the clime of delight, Sirs,
So Western Australia for me.

No lions or tigers we here dread to meet,
Our innocent quadrupeds hop on two feet;
No tithes and no taxes, we here have to pay,
And our *geese* are all swans, as some witty folks say.

Here we live without trouble or stealth, Sirs,
Our currency's all sterling wealth, Sirs,
So here's to our Governor's health, Sirs,
And the Western Australia for me.

Although the colony had so far been known as Western Australia there had been considerable discussion on the subject of finding a more euphonius designation. Stirling himself is believed to have favoured 'Hesperia'—a land looking west—but Moore's song is said to have swayed opinion in favour of retaining the original name.

At the punning tribute to His Excellency in the last chorus, the guests bowed or curtseyed in his direction and the ladies thereupon withdrew. Eliza writes:

> If we might judge of the uproarious hazza-ing after we left the room, there were many toasts given and rapturously drank, but withal, when the gents again joined us, there were no marks of excess. Dancing again commenced and continued till dawn ...[8]

Long before this Eliza had made moves to leave but had found it quite impossible to get away from the merry company, all anxious to compare notes on the progress of the settlement, the mood, for that night at least, being one of general optimism.

> As for my little demoiselle, she was almost intoxicated, not with champagne, but with delight; the scene was altogether so novel and different from anything she had been accustomed to that all appeared enchantment to her. Several gents asked permission for her to dance, but of course she did not attempt such a thing. Two or three times Mrs Stirling in passing shook her by the hand and said 'You shall dance next ball. I'll teach you quadrilles myself.'[9]

At four in the morning a second supper was served and it was not until six that Eliza was at last permitted to tumble into bed. Elizabeth declared she was not in the least tired but even before her mother she was sound asleep—dreaming no doubt 'of book-muslin frocks, long sashes, music etc, etc!'

Only four hours later breakfast was served in the Browns' dining-room where Eliza, Mrs Brown and Miss Leake assembled to talk over the festivities.

> What was very singular ... there was neither quizzing nor scandal. Happiness and good feeling, one towards another, seemed to have taken possession of all and no ill will or ill nature dared even to shew their noses in Perth during the time we staid there.[10]

One cannot but admire the stamina of those early settlers— whether at work or play. Next day the Browns gave a large dinner party which was kept up until four o'clock the following morning!

Eliza, off-colour at the beginning of the journey and at one stage in half a mind to excuse herself from the festivities, returned to Belvoir refreshed in spirit and lighter at heart. She had left Elizabeth being made a great fuss of at Government House and although pressed herself to remain longer, had felt with Mrs Brockman and Mrs Tanner, each with a baby son, that 'real happiness to a mother was at home more than anywhere else, even if that home were but a mud edifice in the wilds of Western Australia.'[11]

Chapter 8

February–April 1832

The Lowest Ebb

Ships bypass Fremantle. Drastic shortages of supplies.
Letters long delayed. Captain Lilburn brings mail at
last. Birth of Lucy Ellen Shaw. Effects of environment
on servants and children. Shortage of women in the
settlement.

I never expected Turkey carpets or marble chimney pieces
to await our arrival in this remote spot. Though, by the
bye, had I been aware of the full extent of all to be undergone in the first instance I might have shrunk from it
appalled ... The colony is now in that state not to warrant
parties even at Government House.[1]

Thus wrote Eliza to the Waghornes in January 1832, when the
settlement had reached its lowest ebb up to that time. The
sad fact was that although over one and a half thousand people
had left the United Kingdom for Australia in the past year
only a handful had stopped off at Fremantle. The rest had
either by-passed the Swan River altogether or, lured by reports of big profits to be made from wool in a free-for-all
squatters' paradise, had sailed on to the eastern colonies. By
the beginning of 1832, where once the arrival of ships at Fremantle had been a commonplace, week after week anxious
eyes gazed out to sea in vain for sight of a sail.

By this time there was no food in the colony except what
could be locally grown and this was procurable only by those
in a position to barter. Stirling, sorely pressed, had dispatched
HMS *Sulphur* to procure provisions from Van Diemen's
Land, but on arrival the Captain was informed—from interested motives it was believed—that the settlement had since

been abundantly supplied by two vessels from Calcutta. Incredibly, the Captain believed this unlikely report and returned empty-handed.[2]

But far worse than their physical hunger was the settlers' hunger for news from home. Swan River mail, with parcels and personal cargo, sent soon after their departure from England on ships that had failed to call at Fremantle would later be found dumped at Hobart Town, while many letters written early in 1831 were to reach them via Van Diemen's Land at the end of 1833!

> Oh! [Moore exclaims, voicing the sentiments of the Swan River community at large] that the tedious, horrible gap of four or five months voyage could be condensed or compressed, or done away with in some way! Eight or ten months clipped out of a man's life at any time of life is unendurable to think of![3]

The Shaws had pinned their hopes on mail being delivered to them in person by Captain Lilburn on the next visit of the *Egyptian* but had been grieved, late in 1831, to hear that their good friend had died near the end of his previous voyage home. He was personally to have delivered their last letters to the Waghornes, advised them when the *Egyptian* was next sailing and picked up dispatches from Thrussington before departure. Now their friends' chances of either receiving mail from Australia or knowing how and when to send it were problematical.

Eliza was later to write:

> How we wondered and surmised whether you would see the advertisement that the *Egyptian* was coming out ... In fact we worried ourselves almost to death with thinking.[4]

Then came a joyful message from Will Brockman just returned from meeting his brother at Fremantle. What had been his surprise to find the *Egyptian* in command of none other than Captain Lilburn himself—not a ghost but robust flesh and blood! It was another ship's captain of the same name who had died of recent months. Captain Lilburn had sent a message by Brockman asking that Shaw proceed to Fremantle without delay and inviting him to take a short holiday on board. Will set off on foot to Fremantle with all possible speed while Eliza, confined to bed by the recent arrival of her first Australian-born baby and almost blind from ophthalmia, awaited his return, hardly daring to hope that he would bring their long-awaited mail.

Shaw did not, of course, stay to enjoy a rest on the comfortable ship, for the Captain had brought not only mail but parcels and boxes of every shape and size. He returned in the utmost haste and at sight of his wife's drawn and anxious face, was completely overcome.

> I could not ask, [Eliza writes] and for many, many minutes he could not tell me he had letters and parcels for us. I shall never forget what I went through. To this minute I have not properly recovered from the excitement. Captain Lilburn has behaved in the most friendly way in everything and I hope he will be here tomorrow.[5]

Thoughtful gifts for everyone emerged from those boxes from Thrussington. There were also letters, not only from their friends at Frisby but from Eliza's sisters Caroline and Sophie to whom Captain Lilburn had conveyed news of the Shaw bereavement. They were, Eliza declared, 'the most sisterly letters that I have received since my marriage', even though Caroline had insisted on referring stiffly to Will as 'Mr Shaw'. 'In fact,' she continues, 'the packets and parcels I have now received from England have been the most welcome, most gratifying and least expected I ever heard of'.[6]

Among them had numbered articles of merchandise purchased for their personal use or barter by Robert Casson, to whom Eliza wrote separately expressing her abundant thanks:

> For a confirmed old bachelor you are the best caterer I know. Your muslin I sold readily for 3s per yard. I could get 2s 6d per yard for calico but I have made it up for necessary garments; the flannel also at 3s ... the needles etc, are a great treasure.[7]

It would appear that the Shaws' friends had rallied to their assistance in a very practical way and that the goods sent out to them had been purchased from the generous contributions of numerous well-wishers. A letter from Will Shaw to Sir Frederick Fowke, written at this time,[8] expresses their profound thanks for favours 'never to be repaid either by acts or words'. He begs Sir Frederick to convey his thanks 'to Her Grace the Duchess Dowager and the Duke of Rutland and to any other lady or gentleman you may have promoted to contribute'. He tells his friends that thanks to the provisions thus supplied they are 'for a time replenished, in not only the necessities of Life but some of its Luxuries'. Nor does he miss the opportunity of again encouraging his friends to join them:

The Cloud which overhangs my Native Land, indeed the whole of Europe, but too often prompts me to wish my Friends were here. The climate upon the whole is beautiful and the land when cultivated will produce most abundantly all the Necessities of life and most of the Eastern Luxuries. Should therefore any of your family feel a disposition to roam I trust this Colony may be their destiny. Our little Band of Heroic Settlers are generally of a class far above mediocrity and indeed though we have had and still have a great struggle to make we must one day be great in the Scale of Nations.

Curiosities: I have none to send you at this time, nor have any here been able to rear the Black Swan or indeed the Kangaroo. Animals and Birds are become extremely scarce.

I propose sending a Power of Attorney in order to raise a few Hundreds upon my property here with either the Official Government Documents or Attested Copies entitling me to my Several Estates in which I have taken the liberty of inserting your name in case anything should happen to my friend Waghorne or Casson coming out to me.[9]

Shaw makes reference in this same letter to some wrong done him by an unnamed 'Revd Gentn,' whom 'God Knows' he has long since forgiven but who now appears to have slighted Sir Frederick perhaps for campaigning on his behalf. Eliza writing to the Waghornes at the same time also refers obliquely to this matter. She thanks her good friends 'for more than life, viz, reputation and refutation of calumny and misrepresentation of character'.[10]

To the Shaws' inexpressible joy Captain Lilburn came up the river to visit them and to take delivery of their mail for England, bringing with him personal presents for his favourite colonial family. The gifts included 'a beautiful Tuscan straw bonnet from his own daughter to Elizabeth ... the handsomest in the colony'.

Eliza, to whom the arrival of mail had been the most effective tonic imaginable, got up and dressed carefully to welcome their generous friend, anxious that he should return with a cheerful report. ('How gratifying to see him and to hear that he has actually seen and conversed with you!') She must have taken it for granted that he would break the news of the recent arrival, then only a week old, for she writes without any preliminary:

> I never was so well in so short a time after a confinement. I fancy I hear you say 'for shame, you have no business with such things at your time of life!' Certainly not Mrs Wisdom, *but such accidents will happen* in the best regulated families, and I am as great a fool with this seventh bantling as if it were my first. Shaw and I have had quite a fight—though no blows have passed yet—on what her name is to be. He says 'Lucy.' I say I have heard you say a hundred times that you dislike your name and I know you loved your mother. I therefore say she shall be 'Ellen'—also after your Ellen *Lucy shall be the next*! Don't you think! I grow worse in my old age?[11] [The child was eventually christened Lucy Ellen.]

She is writing with the wing feather of a wild turkey recently killed by Nat for the family pot, and there being no ink available in the colony she has concocted some from her own recipe—'the sap of a tree mixed with rust from nails, a little sulphate of zinc etc'. Her letter, rambling on over many pages, continues to make light of their difficulties: 'We have now no servants, male or female. Vive la Liberté!'[12]

Markram, she explained, was then working his passage back to England and if he were to visit them on arrival with a tale of woe he should not be believed. He had 'behaved very ill'.

Nor had she any kind words for the 'good for nothing' Anne Haggs. She had run away once, for no given reason, soon after the loss of the two boys. The next time she had gone off 'after a lover or fancied lover'—a young soldier of the 63rd Regiment who had died while she was making her way on foot to visit him at Fremantle. Eliza, warm-hearted and tolerant enough in many respects, shows little sympathy for the unhappy girl, who had all this time been awaiting a letter from her mother with no doubt as much longing as her employers for news of their own dear ones. Picked up at last, destitute and friendless, she had been brought before the Magistrate who had frightened her into returning, though she had since made off with yet another soldier man, and what became of her in future was her own business. The only concession Eliza was prepared to make in the case was that 'a parish workhouse is a bad school'.

There is only one instance in the documents of early Western Australian settlement of a servant girl's relating her own story. She was Amelia Blagg, aged fourteen, daughter of a struggling school-mistress of Greenwich, engaged as nursemaid to the six children of the DuBois Agetts. She wrote to her parents in May 1831: 'Soon after we came on shore two of our men and women servants left us, consequently I was made a slave to all the family not only suffering from their ill treatment but all the clothes you gave me they made me cut up because they were too fine for me as a servant ... One day I was cooking and some straw caught fire owing to the wind blowing that way but was put out. Mrs Agett immediately called me the most scandalous names. She persuaded Mr Agett to send for the Constable to take me to prison but he was so shocked at her brutality that he allowed me to remain with his wife that night. Next day I was brought before three magistrates and a great concourse of people. I was cross questioned and all were much surprised at Mrs Agett's brutality. Mr Leek [Leake] the head Magistrate said I was pronounced not guilty and that if he had not already engaged with a servant he would have taken me into his family. I was taken in by a perfect stranger'.[13] At the time of writing the girl was hoping to get another situation and explained that she had been prevented by her employers from writing before. This letter was forwarded by Amelia's mother to the Secretary of State for

Colonies with a covering note explaining why she was unable to afford her passage home. The outcome is unknown.

While on the subject of servants, Eliza asked the Waghornes to remember them to those splendid people who had served them in England—'the worthy Alice Brown of Thrussington, Bet Bradshaw, our good washerwoman, Martha Horner and her husband of Belgrave—old and faithful servants. I wish,' she adds, 'that they would come out to us here. It would be a fortune to them and they would be well provided-for for their lives'.[14]

It did not occur to Eliza that these admirable retainers would have probably undergone the same sea change as other servants in the colony, for the old régime was hard to maintain where master and servant lived under the same roof and often shared the same table. Here for the first time people of 'the lower orders' conceived the blinding vision of an egalitarian state in which opportunity might be the same for all and where not only members of the gentry were entitled to acquire land. Already there were some in the colony soon to become more affluent and influential than the families they had come out to serve.

Nor were servants the only ones to be curiously affected by the new environment. The Shaws, like other settlers, had become aware that their young people were showing signs of a precocious maturity. Of Nat Eliza wrote that he had no sooner turned sixteen than he was 'setting himself up as seventeen as though anxious to rush from youth into the cares and trials of manhood'.[15] One gathers that Nat's own accounts of life in the colony, passed around by Johnnie Gamble, had caused their friends some concern. Having promised to write the truth as he saw it, he must have done so with a lack of the restraint and perspective that his parents were so careful to observe.

'Young people,' Eliza writes, 'are always apt to see things in a different light to what is intended.' In this she was no doubt referring to Nat's resentment of his father's criticism. What, he asked, if he should lack the pretty ways of British gentlefolk, if his manners were gauche and his speech had developed a cockney turn? How could his parents expect otherwise, since when they visited their fine friends he must stay at home with the servants and feed the pigs? When the Shaws had visitors he was lucky to receive as much as a nod, being usually mistaken, in his rough working-clothes and bare feet, for a hired man.

> At one time, [his mother writes] nothing in the colony pleased him. Even now he does *not think that hard work is easy* ... Upon the whole he has not done amiss since he came here, though he is now just entering his puppyhood and sometimes gives far more trouble than his poor old dad, who takes things very coolly and will not be diverted from doing as he thinks proper by sometimes rather stormy remonstrance when things don't exactly please my *Royal Highness*.[16]

Elizabeth, too, had developed surprisingly. A thoughtless child on her arrival in the colony only two years before, she was now, though still barely thirteen years old, almost a grown woman, with opinions of her own—not always shared by her parents—and a sense of responsibility beyond her years. After the grand ball of August 1831, she had stayed on for two months with the Governor and his wife who were genuinely attached to her and she to them. In fact she had been pressed to remain indefinitely, taking lessons from Mrs Stirling and accompanying them on their journeys to outlying settlements. Tempting though the proposal had been, the girl, knowing her mother to be near her time, had elected to return and had since taken on the task of nursemaid as a matter of course.

This, while a comfort to Eliza, was also the cause of some apprehension, for how long, she wondered, might she count on her daughter's support with marriageable women the scarcest commodity in the colony? She wrote home of the problem lightheartedly enough, but as everyone in the settlement knew it was a very real one:

> As soon as I get about again I mean to set about a *Ladies' Memorial* to King William asking him to *award a handsome premium as well as a pension* to all of us who, for the good of the colony, have presented it with young females. They are so scarce here that Mrs Tanner and myself have promised to get the gents a cargo of young ladies sent out!

But lest her friends might take this remark too seriously she then made haste to add:

All the neighbours round here are men of good family, have moved in the first circles in England and Ireland—yet I should be sorry, for some time at least, to see any young friends of mine out here, for upon the prudent and well selected choice of a husband depends entirely the happiness or misery of a girl's life ... Love in a cottage reads well in a novel but is not quite so pretty when reduced to every day practice.[17]

In the meantime the young men of the colony must look for their women elsewhere. Already black mothers in the outlying camps, puzzled by their pale-skinned babies, were rubbing them with charcoal and when this proved to no avail sadly returning them to their spirit ancestors.

Chapter 9

1831–1832

Yagan—'The Wallace'

Aboriginal population. Customs puzzling to settlers.
One-sided nature of new régime. Raids and reprisals.
R M Lyon defends tribespeople. Governor Stirling
returns to England at settlers' request. Yagan—Abori-
ginal 'Wallace'. Lyon reports to Downing Street. Joins
Yagan and fellow prisoners on Carnac Island.

Up to this time Eliza had made little reference to a problem
that was every day increasing in complexity and could no
longer be thrust aside. This was the relationship between the
settlers and the Aborigines.

Early estimates of the Aboriginal population were soon seen
to have been greatly exaggerated. Instead of numbering up to
13,000 as at first suggested, it was later thought more likely
that the tribes around Swan River, Augusta and King George
Sound did not exceed 1,000 people all told.[1]

Fears for the safety of their womenfolk that had preoccupied
the settlers during the first year or so were set aside as it began
to seem that the tribesmen wanted no more from the white
women than food and cast-off clothing. Nothing in the Aboriginal culture as yet made sense to the average settler, their
sexual behaviour least of all. On the one hand it seemed that
the gratification of sex in this curious society was subject to
tribal disciplines that made the European system appear hap-
hazard and permissive in the extreme. On the other hand it
was apparently the custom for an Aborigine to offer his wife
to another—black or white—as a gesture of trust and friendship or as an article of trade.

Having welcomed back their 'jumped-up white' relations to
the haunts of their previous existence, they had hospitably

withdrawn from the river frontages, returning occasionally only to visit or to fish, and it had seemed to the settlers that they would soon reach a satisfactory *modus vivendi*. Early in 1831 George Fletcher Moore wrote to his family:

> The natives are not so despicable a race as was at first supposed. They are active, bold and shrewd, expert in thieving, as many have experienced; they are courageous when attacked; however they are not very numerous, and we are on good terms with them. I walk occasionally to and from Perth, through the woods, alone and unarmed; so you may perceive ... we are not in much dread of them.[2]

Before long, however, the distinctly one-sided nature of this black/white relationship began to worry the easy-going sons and daughters of the Bibbulmun tribe. It seemed that the white man considered himself entitled to everything the black man possessed—not only his sacred waters and his ancient hunting grounds but all the wild life that had been maintained through the ages by the sacred increase rites of the tribal elders. He even found himself forbidden the ancient custom of firing portions of the bush during the summer months—a process by which the hunters not only flushed out the kangaroos and lizards from the thicket but encouraged new growth and hence more game in the coming season. In return for such loss of land and liberty the native had been guaranteed the protection of a law he did not understand and the benefits of a civilization he did not want. He soon discovered however that he liked the taste of the white man's food, whether the stores that arrived by magic from somewhere far away or the good things that sprang from the seeds he had sown in the ground. But even here there was a catch that the black man could not have foreseen, for to obtain these benefits he was forced into the roles of either beggar or servant that were never played in tribal life. If he refused to beg or to serve he must either go without or he must steal—*queeple*, as he called it—an act uncommon in tribal life, since, except for his women, no man had anything much another might desire.

In order to make himself understood, the black man tried hard to pick up the white man's tongue. Living as he did in a multi-lingual society he had an aptitude for languages, but the process, with a minimum of co-operation—the white man mistaking this eagerness to imitate the new sounds as aimless 'mimicry'—took time. The white man did most of the talking, anyway. Having picked up an Aboriginal word here and there and acceded the black man's difficulty in coping with the latter 'S', a spokesman for the Governor, as recorded by George Fletcher Moore, addressed the tribespeople in this way:

> Blackfella pear white man, white man poot. Blackfella queeple no good. Blackfella pear black fella no good ... Blackfella give him white man wallabies, water come here, wood come here [fetch wood and water] white man plenty shake hands black man, plenty give him bikkit, plenty ehtah, plenty blanket, rice, tomahawk.[3]

It was all very well for the Governor to make such promises but the truth was that the settler could not afford plenty food, blankets and tomahawks in return for peaceful behaviour or the occasional odd job. Still, it was only after a teen-age Aboriginal boy was shot dead for attempting to steal a melon that real trouble flared up. Vengeance was immediately exacted by a party of natives, unfortunately against the wrong man who was discovered in the cottage from which the shot was fired. The military was called out and stealthily surrounded the natives' camp at night—only to find it deserted when they closed in upon it at dawn. After that the natives, who had hitherto moved freely about the township and outlying settlements, completely vanished. The settlers hoped they had removed themselves to some remote back country where they could pursue their tribal lives without disturbing the white community. It was not understood that the local groups were being forced to encroach on their neighbours' boundaries, causing a breakdown of the finely-balanced tribal ecology. This process had already become the cause of a good deal of fighting among the natives themselves who, fortunately for the whites, made no attempt to stand together in their grievances.

Before long the sporadic raids on the settlers' stock became commonplace, and it was realized that the dark people, if seldom seen, were never far away. From early in 1832 Will

Shaw and son Nat, sometimes joining forces with indignant neighbours Tanner, Brockman, Moore and the brothers Burges, spent a good deal of time and energy trying to catch up with natives who had got away with sheep, pigs and poultry. Their efforts, however, seem to have resulted in nothing more satisfactory than a good hard ride and the occasional discovery of evidence. Moore describes one such chase in company with Will Shaw, when after a two hours' ride they found '*horresco referens*—the Bloody Head—of one of the missing pigs'. To this he added, with more tolerance than was displayed by the average settler, that 'Perhaps these uninformed creatures think they have as good a right to our swine as we to their kangaroos; and the reasoning, if such there be, may be plausible enough; however if we had caught them *flagrante delicto*—in the act of slaughtering them—I would not answer for the force of it.'[4]

In May of that year a meeting was held in Guildford to discuss what was to be done about the natives whose depredations were declared to be 'truly alarming and disheartening'. As a result, strong resolutions were presented to the Governor whose lenient policy towards the Aborigines the settlers felt was at the expense of their property and their personal safety. In answer to previous protests the Governor had appointed additional Magistrates and had established a military barracks with a small party of soldiers at the head of the Swan, but these measures the settlers held to be more or less ineffectual. Some even declared that they would have to abandon the colony if not permitted to defend their interests. The Governor heard their plea with sympathy but refused to rescind his policy of Aboriginal protection, which was indeed a firm direction from the Home Government.

It was at this stage that R M Lyon entered the arena in defence of the indigenous people. He delivered at a meeting of settlers what Moore describes as 'a grand palaver', and propounded a scheme by which he believed the natives would soon embark on a new life of Christian civilization and usefulness.

Lyon's eloquence was not to be despised:

Gentlemen, [he said] have you a Fatherland? So have the Aboriginal inhabitants of this country. Have you the rights of men? What has expunged theirs from the book of nature? Their lands have descended to them from time immemorial and their title deeds require not the wrangling of lawyers to prove them correct. They have the Seal of Heaven, the sanction of Him who divided unto the nations their inheritance ... Reflect! ... Beware! ...[5]

But the speaker would seem to have known that while emotional appeals to fair play might not make much impression on the harassed settlers, a possible solution to their labour problems must surely interest them. He proceeded therefore to prophesy that the Aborigines properly handled, could become in time 'a useful peasantry, thus defraying the expenses of bringing the labouring poor from English villages'. His proposal that a request be sent to the Church of England Missionary Society for the help of teachers to instruct and train the Aborigines gained the support of the meeting.

In July 1832 another meeting was called, this time resulting in a request to the Governor to proceed to England and put in person to the Colonial Office the truth about conditions in the colony. Among the complaints he was asked to voice were lack of labour, lack of funds or other support from the Home Government, and of endless delay caused by Stirling's having to refer every matter to London rather than make decisions on the spot. To this Stirling readily agreed, for although his commission as full Governor had been granted in the previous year, the Home Government still allowed him little freedom of action and showed no more understanding of local problems than before. He sailed the following month with his wife and family, leaving Captain Irwin, Commander of the local military detachment, to act for him during his absence.

Irwin not only inherited the full weight of the Governor's ordinary duties but also a particular problem that had been building up over the past year—namely, what to do with a formidable and intelligent Aboriginal named Yagan. This man was the son of Midgigeroo, leading elder of the tribal territory of Beeliar, bounded by the Swan and Canning rivers and extending south of Perth to Fremantle. His mother was a powerful matriarch known as Moyran who had warned her people from the beginning that no good would come of their extending a welcome to these 'Djanba'—white spirits of the dead—in whom she for one recognized no trace of Aboriginal origin. Day and night from the time the settlers arrived her wail had gone up from the river banks: *'Djanba meenya boomiggur.'* ('The smell of the Djanba is killing us!')

It had been Yagan and his parents who exacted vengeance for the boy shot in Mr Butler's melon patch, and who had some time later avenged another death by spearing an innocent farmer on the Canning River. At the insistence of the settlers, Yagan and his father were thereafter deprived of protection and a price was put on their heads. This worried neither of them since they knew that no white man could catch them while they were on their guard. Yagan, however, jeopardized his position by placing complete trust in the loyalty of certain settlers whom he had elected as friends or relatives. As a result, not long after the Governor's departure, he and two companions were lured into a boat by a couple of supposed white friends who promptly delivered them into an ambush of the 63rd Regiment.

Hearing of the capture, Lyon wrote immediately to the *Perth Gazette* explaining that the two murders in which Yagan had been implicated were matters of tribal honour and carried out in accordance with his threat to take a life for a life. 'He must,' Lyon contended, 'be ranked among the princes of the country. He has greatly distinguished himself as a patriot and a warrior. He is in fact "The Wallace of the Age".'

Writing to the Secretary of State for Colonies about this time, Lyon had expounded at length on the character of the Aborigines declaring that 'in simplicity of manners, generousness of disposition and firmness of character, they very much resemble the ancient Caledonians, and were the disbelievers in the authenticity of Ossian[6] to become acquainted with them they would almost be persuaded to adopt the opposite opinion, so much do the inhabitants of the Australian forests resemble the race whose songs were sung by the bard of Morwen.'[7] Lyon had also much to say in the same letter of the absurdity of pretending to govern a people 'not only without their consent but without a knowledge of their language and without any person to act as interpreter'. In an attempt to remedy this need he had set about a study of local customs and languages that had won him some respect in the colony, and even though Moore remarked of his careful list of 'lost sounds' that 'it would be a pity if some were ever found again', he was none the less impressed by Lyon's erudition. In his correspondence with Downing Street Lyon announced that he had come to the conclusion that twenty-two characters were requisite to form an Aboriginal alphabet—'precisely the number of characters which compose the Hebrew alphabet. The *ain* of the Hebrew, the genuine pronunciation of which has been so long a desideratum of the philologists of Europe, these people seem to possess in perfection. But they have neither the *zain*, the *samech* nor the *shin* of the Hebrew ... I have reason to fear the existence of a good deal of irregularity both in the declension of the nouns and the conjugation of the verbs. The task therefore of moulding this strange language and giving it a niche in the temple of literature does not promise to be an easy one.'[8]

In the course of his research he claimed to have learned from the natives of rich lands, lakes and rivers to the north and had actually written to Downing Street offering his services— at £200 a year—to lead a party of exploration in that direction:

> Tell the King, my Master, [he had bidden the Prime Minister] that one who served his father and his brother is now employed in subduing to the British Sceptre an Empire of Natives in Australia and though it be sable, when adorned with the virtues of Christianity, will be one of the brightest gems in the British Crown ... (Pray excuse pen, ink and paper, we have no better in the colony ...)[9]

Lyon did not, of course, restrict the subject matter of his correspondence to the Aborigines. He had advice to offer on every aspect of colonial development and devoted many pages to such matters as the superior potential of Western Australia to any other of the British colonies, to the type of migrants who should be sent out and the finance required for their efforts to flourish:

> Here, [he informed the Secretary of State] is employment for the millions of your dormant capital. Here is an outlet for the surplus population of the British Isles ... You but waste your time in legislating for the accumulating evils of a redundant population ... Every pauper you send here in-

stantly ceases to be a burden to the mother country, exchanges his poverty for wealth and becomes a consumer of your manufactures. But ... send us none of your quacks in morals, philosophy or politics. Send your Malthuses to the deserts of Africa or the jungles of India and let them herd with the lions of Biledulgerid or the tigers of Bengal. It will be a just punishment for the insult they have offered to Heaven by libelling the wisdom of the Supreme. Your O'Connells, your Shields and your Cobbetts I would send to Rome, Vienna and Constantinople, and there, if they can manage to keep out of the hands of their friends, the Pope and the Sultan, there will be abundant scope for their oratorical powers.[10]

The writer then launches into an elaborate proposal by which he undertakes to disburden his mother country of 500 of her surplus population annually for the sum of £10,000 a year which he guarantees to repay with interest in twenty years' time.

Give us the loan of bank notes at a reasonable rate of interest on the security of our land and we will ... turn them into gold. Many of those for whom you are solicited to do this have watched Messina from the lines of Torres Vedras, chased Soult through Spain and fought at Corunna, Salamanca and Vittoria and they will leave a race behind them here who inspired by the spirit of their fathers may fight for Britain as well in the East and in the South ...[11]

After several letters of this description Lyon had received a curt reply to the effect that 'Captain Stirling having, since his return, furnished the Department with ample information on every subject with the settlement, Mr Stanley thinks it no longer necessary to give you the trouble of continuing your correspondence ...[12]

Truth to tell, Stirling had grown weary of Lyon's loquacity and his grandiose schemes, and had no doubt warned the Secretary of State not to take him too seriously. Captain Irwin, however, had given him a good hearing when he sought an interview to discuss Yagan's arrest. He suggested that he be allowed to accompany Yagan and his two countrymen to some place of custody where he could introduce them to the tenets of Christianity and the white man's law. The idea appealed to Irwin, himself a man of deep religious principles, and he agreed that the Aborigines be sent to a prison that had been set up on Carnac Island a few miles south of Fremantle.

Chapter 10

1832–July 1833

Death of a Patriot

Yagan escapes and makes truce with Lieut-Governor Irwin. Lyon reports on Colonial Secretary's 'hostility'. Further shootings and reprisals follow short-lived peace. Arrest of Midgigeroo. Yagan interviews G F Moore. Midgigeroo executed. Yagan takes revenge. Yagan shot by W Keates for reward of £30. Apprehension mounts.

Over several weeks Lyon reported at length to the Lieutenant-Governor who transmitted the information to the anxious settlers. The experiment he declared to be growing every day more successful, his charges' savageness of disposition becoming mollified, their appearance orderly and their conduct at Divine Service most edifying. While being instructed in the English Language, Yagan in turn instructed his teacher in his native tongue. 'I have,' Lyon declared, 'my hand on the key that will unlock its hidden spring and disclose its treasures.'[1]

The next news from Carnac was not so reassuring for the three prisoners, while walking one day with their tutor, had espied at the water's edge a small dinghy in which they had contrived an escape to the mainland. Since none of them had ever handled a boat before, this was no mean feat, but what astonished the settlers still more was the nonchalance with which Yagan then strode into Perth and presented himself to the Lieutenant-Governor. In a quaint mixture of Aboriginal and his newly-acquired English, helped out by a wealth of eloquent gesture, Yagan laid down terms of a truce by which he guaranteed that black and white could live in harmony. He was not, he implied, among those of his countrymen who believed that the white people should be forced to return from whence they came; nor could he agree that the Swan and Canning natives should retreat to join other tribes beyond the outer limits of settlement. He had at once recognized Stirling as his long dead brother, James Drummond as the reincarnation of a tribal father, and Mr Bull and Will Shaw as other relatives, while George Fletcher Moore he respected as an important keeper of a law which should serve both black and white. Yagan explained his having previously thrust a spear through Moore's window, narrowly but deliberately missing his head, and another into his window-sill, as a warning that he should attend no more meetings such as one held in Guildford, at which settlers had spoken against the Aborigines.

Yagan's terms, as expressed to Irwin, were that his people were to receive regular rations in return for their lost hunting grounds and that they were not to be denied entry to the township or the fishing rights to their river frontages. The rations were to be given not as charity but as rightful payment and to be collected and distributed by himself. The tribespeople would then have no further need to raid the settlers' gardens or spear their stock. Despite current shortages, Irwin agreed to these terms and as a result the colony entered upon a short period of peace and harmony.

Yagan, now generally known as 'the Wallace', was often to be seen about the town, very fine in his red soldier's coat, sometimes offering to chop wood or cart water for his friends, once organizing his people to save a burning house. The *Perth Gazette* made frequent mention of his doings, remarking his good nature but warning the townsfolk that it could quickly turn to umbrage at the merest suggestion of an insult to himself or his people.

R M Lyon meanwhile continued to write at length to the *Perth Gazette* and to the Colonial Secretary giving advice and proposing schemes for the advancement of the natives. These suggestions included the removal of leading Aborigines and their families to Rottnest Island where they should be educated and trained in agricultural pursuits. His comments were apparently received with anything but appreciation by Peter Brown, for Lyon wrote again to the Secretary of State complaining of his attitude:

It remains for me [he declared] to name the only cause to

which the hostility of the Secretary is assignable. When Lieutenant Shaw, formerly of the 95th Rifle corps, arrived in the settlement—the mountains not having then been passed—the Governor had no land to give him unless he went to the south. This was impossible. He had not the means. In this distressing case Shaw had a large family and limited resources. I presented him with about 4,000 acres, a much admired grant on the Swan. Mr Shaw was a stranger to me but I felt for a man with so large a family who had served his country. The Secretary expected me to present *him* with the grant and consequently felt disappointed. I regret to say that no other reason can be assigned ... as the cause of the strange and impolite conduct of the Colonial Secretary in opposing my endeavours to pacify and ameliorate the condition of the native tribes ...[2]

In April 1833 Eliza Shaw, when sending the Waghornes some native artifacts (described by her little Mary as 'curiousosities'), wrote that their relationships with the Aborigines had greatly improved. The natives now came with offerings of kangaroo and wild game in exchange for 'wheat, bread or rice —whichever is convenient—and for which they are very grateful. I do trust,' she concludes, 'that we may from now on form a friendly communication. From my own personal knowledge I have discovered traits of character in them which would do honour to any European.'

But too soon again, overshadowing all other topics in the colony, was the fear of the Aboriginal and his well-aimed, if often mistakenly directed, spear. Yagan, the friendly 'Wallace', was once again the terror of the settlement. The period of truce had ended abruptly at the beginning of May when a visitor to the settlement, seeing a group of unoffending natives on the Canning Road, had drawn his rifle, remarking to his companion: 'Damn the rascals, I'll show you how we treat them in Van Diemen's Land!' He had thereupon opened fire, killing or wounding every member of the party. Yagan and his father, leading about fifty others of their tribe, had followed the fresh tracks of the returning cart and attacked the two occupants (neither of them the villain of the piece). A settler named Phillips described how, following in another cart, he heard from afar the angry chanting and stamping of feet that accompanied the blood dance of the outraged Bibbulmun. Peering through the trees he saw that Yagan, almost unrecognizable in his rage, had cast aside the body of his first victim and was plunging his spear again and again in that of the second, his old father Midgigeroo, blood-stained spear in hand, prancing in savage frenzy at his side.[3]

It was at this stage revealed that a young native who had been shot a few days before at Fremantle while making off with a loaf of bread had been none other than Yagan's brother Domjuim, to whom he was known to have a strong attachment. There was panic in the settlement for it was believed by many that Yagan was now capable of any outrage, and under pressure from the settlers, Lieutenant-Governor Irwin placed a price of £30 on his head—dead or alive—and £20 on that of Midgigeroo. The peaceful days were over for the settlement. There were no natives to be seen in the township, and week after week soldiers and settlers combining to flush them from the outlying bush beat about in an apparently deserted waste. Fears were by no means allayed when it became known that Midgigeroo had at last been captured and that Yagan had threatened to take three lives should any harm come to him.

At a trial, of which the defendant understood nothing, the old man was identified as having been implicated in at least four murders and sentenced to death. Some settlers recommended that his body be left hanging from a gibbet as a fearful lesson to his countrymen, but others gave timely warning of Yagan's probable reaction to news of the old man's execution. Midgigeroo, calling in vain for his son to his last breath, was discreetly shot and every effort made to keep his execution from reaching the ears of his countrymen.

Meanwhile Yagan, defiant in his peril, continued to visit his friends in the Upper Swan, questioning them closely concerning his father's whereabouts, and laughing over the many fruitless and clumsy efforts to lay hands on himself. In view of his threat to take three lives for that of his father, no one dared enlighten him, nor could those he trusted bring themselves to betray him. Towards the end of May he appeared one day at Millendon, in company with eight other tribesmen to interview George Moore, who interpreted his words as being to this effect:

You came to our country; you have driven us from our haunts and disturbed us in our occupations; as we walk in our own country we are fired upon by the white men; why should the white men treat us so?[4]

The scene, Moore said, reminded him of a chorus in a Greek tragedy, the other natives standing by as subordinate characters to their leading spokesman. Finally came the loaded question: 'Midgigeroo shoot?—walk?' When Moore evaded the question, Yagan repeated his threat to kill three men if harm had befallen his father.

During the later part of this conference, [Moore continues] he held a beautifully tapered and exquisitely pointed spear, grasped like a stiletto ... while the shaft lay over his shoulder with seeming carelessness. He evidently suspected treachery and was on his guard against it, taking care not to let my men press him too closely ... Nothing short of an overwhelming force (which I did not possess) or a cold-blooded, deliberate treachery (of which I was incapable) would have enabled me to secure him as he stood ... In the meantime this proclaimed and dangerous outlaw, with a price on his head and threats (not idle) on his tongue ... was suffered to escape unmolested. The truth is everyone wishes him taken but no-one likes to be his captor. There is something in his daring that one is forced to admire.[5]

Soon after this Yagan made it known that he had learned—or guessed—his father's fate and the *Perth Gazette* issued a warning:

Every man should now be on his guard. Yagan seems to possess the power of ubiquity. He has declared, and his are not idle threats, that he will take three lives for that of his father.

Within a week two soldiers connected with the arrest of Midgigeroo were found speared on the edge of the settlement. Still Yagan continued to visit his friends—the Bulls, Drummonds and Shaws on the Upper Swan—to all of whom he openly admitted the murders and wept when they begged him to refrain from taking a third. In mid-July, 1833, he agreed to the proposal of Mr Bull's two apprentices, James and William Keates, to go hunting as they had often done in the past. They killed and ate a kangaroo, and when the natives had lain down to sleep the older brother crept forward and shot Yagan through the head. The boy was speared instantly while the younger made his escape and conveyed the tragic news to his master. Lieutenant Bull called on George Moore and Will Shaw to help him with the burial of the dead youth. The body was conveyed to Belvoir and buried somewhere close to the property—possibly near the grave of the two Shaw boys. Will Shaw as JP for the district had been expected to read the burial service but the memory of his own lost boys was still fresh in his mind and, pleading the need of spectacles, he relegated the sad task to Moore.

After all, however, it was Yagan's death, or the manner of it, that was the more regretted by those who had come to respect, if not to understand, him. The *Gazette*, which had at first expressed some satisfaction at the news of Yagan's death,[6] was soon to have second thoughts, and to regret that his end should have come as a result of a 'wild and treacherous act'. Misgivings were expressed that what was in fact a 'rash and unadvised adventure of youth' should be held up as an example of courage to a rising generation. It was also remarked that Yagan, though undoubtedly vindictive, had shown certain noble tendencies and had never been known to abuse a confidence or betray a friendship.

The thirteen-year-old James Keates, with the £30 reward his elder brother did not live to claim, was promptly sent back to England.

On the day after the funeral Moore visited the home of Mr Bull, where he saw the head of Yagan which one of Bull's men had cut off in order to preserve it for the British Museum.

The features [he writes] were not in the least changed. He must have died instantaneously ... Yagan had a very particular mark of tattooing extending over his right shoulder and down his back, by which many settlers recognized him. He wore a soldier's old coat under his kangaroo cloak to hide this mark, as he had been often warned of its danger. This peculiar cicatrice was flayed from the body by the man who is preserving the head. I have rudely sketched this 'caput mortuum' which was ornamented by a twisted cord round the forehead.[7]

Once again settlers everywhere began reporting the killing and chasing of stock, and for the first time the deliberate firing of crops and outbuildings. Young Nat Shaw, pursuing a party of marauders, was speared through the thigh, causing him to be laid up for two weeks and to sustain a jagged wound.

A few weeks later the *Gazette* reported sadly:

> Contrary to expectation there is no relief felt at the passing of Yagan. Rather, among the more thoughtful elements in the community, there is regret and apprehension, for with his passing it is believed that we may bid goodbye to any hopes we have entertained of coming to reasonable terms with the local tribespeople. The power which this man wielded is now known to lie in the hands of his mother, a vindictive old harridan named Moyran who now incites her people to wholesale revenge, theft and larceny ... This state of affairs can only result in the final subjugation or virtual extermination of the south western Aborigines. Already the settlers are demanding stern protective measures that the Government cannot long deny them.

A sketch of Yagan's head was included in a small book by Ensign Dale published in England in 1834. This must have been seen by members of Moore's family as he comments in November, 1835: 'Of course you must be aware that the smoke-dried face of Yagan cannot have the slightest resemblance to his living face which was plump, with a burly-headed look about it. I defy his very mother to recognize the face of her own son now and I do not think she's craniologist enough to recognize his head.'

1832–1833

Future in the Balance

Swan River population in decline. Convict labour
advocated. Shaw raises crown mortgage. Christmas
mail. Sad news from home. Shaw and Brockman write
of the local scene. The Brockmans' house destroyed
by fire. W Tanner leases Baskerville to Shaws. Shaw
and G F Moore discuss the servant problem. Moore's
varied activities. Moore and Nat Shaw explore new
country. Aborigines rob Shenton's Mill. Attack on
Upper Swan Garrison. Report of shipwrecked survivors
on north coast. Governor Stirling (now Sir James)
about to return.

The Aboriginal people little knew that it needed only their
organized resistance, added to the other problems of that time,
to have tipped the scales against continued settlement. Immigration that had virtually ceased at the beginning of 1831 had
not picked up again, and most of those who had come out
determined to settle in the west had begun to lose heart. By
the time Stirling left to interview the Colonial Office, the
settlement had lost some 3,600 of the 4,000 maximum population it had boasted in 1830.[1]

The settlers blamed the Home Government's having tight-
ened up on the colonial land policy. According to the original
terms landholders were to be allowed twenty-one years for the
improvement of their grants, but this had quickly been reduced to ten and it was then announced that confirmation of
grants in fee simple was to be withheld until improvements
to the extent of 1s 6d an acre had been carried out. The end
of free grants and the 5s an acre minimum price for crown
lands had certainly put off many potential immigrants. The

frustrated settlers also looked for scapegoats in other directions. Some maintained that too-easy access to alcohol was the curse of the colony and others that it was the isolation and general disappointment in the quality of the soil that caused so many to seek solace at the 'shrine of Bacchus'. Others blamed the exorbitant cost of labour in a situation where ready cash was in chronically short supply. This was a very real dilemma, for not many settlers could pay their servants other than in kind and the majority of workers who were worth their salt were either hiring themselves out to the few who could pay them well or were claiming land for themselves.

A number of people, including the articulate R M Lyon, now declared that the fine ideal of a free colony had been after all impractical, for without convict labour how were they ever to have roads, bridges and public buildings? How were any but a few rich families to achieve an acceptable standard of living? And without these things how was the colony ever to attract 'the right kind of people' in sufficient numbers to establish a healthy economy?

But now the Governor was in England and could put all these problems to the Colonial Office in person. He could explain why Western Australia, by virtue of its enormous size, emptiness and isolation from the eastern colonies, should be exempt from the new upset price of land. He could reveal the true, destitute state of the settlement, its government impoverished and powerless to implement the public works necessary for its survival.

Will Shaw, writing to Robert Casson at this time, presented as bright a picture as possible, for he did not want his good friends to think they had invested in a failure, or to put Casson off coming out. The deserters, he declared, were after all 'people of little importance to the colony, generally storekeepers, or what I term "half-merchants", of whom we have a superabundance.'[2] It would never have done to admit that most of those who stayed had no choice in the matter and that many who left had made an intelligent enough appraisal, for these times at least, of the real potential of the colony.

Truth to tell, however, Will Shaw, while claiming to have every faith in the outcome of Stirling's representations to the Home Government, was sadly despondent. Like so many other colonists of this time, the Shaws' difficulty lay not so much in obtaining labour as in paying for what was available. They had little or no cash and barter was not the answer to their every need. Stirling appreciated this difficulty and had agreed that the government might lend needy settlers small sums at interest for limited periods on the security of their holdings. Shortly before his departure Will Shaw had raised a crown mortgage on Belvoir for the sum of £125 9s 7d.[3] This arrangement had been entered into with the Colonial Secretary operating as government agent, for since there was no banker in the colony Peter Brown had undertaken this function as a temporary measure. As will be seen it was a service he would live to regret and for which he would be bitterly criticized, particularly by Shaw himself, whom Brown would be chasing to the end of his days for repayment of his debt to the Treasury. In the meantime, however, the Shaws pinned their hopes on receiving word from home of the payment of Eliza's legacy which, although now reduced to £180[4] was of great importance to them.

On Christmas Day 1832, a message reached the Upper Swan that local mail had been found aboard a vessel that had arrived from Sydney some days before. All suspected this to have been a trick—as Moore expressed it 'a frequent and inexcusable one'—to keep the mail and private parcels until the other cargo had been disposed of, lest the settlers should receive goods they would otherwise be forced to buy.

Eliza reports that the news reached them as they were sitting down, in a temperature of 103°, to their midday dinner of roast kid and plum pudding, and that Nat, without waiting for a bite to eat, set off post-haste to Fremantle. He returned at 11 o'clock at night with mail and packages which were opened in the usual atmosphere of feverish excitement.

> So intent were we in opening our mail, [Eliza writes] that the black seal did not attract our attention; all our anxiety being to learn its contents, but melancholy indeed they were ...[5]

To Eliza the news, conveyed by the Waghornes, of her mother's death, would seem to have been even more of a shock by reason of their long estrangement.

It is odd [she remarks] that my sisters Caroline and Sophie did not write to me ... I don't know what they will do without her, but I hope they will now marry and settle comfortably ... [Mother] ... had saved something and I hold her too just to die and not leave me a trifle, were it but a button off a garment she had worn.[6]

Further melancholy news was of the death not only of the Rev Casson and several other friends, but also of the ill-health of both Mr and Mrs Waghorne. Will Shaw wrote sadly to Robert Casson:

With regard to your leaving England, it is a matter of too delicate a nature for me to say one word more upon ... I feel the loss of my friends so great that I often wish I had not left. My wants keep more ahead of me than I can well manage to surmount ... I fear if I do not make some show of cultivation on my large grant near York, I may have the Government calling me to fulfil my location duties, but if you can raise me the few hundred pounds I have named to you I shall soon be able to extricate myself from my present difficulties. I believe, my old friend, that no two were cast in a much nearer mould in ideas than ourselves. Though we have bandied words at times, would we could do so again over a good pudding as we used to do, even in our angry moods, rather than never meet again. I can never forget the happy hours we have spent together, in those days when the best of men lived. But I must not dwell upon days of old. Of the dear Waghornes I live in fear and apprehension for their existence. Would that I could once more shake you by the fist! ...[7]

He still tried however to strike a note of confidence in the future. They had gained the reputation of being among the settlement's most progressive farmers and although much of their land was poor quality it included several hundred acres equal to the best in the colony. Their last harvest had been most satisfactory and they had a supply of seed wheat 'that would do credit to the best farmer in England'. Their stock was increasing, their vegetables flourishing and they had come to an arrangement with a well-to-do farmer named Marshall

McDermott, by which he supplied agricultural labour in return for half Shaw's yield of hay.

In their neighbours they considered themselves truly fortunate, and all these early letters convey the impression of generally helpful and amicable relationships. The Brockmans, their first close friends in the Upper Swan, had met with a serious setback in the summer of 1832, when the blackboy thatch of their roof had caught fire and their house with all their possessions was burned to the ground. They would have been in a sad plight had not the Stirlings, shortly before their departure for England, offered them the use of the 'cottage *ornée*' at their Guildford property, Woodbridge. Will Brockman's letter of thanks to his brother-in-law, the Rev Thomas Du Boulay of Dorset who had lent him money to rebuild at Herne Hill, shows something of the determined optimism of the Shaw neighbours:

> We have [he wrote] as poor, and as rich soils as any perhaps in the world, but plenty of the latter for all our purposes ...
>
> We suffer much inconvenience here for the want of a Bank. Any capitalist starting a banking establishment on a liberal scale would be certain of realising a large fortune and the Colony would be most materially benefited by it. At present, whatever your amount of property, it is next to impossible to raise money upon it, whatever amount of interest you offer ...
>
> Left as we have been to fight our way unassisted thro' innumerable difficulties, this Colony has made most rapid strides, and its success is now complete.[8]

This rather over-sanguine summing up may have been inspired, like Will Shaw's letter to Casson, by Brockman's desire to reassure his generous friend of his security.

While the Brockmans were at Woodbridge the Shaws saw less of them than previously, but the Tanners they saw almost daily. Eliza had delivered Mrs Tanner of her second child and had nursed her through distressing attacks of asthma that, late in 1832, decided her husband to return with his family to England for an indefinite period. As it happened this move had fortunate repercussions for the Shaws, who were granted a three-year lease of the Baskerville property. This included the use of the fine house, outbuildings and everything accruing from the produce of the estate. The transaction also allowed the purchase of some stock to be had on credit until the termination of the lease.

> Money is so scarce here, [Eliza wrote] it is still impossible to do business in any way except barter. I know not how we would have managed, but certainly through the merciful Goodness of Providence in raising us up the best of friends, we have struggled through most wonderfully ... I shall regret leaving our humble mud edifice to go to the great house. It is not more than eight hundred yards from our own door, but one becomes attached to home, be it ever so humble.[9]

After all the Tanners were forced to postpone their journey since the doctor had pronounced Mrs Tanner temporarily unfit to travel. In the meantime, having leased Baskerville to the Shaws, however, they took over tenancy of Woodbridge and moved with some of their servants into the main house on that estate.

The Shaws now had on their hands two homes and three properties, including the untouched Avon grant, to develop which they were anxiously striving to acquire capital and labour. They no doubt hoped that this would be provided by the combined output of the Belvoir and Baskerville estates, especially as they had inherited with the latter property about ten farm labourers. The Tanners, however, had been among the few people in the colony able to pay their servants in hard cash, whereas the Shaws found it increasingly difficult even to keep them in the perquisites to which they had been accustomed.

One of the touchiest aspects of the servant problem had always lain in controlling the ration of alcohol, without which few workers in the colony would continue to operate. This was a matter on which the Shaws had much conversation with their neighbour, George Fletcher Moore, who called on them frequently to discuss problems confronting the Guildford Agricultural Society, of which both Will Shaw and Moore were executives. Lingering many an evening over their dinner wine, both men deplored the process of decline they were powerless to stay and the circumstances that had made alcohol so great a part of colonial life. From the beginning of settlement it had been laid down that in all circumstances servants were to be adequately clothed and housed and to receive one meal a day of meat, vegetables and pudding, two meals of bread and tea and a glass of wine or rum. 'If this be not improvement in their condition,' Moore writes, 'I know not what their condition was; and yet they are dissatisfied.' Before long they were demanding two glasses of wine and two of rum a day—*not* as Moore points out the usual proportion of spirits and water but 'unmixed, ardent spirits'—and this with rum at £27 a cask! 'To the use of "grog",' he complains, 'I attribute all my troubles with my people ... I feel they are no longer my friends as I fondly hoped they would be ... for they look upon one in no other light as that of one who is *bound* to feed and clothe them and give them grog, and for whom they are not under obligation to do anything willingly ... I approach the subject with reluctance and dwell upon it with sorrow and pain ...'[10]

Moore, a remarkably energetic man, had by this time a finger in every local pie. Besides secretarial work for the Agricultural Society which had its headquarters in Guildford, he had undertaken the work of Commissioner of the Civil Court and was a member of the Legislative and Executive Council. These latter activities required his setting up a Perth office, to which he walked seventeen miles from his Swan property at least twice a week. He never complained about the journey on which he invariably read as he went along. In fact, apart from missing his family, the great distance that separated them and the unreasonable demands of his servants, Moore found, at this time, very little to complain of in his situation. He remarks, to be sure, on the sad lack of population, the retarded economy and the disappointing increase of stock, but for the rest he found life surprisingly civilized and full of pleasant diversions. He writes about this time:

How different my rural life from that which I had imagined it would be! Instead of being demi-savage and romantic it is civilised (often ceremonious) and uniform; with less privation and much more occupation for mind and body than I had anticipated. But where are all the flocks and herds? Where?[11]

Himself an urbane and bookish man, Moore had found common ground over this period with the comparatively unlettered Nat Shaw, who frequently joined him in hunting kangaroo, searching for missing stock or miscreant natives, exploring outlying country and collecting botanical specimens to be shipped to England to Captain James Mangles, a cousin of Mrs Stirling, who had visited the Swan in 1831.

Botanical artists 'at home' were at this time actually painting many of Western Australia's wildflowers that had flourished under hothouse conditions in the Kew, Birmingham and Mons Cels [Paris] Gardens as well as in the elegant conservatories of wealthy families.[12] Some of these, including a type of Kangaroo Paw, Hardenbergia, Pimelea and a handsome shrub variety of Hovea, had been introduced to European soil by members of the French expedition that sailed under Captain Baudin in 1800. Others had been collected by Robert Brown, a botanist who had arrived with Flinders in the *Investigator* and who was later appointed Chief Plant Collector at Kew Gardens. Many other species had been transported by Allan Cunningham who came out as Botanist on the ship *Surry* in 1816 and continued collecting plants when with Philip Parker King on the ship *Mermaid*. After the establishment of the Swan River Colony, innumerable local plant specimens were sent to James Mangles not only by his Stirling relatives and George Moore but by James Drummond and his sons, by Georgiana Molloy of Augusta[13] and several other enthusiasts.

In May 1834 Moore, having heard from the natives of a big freshwater lake immediately to the north, set off with Nat Shaw and an Aboriginal guide in the direction of what was later to be known as the Moore River. They had been given the impression that their destination was a mere fourteen or fifteen miles away but it turned out to be thirty-three—'a long winding valley of bays, swamps, lakes and shrunk up pools surrounded by tea-tree, spear-wattle and bulrush.'[14] The country, recently burned by the local tribespeople whose reception of the strangers was 'rather indifferent than friendly', proved disappointing, but it provided a good chance of observing the wild life of the area and the habits of the Aboriginal people which never failed to intrigue them. From earlier times when 'the natives' had appeared to the newcomers more or less indistinguishable, they were now being seen as individuals with particular characteristics and sometimes even a beauty of their own. Moore, from this time on, makes reference to the pretty young wives of tribesmen visiting his house, and to the charm and grace with which they disported themselves in the river laughing merrily as they sucked honey from the gum blossoms and, no doubt, casting seductive glances at the women-hungry white men watching from the banks.

Moore had formed a friendship of a kind with an elder of the Upper Swan area named Weeip, an attractive personality, evidently determined to survive in the new régime even if it sometimes meant running with the fox and hunting with the hounds. Weeip had a habit of appearing out of the thicket to interview Moore on matters concerning himself or his people, a case in point being a situation that arose in May 1834. A group of Aborigines from the Murray River area, had that month descended on the mill then operating across the river from Perth, and holding the caretaker, George Shenton, at spear's point, had made off with 980lbs of precious flour. The settlers, already irritated by thefts of stock and vegetables and the burning of their hay stacks, were up in arms at this outrage. Irwin was persuaded that the military must act. As a result one of the thieves was shot and four others arrested and sentenced to flogging and imprisonment.

It was not yet realized in the colony that flogging, that time-honoured remedy for crimes of any kind, would prove the opposite to a deterrent where an Aboriginal was concerned. It was an aspect of the white man's culture that shocked and enraged the Australian 'savage' far more than the swift reprisal by bullet or hangman's noose. Heavy blows with clubs or wounds with knife and spear he accepted in the enactment of tribal justice without complaint—in fact a man would unflinchingly present a thigh, calf or buttock to be pierced with the spear of the law. But to be tied and flogged, or to see another treated in this way, would rouse him either to immediate and defiant repetition of his offence or to vengeance on behalf of another.

The Swan River people, not usually given to fighting battles for neighbouring groups, were roused by this action against their Murray River countrymen to angry demonstrations. When the news reached the Upper Swan, Weeip immediately took it upon himself to lead an attack against the local barracks. A young soldier, supposedly on guard, was surprised and killed and the building, with the rest of the contingent inside, was about to be fired when Will and Nat Shaw happened on the scene. They quickly routed the natives, who made off into the bush so angrily that it was feared they intended rallying for a more formidable attack, and everyone in the neighbourhood was alerted to be on guard.

Shaw, in an addenda to one of his appeals for justice, was later to remind an ungrateful government that: 'but for this timely assistance the whole detachment, with women and children, would in all probability have been sacrificed ...' Nor, he pointed out, was this a solitary instance of soldiers being rescued by those they were appointed to protect. 'Did the government of that day offer the settler any protection?' he asked. 'No, that very detachment received orders to defend themselves and their barracks ... and the settler must defend himself and stock as best he could.'[15]

We are all in indecision as to what is the best course to pursue [Moore writes]. Our government seems so nervous as not to know what to do but I am sure no settler will now feel any compunction in putting Weeip or his associates to death if they can be found. They have all vanished now as if there were no such inhabitants in this country.[16]

Not long afterwards rumours were circulated by the natives that a number of white people had been shipwrecked on the coast somewhere north of the Moore river. The story seemed sufficiently convincing to warrant sending off a search party by ship and also a message to be delivered to the castaways by native couriers. The latter manoeuvre had been suggested by Moore, who prevailed upon the Lieutenant-Governor to offer, as a reward for carrying out this service, the liberation of Weeip's son Billymerra who was then in custody. Weeip himself, who had been outlawed since the barracks raid, got wind of this suggestion and materialized out of the forest to inform

Moore that he and a native named Tomghin would undertake to deliver a letter to the supposed survivors.

The ship returned at last, having sailed as far north as Shark Bay without sighting any evidence of a wreck. The natives also reported back in due course that, having followed the coast for several weeks and made exhaustive enquiries from tribe to tribe, they had come to the conclusion that the story had been 'a lie properly'.

For the settlers the report of the wreck had provided a welcome stir of excitement, and the disappointing outcome was regarded as further evidence of the unreliability of Aboriginal information. No one at that time suggested that the story might well have been a true enough account of a bygone happening perpetuated by word of mouth and interpreted, on at last reaching the Swan River tribes, as a contemporary incident. Chronology was of little consequence in an Aboriginal context, in which one year ago or a century were simply 'the time past'. Wrecks had been many on that treacherous coast—one of them, the Dutch vessel *Gulden Draak* (Gilt Dragon) had gone down some sixty miles north of Perth in 1656. The story, as told by seven survivors who reached Batavia in a small boat, was that seventy-five men, women and children had made ashore, though subsequent search parties found no trace of them. Then there was the *Zuytdorp*, wrecked fifty-six years later north of the Murchison river,[17] which must also have had a place in Aboriginal memory.

But despite the fruitlessness of his mission, Weeip was granted a reprieve for having faithfully carried out his commission and his son Billymerra was released from the Fremantle gaol.

It the meantime, compensating for this anti-climax, a dispatch had reached the colony to the effect that Governor Stirling and his family were due back at any time, and that His Majesty had seen fit to honour him with a knighthood in recognition of his work as founder of the western colony. The settlers, in their slough of despond, read great significance into this news. In honouring their Governor it seemed that the crown was surely honouring them all, and was at last to acknowledge the importance of their neglected outpost of Empire.

Chapter 12

1834-1838

The Governor's Dilemma

Return of Sir James Stirling. Orphan apprentices. Unemployed and unemployable. Shaw's mounting debt to government. His claims for damages. Settlers hardened against Aborigines. The Battle of Pinjarra. Shaw hires Aboriginal shepherds. Missionary experiments unsuccessful.

Late in June 1834 a horseman dispatched to Perth from King George Sound brought the welcome news that the Governor and his family had arrived in Albany in the ship *James Pattison*, and would be proceeding to Fremantle as soon as the weather permitted. This announcement emphasized one of the main drawbacks of the Swan settlement, for the exposed entrance off Fremantle, in which many vessels had run aground and a number had been wrecked, had become the terror of ships' captains especially during the blustery winter months. Albany, with its safe harbour, had therefore become the colony's main port of call and was to continue as such until a proper harbour at Fremantle was completed in 1897. The clearing of a road and erection of bridges between Albany and Perth, in 1852, would help to overcome the inconvenience of passengers and the impatience of settlers awaiting their mail, but before this time there was no alternative but to await favourable sailing conditions.

It was two months before the ship reached Fremantle and during this time the three main Swan settlements—Fremantle, Perth and Guildford—had been busy composing separate speeches of welcome and congratulation. The writers of the Perth address certainly excelled themselves in hailing His Excellency's return 'as in every possible respect, moral and political, pregnant with the most beneficial consequences'. There were a few veiled references to 'existing evils' (to be gone into more thoroughly later on) but the general spirit of all three orations was one of confidence and gratification at the recognition of the colony's importance implicit in the honour His Majesty had seen fit to bestow upon its founder.

Stirling's reply was in like vein—optimistic if somewhat vague regarding the actual benefits accruing from the long siege he had waged on behalf of the struggling colony. Later it would emerge that his reception by the Home Government had been decidedly cool. His not having asked permission to leave his post had been frowned upon, and he was criticized for his lack of system in the allocation of land grants and for allowing 'capitalists' to take up what seemed extravagantly large areas. As time went on, his obvious dedication to the cause of his settlement struck a note of sympathy in at least some official breasts and he was granted, along with his title, a few minor concessions. It was not long, however, before the settlers began to suspect that his representation had achieved little. They detected, too, a growing reticence in his pronouncements on the potential of the land and local enterprises in general. He was never discouraging—merely cautious. He had tried hard while away to obtain suitable labourers and tradesmen, but there had been too much adverse publicity about Swan River to attract those who could make a reasonable living at home. He did not, however, return quite empty-handed for the Parent Society of London had placed in his charge twenty-two orphaned or deserted children to be hired as apprentices on very liberal terms. The Society had provided £6 a year towards the keep and 'proper instruction' of each child, while stipulating that all should be treated as members of the families by whom they were hired. Some colonists no doubt lived up to this undertaking, while others through neglect or over-diligence were to contribute to the growing burden of colonial misfits and petty criminals.

But strange to say, one of the main problems awaiting the Governor's return was not lack of labour so much as an embarrassing number of unemployed. These included the less skilled and enterprising of Peel's followers, and a number of men who had broken or finished their terms of indenture and whose masters were either unable to pay them or were willing enough for some other reason to let them go. The settlers complained that the colony was in danger of being over-run by vagabonds and scavengers if the government did not find some means of controlling the situation. Stirling therefore quickly devised a scheme by which he hoped to keep them employed to the benefit of understaffed but impecunious landholders.

Will Shaw was quick to take advantage of this arrangement, at once engaging three men to clear and generally improve the land that had come as a bonus by reason of the boundary survey of 1831. By the time the job was completed he reckoned that the bill for their rations was at least double the cost of wages for competent workers, for as he complained to the Governor, one of the men was suffering from a double hernia and was quite unfit for labouring work while the others were insolent, in need of constant supervision and loudly insistent on their entitlement to the same allowance of grog as regular labourers. Pressed for payment of the £149 11s 3d owing for the government stores supplied for them, Shaw's request that he be allowed to settle up in wheat at a rate of 15s a bushel[1] was refused, in a curt note from the Colonial Secretary to the effect that his office was not a trading post and that the collector of revenue had 'no authority to receive hay in payment for Crown debts'.

Shaw was not of course alone in owing money to the government. It fact his debts were small compared to those of other leading citizens, including the Colonial Storekeeper, Thomas Peel, and the Colonial Secretary himself, but he must surely have out-done them all in the persistence of his claim that the government was, in point of fact, in debt to him. It was his contention that losses he had sustained from Aborigines firing his crops and haystacks and thieving his vegetables and produce, which he valued at £680, should be deducted by way of damages from his crown debts. Having failed to get satisfaction on the matter from the local government, he wrote through the Colonial Secretary to the Secretary of State for the Colonies in England, who replied in due course that in the opinion of Governor Stirling 'the Calamity arose entirely from the Periodical Conflagrations to which the Country is subject during the dry Season'.[2] Shaw wrote again to England, stating that His Excellency was acting under a misapprehension since the land around the stacks had been carefully cleared to prevent such a disaster. He named the culprits and cited witnesses to the sudden and localized nature of the blaze. The claim was only one of the wrongs that Shaw was to protest with dogged persistence, but to little avail, over the years.

Of the many and various complaints that had awaited Stirling's return from England, by far the strongest had concerned the settlers' lack of protection against such Aboriginal molestations. Was the Governor content, he was asked, to allow this behaviour to go on unchecked; lives threatened; stock speared; crops fired; until his settlement lay about him in ruin and desolation? Or was he prepared to demonstrate once and for all that the white man was now master in this land?

Among all matters on which he had been urged, from the beginning of settlement, to take positive action, this was the one Stirling had been least inclined to tackle. A man of liberal and moderate mind, he had seen many good qualities in the native people and their way of life, and had always conceded them a point of view. He had hoped no doubt that by proceeding as quietly and reasonably as possible the problem would, in some way, solve itself. The tribespeople would either retreat to unsettled areas, of which there would surely always be sufficient in this vast land, or they would accept the blessings of civilization. They would don the white man's clothing, attend his schools and his Sunday services and become part of the work force of a colony that God had ordained to take the place of the black man's uncultivated hunting grounds. Before the Governor's departure many had shared this opinion, but after his return he realized that the mood of the settlers had hardened against the natives and that few any longer believed in their ability to integrate with a Christian culture. Even the moderate G F Moore reported that 'the natives are becoming everywhere more bold, the colonists more uneasy, the Governor more puzzled, and I fear a rupture if the offending natives be not removed wholesale to some island—which might be done.'[3]

The settlers were angered to hear that Stirling had been criticized by the Home Office for the mild disciplinary measures he had taken in the past, and that news of the execution of Midgigeroo and the shooting of Yagan that came while he was abroad had been most sternly censured. How dare they—safe in their beds at home—lay down the law on how people should deal with a problem of which they had no experience! Let the Secretary of State for the Colonies or any of his sanctimonious minions come to Australia and see what they would do when confronted by tribes of Godless and murderous savages!

It was in just such terms that settlers in the untamed north of the colony were later to defend themselves against their critics in the south, where the war songs of the Bibbulmun had been long since silenced and their weapons annexed for souvenirs!

Most insistent of all in urging the Governor to forthright action was Mr Thomas Peel, then living on his Mandurah grant and for whose misfortunes Stirling, though not holding himself responsible, had considerable sympathy. Peel complained that the Murray River group, about seventy strong and more aggressive than those of the Swan or King George Sound areas, were now attacking not only the stock but the settlers themselves. Within a few weeks his son had been threatened, another boy wounded and a young soldier killed. These deeds were said to have been carried out in revenge for the flogging and imprisonment of the four tribesmen following the raid on Shenton's Mill.

Convinced at last that his lenient and tolerant policy had been interpreted as weakness by the Aborigines, Stirling agreed to take action. He immediately established a corps of mounted police in charge of Captain Ellis 'to afford a most substantial protection of the colonists against the natives'.[4] A few days later he set off with a party of twenty-five, including J S Roe, Thomas Peel, Captain Ellis, and five mounted police who surprised the Kalyute tribe in their camp on the Murray River near Pinjarra.

'The men,' Moore tells us, seized their numerous spears and showed a formidable front, 'but as the whites approached suddenly broke their ranks and ran.' Moore's usually admirable objectivity falters at this stage in his anxiety to justify what followed. 'The word "forward" from the leader of the gallant little party brought the horsemen in about half a minute dashing into the midst of them, the same moment having discovered the well-known features of some of the most atrocious offenders of the obnoxious tribe.' At the river bank the natives turned and stood their ground but when four or five fell dead they took to the river. Here they were exposed to the cross-fire of mounted men on either side until fifteen to twenty natives were left dead in the water or on the banks. 'Despite some care taken to fire only on the men, it cannot appear surprising,' Moore continues, 'that one woman and several children were killed.'[5] During this skirmish Captain Ellis received a wound from which he was to die two weeks later.

Stirling's firm stand met with the warm approval of the settlers, who believed it to have exercised a salutary effect, not only in that area but further afield. They were to prove right enough in this surmise, for although there would be trouble in one area and another as settlement spread, never again would a son of the Bibbulmun walk in his country with the pride and confidence of 'the Wallace', whose pickled head was then on its way to England to advance the cause of science.

Meanwhile George Fletcher Moore had been tackling the problem of marauding natives in another way. In order to sponsor good relations and to assist in the compilation of his local vocabulary, he had engaged a number of native helpers whose antics he records so amusingly in his journal. Moore was fascinated by the reactions of the tribespeople to new situations, and had found that encouraging their friendship, while expensive from one point of view, paid off in another. He advised Shaw to take on two Aborigines named Tomghin (the same man who had accompanied Weeip in search of the rumoured castaways) and his friend Coroor, both of whom he had found reasonably intelligent and trustworthy, to act as shepherds and watchmen on the Belvoir property. This worked well for some time, and the Shaw family became quite attached to their native helpers, though at first it had been feared that they were allowing the sheep to wander on an irresponsibly wide range, often well out of hearing of the bells. It was soon found, however, that they never lost an animal and that the flock had improved from the greater choice of pasture. The two men also served the purpose of night-watchmen around the Belvoir house—one electing to sleep in the barn and the other in the kitchen. Shaw was beginning to think that, perhaps after all, even though employing two men meant feeding at least six others, native labour might prove a solution to one aspect of his problems.

No doubt Moore was congratulating himself also, when one day in February 1835 Shaw arrived at Millendon in some agitation to report an 'extraordinary circumstance' that had just occurred at Belvoir. He described how early that morning he had entered the kitchen where Coroor lay asleep, as usual, on the floor. Shaw was about to wake him and dole out his rations when a spear flashed past him and pierced the slumbering native through the heart. Shaw looked quickly around to find Tomghin standing in the doorway, seemingly quite unconcerned. He had, he explained, been obliged to kill his friend in revenge for the death of his brother who had been shot not long before by a party of soldier-men. When Shaw protested the callous injustice of the act, Tomghin, with a gesture that betokened the hopelessness of joining argument with a white man, had taken himself off into the bush. 'Are they not an extraordinary race?' Moore asks of his Journal. 'No wonder they are not very numerous!'[6]

Tomghin may possibly have nursed a secret grudge against Coroor and have come up with the first explanation of his action that entered his head. It is more likely, however, that he had been sincerely troubled in conscience about his brother's unavenged death. A life for a life, however haphazardly taken from a white man's point of view, was the inexorable law of his people but, having pledged himself to the white man, and no doubt afraid to act in that direction in any case, it would not have seemed to him illogical to kill his companion. Besides, he had not acted without human consideration, in the Aboriginal sense. He had placed his spear skilfully and the man had died quickly in his sleep. His victim had feared nothing and felt nothing, and the law had been satisfied.

From the beginning of settlement R M Lyon had forthrightly advocated the introduction of missionary teachers to civilize and Christianize the Aborigines. In this he had the support of Captain Irwin who, while in England between 1833 and 1837, had engaged an Italian named Dr Giustiniani to minister to both whites and Aborigines at the Upper Swan. He arrived with his wife in September 1836, took over a house and put up a small church in Guildford. The settlers were somewhat disconcerted to find that of the many languages in which the doctor was reputedly so fluent, none of them was English. Nevertheless they welcomed him warmly and, since the behaviour of the Aborigines had considerably improved, expressed pious hopes of their being soon gathered into the Anglican flock. Before long, however, they began to suspect that Dr Giustiniani was in at least as much need of spiritual guidance as the savages he had come to save. It was found that he had been in his time a Jesuit priest, a Lutheran and a Methodist minister, that he was of a highly unstable disposition, given to uncontrollable rages and disturbing flights of imagination. True, he mustered up a number of Aborigines to attend church services and taught them to sing hymns, but he made no attempt to train them in any practical skills. He had not been long in office when, claiming to be the natives' protector and confidant, he reported a 'conspiracy' on the part of the Avon River settlers to wipe out all the tribespeople in that area. The rumour was at last dismissed as being without foundation, and soon afterwards Giustiniani's inauspicious career in the colony came to an end. He was replaced by the Rev William Mitchell, a self-disciplined and scholarly man of unassailable rectitude, whose efforts on behalf of the Aborigines were of little more avail.

Stirling had in the meantime established another institution for the protection and instruction of the Aborigines at the foot of Mt Eliza. This he put in charge of Francis Armstrong who had come out in the *Gilmore* as a boy, his family having numbered among the free settlers included in Peel's scheme. He had later been employed by G F Moore, whom he had helped in the compilation of an Aboriginal vocabulary that was published in London in 1842.[7] He showed great dedication to his work at the Mt Eliza Institute, but as time went on the contradictions that have frustrated every missionary, teacher or welfare worker from that day to this, began to overwhelm him. One could shield the people from the more obvious abuses at the hands of the whites, but how protect them from themselves? How far was one to tolerate the tribesmen's brutal beating of their wives, the casual disposal of unwanted children, the vendettas causing the wheel of massacre to turn perpetually? In how far was one justified in confining a people used from ages past to the freedom of their open range? How serve the hunter food he had not caught himself and keep his pride? Of what use was the provision of a man's every material need if the spiritual meaning of his existence lay within the fenced-off waters, buried in the ploughed paddocks and under the felled trees?

The closing of the Mt Eliza establishment at the end of 1838 was to be one of the last actions Stirling felt compelled to carry out before leaving the colony.

Chapter 13

1835–1836

Hot Words in High Summer

Home life at Baskerville. Birth of Robert Casson
Shaw. Financial problems. Bills of exchange. Shaw
summonsed over boundary. Taken to court for defam-
ing Peter Brown. Brown gives evidence of his banking
activities. Wins case against Shaw.

For a woman who had never wanted anything so much as to
have her family about her, this was a happy enough period for
Eliza and one that she would look back to in time to come—
forgetting the gloomier aspects—as 'those dear old Baskerville days'. Living in the Tanners' fine house, the family must
have presented to their many callers an impression of rustic
prosperity. The large staff of farm and domestic helpers had
soon dwindled to a minimum, but due to Eliza's good management and the help of her family their standards of living remained very comfortable. They were notably hospitable and
kept a good table from which meals were served on spotless
linen with polished silver cutlery and good china.

The family had been increased in March 1835 by the birth
of a son, named Robert Casson for the friend they still hoped
would turn up in the colony and bring his legal mind to bear
on their problems. Nat was still at home, restless to be sure
but a good worker, fond of his family and, despite the lack of
social graces of which his father complained, popular enough
with the local gentry.

For a few months in 1834, Elizabeth had attended a little
school in Perth run by a cultivated gentlewoman named Miss
Helm, under whose direction she had striven diligently to
improve her handwriting and to appreciate excerpts from the
great writers. She was home again before the birth of her baby

brother, and was to have no more schooling, though Eliza taught her to play the Tanners' grand piano, at which, like most things to which she applied her capable young hands, she displayed some aptitude. Her younger sister Mary, then ten years old, had meanwhile taken on almost sole charge of little Lucy Ellen, who had become her shadow and was to remain her precious responsibility for the rest of her life.

The six-year-old George, his father's inseparable companion, had been calling himself a workman for the past two years when he began, as Eliza told her friends, trudging into the fields, pulling up weeds, fetching and carrying spades and hoes. Strangely enough, it is of this son who remained at home and was to become his widowed mother's 'staff of life', that we have been left the sketchiest picture of all. Certainly the most reliable of the three boys, he seems to have been the least popular with his sisters who would refer to him offhandedly in the years to come as 'old bachelor George'.

For all their set-backs, the family had come a long way from their beach tents of six years before, but that is not to say that their difficulties were at an end. In many ways, as we shall see, they had hardly begun. Their being unable to afford adequate labour had limited the use of their land, and while leasing the Baskerville property had improved their domestic standards it had considerably complicated their finances. Their debts, although trifling enough by present-day reckonings, were steadily mounting and they now owed money not only to the crown but to private individuals as well.

Before the Tanners eventually sailed for England in March 1835, they had agreed to lend the Shaws the money expected from Eliza's legacy which had not yet been released from her father's estate. In default of their payment of a 10% annual interest, Tanner was empowered to take over the Belvoir property, though it was obviously thought unlikely that so generous and sympathetic a friend would do any such thing.[1]

A state of indebtedness was so common in the colony that there was no social stigma attached to the complaint, and people in the best circles freely aired the complicated juggling of their finances. They also seem to have thought little of taking each other to law, often causing local magistrates to remonstrate against the time spent in court over trifling matters that could surely have been settled outside. This state of affairs was largely brought about by the chronic lack of cash, which caused merchants to accept produce from farmers in return for other goods, often allowing accounts to run on until after harvest time. Indeed, but for this system the settlement could not have carried on, but difficulties inevitably arose and Will Shaw for one had his full share of them.

In 1835 he was brought to court by two men wishing to clear up their affairs before leaving the colony, who demanded that he immediately honour their bills of exchange. One plaintiff sued him for £10 10s 0d, being the value of a cask of pork, the other for £55 for other goods. Shaw, in answer to the challenge, had proffered bills made out to himself by one Harrison Blechynden. These were accepted by the plaintiffs, but when Blechynden was unable to meet them they were immediately returned to Shaw. When he failed to respond within a week he was summonsed and ordered to pay the sum owing, plus interest.[2] He objected strenuously and even called upon the Governor for redress but was at last forced to find the money.

He was still smarting from this injustice when, in January 1836, he received a far greater and more bitter blow. This was the advice, quite out of the blue, that the 270 acres of rich alluvial flat that had been awarded him as a result of the special survey of 1831 had been found after all to come within Brown's Coulston boundary. Brown claimed to have come by this information accidentally, after engaging a contract surveyor named Smythe to ascertain one of his boundaries for a tenant. Brown declared that in the process of this work an error had been chanced upon in the Coulston/Belvoir boundary. He had thereupon applied to the Surveyor-General, J S Roe, for the services of Alfred Hillman and an assistant from the Survey Department who showed the existing line to run 5.20° too far to the north. Brown then determined to contest this matter again, for not only would the area involved increase the value of his personal securities at a critical stage of his career, but the boundary as originally drawn caused the river to divide the best part of his land into two detached portions. This meant that no communication could be kept up between the divided areas other than by crossing the river or trespassing on the Shaws' property.

Will Shaw had been outraged to find his boundary being

again assessed, with the Surveyor-General himself, no good friend of his he believed, setting the starting point. Informed of the result, his reaction must have indicated that he had no intention of conceding the point and convinced Brown that his only hope of a settlement lay in taking him to court.

When issued with a writ, Shaw's indignation knew no bounds. He did not believe for a moment that Brown's case, after the evidence he would bring to bear, would stand up in a court of law but he was nonetheless resentful that a man who had called him a friend, with whom he had happily engaged in barter over the years and shared many a convivial occasion, should see fit to issue him with a summons. If the boundary was still a matter of dispute then Brown, he contended, should have confronted him as an officer and a gentleman and had the matter out in decent privacy. It was not long before he had convinced himself that the whole affair was a carefully constructed plot, aided and abetted by Roe, to help the Colonial Secretary overcome the unhappy results of his dubious financial deals.

The more he thought about it the more his ire rose, and when he soon afterwards encountered Brown talking to—or as he no doubt saw it, 'conspiring with'—Justice Mackie who was to try the case, his self-control deserted him. In answer to their polite 'good morning', he had raised his stick and shaken it about Brown's shoulders bidding him to consider himself 'horse-whipped' and naming him 'a blackguard and a scoundrel'.[3] It seems that Shaw had by this time conceived the romantic idea of thereby provoking a duel with Brown, which would bring his wrongs dramatically to the attention of the public. At all events, it was in almost the same terms that solicitor William Nairne Clark had addressed merchant George French Johnson in the streets of Fremantle four years previously. ('You are a scoundrel and a blackguard, and if it was not from motives of prudence, I would give you a sound drubbing.')[4] This encounter had provoked a duel in which Johnson, in the course of the traditional procedure, was fatally wounded. As a result, Clark and the two seconds were tried and acquitted.[5] Brown, however, instead of taking up the challenge as had young Johnson, at once lodged a complaint against Shaw who was immediately summoned to appear before Captain Whitfield and the Rev Wittenoom at the Guildford court. Both officials, being friends of the two parties, must have suffered some embarrassment. At all events they hastened the matter to a close, having fined Shaw 5s with costs and cautioned him to avoid such offences in future.

His emotions, however, were by this time thoroughly roused and on 22 January, the day before the case on the land issue, he was again in court, this time before Judge Mackie and a special jury of twelve prominent citizens, including his friends W Habgood who had travelled out with him from England, Will Burges and George Moore's brother Sam, who had come out in 1833 and taken up a property called Oakover on the Upper Swan.

J S Roe gave evidence of Shaw's having stopped him in the street to declare that Brown was a disgrace to his position, a liar and a cheat and quite unfit for the society of gentlemen. Other prominent people testified to Shaw's having accused Brown of defrauding both government and public by his nefarious banking activities. Mr Trimmer quoted the defendant as having told him that 'there is a person called a gentleman who is no gentleman, a friend of yours, over whose shoulders I have just dropped a whip in the presence of Mr Mackie, and I told him he was a scoundrel, a rascal and a liar and that he had deceived every person in the colony.'[6]

Shaw then called witnesses to attest to Brown's dubious banking methods, but these men succeeded only in showing that although Brown's business procedures had been extremely involved, there was hardly any other way he could have operated in the circumstances. In fact the case gave Brown a chance of publicly explaining the difficulties in which he had been placed by reason of the authorities having neglected to include in the official entourage of 1829 a person qualified in book-keeping and the handling of finance. Since there had been no one to take charge of the settlers' surplus cash, this task had fallen to himself and when a treasurer had been appointed in 1832 he had continued to operate a form of banking business more or less for the convenience of the settlers. He was unfortunately not qualified to meet the hazards of this undertaking, and before long had found himself enmeshed in the dicey colonial practice of dealing in bills of exchange, otherwise 'shin-plasters', which, owing to local conditions, would often be floating about the country, passing from hand to hand for up to six months, and sometimes disintegrating in the process.

In 1835 Brown had found himself forced to borrow £70 from a friend in order to make up his deficit. This news soon got around, and although most of the settlers had had confidence in his being able to overcome his problems these naturally became the subject of local gossip and speculation. His affairs were soon afterwards straightened out, with the help of colonial funds in return for which he agreed to assign a fourth part of his income. This meant the selling up of his Bassendean estate between Perth and Guildford, a necessity that must have caused him further regret over the acres previously lost to Shaw on his Upper Swan boundary, and that may, as Shaw suspected, have caused him to connive with Roe for a professional survey.

After this account of Brown's problems Will Shaw, unable further to uphold his aspersions, entered into a defence of the time-honoured practice of duelling which he suggested as the only honourable way of settling such a dispute. He had not gone far with this oration before Justice Mackie ordered him to sit down.

All the jurymen were more or less closely acquainted with the parties concerned. They were aware that both were in financial difficulties and that, although Shaw's hot-headed conduct and ill-considered public statements had lately alienated some degree of sympathy, it was not to be forgotten that he had an honourable military record, an excellent wife and six children to support, and had sustained a shocking personal loss that might well account for a certain measure of imbalance.

The matter was debated for several hours in the extreme heat of a January day that caused the windows of the room to be opened on all sides. Meanwhile the dispute involving two such prominent local personalities had aroused wide interest in the gossip-loving little community, and eager ears were cocked outside during the course of the discussion. Before the jurors reappeared it was general knowledge that the verdict had gone in favour of Brown, but that although damages had been fixed at £50 the jury intended adding a rider to the effect that they hoped he would not claim the money.

Judge Mackie, already fully informed on the matter before

the court reassembled, was much put out by this hill-billy turn to the dignity of the law and 'expressed himself with much warmth'[7] in condemnation of the jurors for their carelessness and the listeners for their curiosity. He dismissed the suggestion that the damages should be recorded but not claimed, and directed that Shaw pay the stipulated sum and mind his tongue in future. It was later stated, however, that Brown, having removed his expenses from the amount awarded him, returned the rest to Shaw.

All in all it was an exciting week for Perth, as next morning was scheduled for the hearing of the land dispute between the same two men. That it was to be a 'special sitting' to be held only three weeks after the re-survey of the boundary in question and at a time of year when one would not anticipate the courts being regularly in session, suggests that the Colonial Secretary may have used his influence to hurry the matter along. At all events, Shaw was of this opinion and had already asserted that if the case should go against him—unlikely though he thought this possibility even in the face of blatant personal prejudice—he would take it to the higher authority of Lord Glenelg, the Secretary of State for the Colonies.

Chapter 14

1836–1839

Disputed Boundary

W Shaw and P Brown in Court over boundary. Justice
Mackie decides for Brown. Shaw pursues case to
Secretary of State for Colonies without success. Depart-
ure from settlement of R M Lyon. Shaw takes out
mortgage with G Leake and sails for Van Diemen's
Land. Returns to Western Australia.

Brown repeated to the court the story of his chance discovery
of the mistake made by the arbitrators in 1831. The referees,
with the exception of Tanner, who was still abroad, then gave
evidence of having done their utmost, with the best instruments available, to mark out the precise due east line which
they understood to have been intended by the government.

Moore put the case for the defendant, pointing out that it
had been Brown's idea to have the survey made by mutual
friends and Brown who had maintained that a pocket compass
would be 'as fair for one as for the other'. He himself had been
led to believe that each party would sustain the risk of any
inaccuracy and abide by the result. He had understood that
both parties had considered the matter finally settled, but that
neither had contemplated any material error or believed that
one would have an important advantage over the other. He
himself had had no idea that a pocket compass could lead to
such a serious error.

Other witnesses called were Lieutenant Bull, Will and Sam
Burges, Alfred Hillman, H W Reveley (for evidence on astro-
nomical instruments) and J S Roe, who said he had no recol-
lection of Shaw's ever having applied, as he claimed, for the
help of a surveyor in 1831.

In summing up, the Commissioner said that it mattered not

whether the referees had unskilfully handled an accurate instrument or skilfully handled an inaccurate one. What he was forced to conclude on expert evidence was that a mistake had been made by the referees, and they had thus acted contrary to their own intention and principle. They had fully understood that the government line was the one they were deputed to set out, and they had failed to effect that objective. He did not believe that any court of law would allow the defendant's contention that the transaction had been in the nature of 'a game or a gambling speculation'. The 'spirit and intention' had been that no material error was ever contemplated, and that if such were detected it should be rectified. Clearly the error had been a material one, giving one party a considerable advantage over the other. The decree was therefore that the boundary line be set aside and that the plaintiff pay the defendant for any expenditure made on the disputed land which was a total loss to the defendant and beneficial to the plaintiff.[1]

The refusal of Shaw's request for trial by jury he felt to have been a flagrant injustice, though the action sought by Brown—namely to have set aside, under the Law of Equity, the mistaken deliniation of a boundary line—was not the sort of case one would normally expect to be heard by a jury. It is, however, possible that a body of men whose boundaries had been similarly assessed might have returned a different verdict, for the Rules and Orders of the Survey Department laid down in the dire exigencies of early settlement, and in accordance with which the mistaken boundary had been marked out, had not so far been rescinded. According to these the direction of an intended boundary and a starting point having been given by the Survey Office, it lay with the individuals concerned to ascertain where their boundaries ran and to abide by their decision. It was certainly bad luck for Shaw that, however legally correct and fair-minded the judge may have been, the contested Belvoir boundary was shared by the Colonial Secretary, who, without abusing his office, could call upon the immediate assistance of the Surveyor-General.

There was no doubt in Shaw's mind that he had been conspired against by a local power group, and he refused to be mollified by Brown's seemingly generous permission for him to continue using the disputed land for two years at a peppercorn rental. He saw these acres as his family's rightful heritage and Brown's gesture as no more than an attempt to show himself up to the public in a favourable light.

He had been disappointed, too, that his usually helpful neighbour George Moore had not come forward more positively on his behalf—that he had in fact been prepared to accept the judgement of a man who, as Moore himself acknowledged, 'had never been called to either the English or Irish Bar.'[2]

Moore had probably conceded this point in answer to Shaw's persistent questions concerning the Judge's credentials. He could hardly, however, have meant it in a derogatory sense, for like most others in the colony he had a great liking and respect for Mackie who, a Cambridge legal graduate, had come out on the ship *Caroline* in 1829. He had been appointed Chairman of the Quarter Sessions and had replaced Moore as Commissioner of the Civil Court when the latter replaced him as Advocate-General in 1834. Mackie was a brother-in-law of Captain Irwin, with whom he jointly owned the Henley Park property on the Upper Swan, and besides this had taken up a 7,000-acre grant on the Avon and had built a house in Perth. He had the general reputation of being a wise, upright and learned man with a ready wit and a kindly ear for the problems of his fellow settlers. Shaw was therefore not likely to have found many supporters in the derogatory insinuations he cast upon Mackie's legal qualifications. Nonetheless he was to continue disputing the issue for many years, not only to the Governor but to the Secretary of State for the Colonies and the House of Lords, some of his memorials running to over thirty pages. In the process he cast aspersions on the integrity, not only of the Colonial Secretary and the Surveyor-General, but on Commissioner Mackie, who, the titles of his own property now safe, 'sits here as personating the Lord High Chancellor of England with far greater powers than are vested in His Lordship'.[3]

As far as Governor Stirling was concerned, Shaw, although sometimes declaring him to have been 'in error' or 'misinformed', never accused him of deliberately unfair treatment or personal prejudice. It says much for the Governor's diplomacy that he managed somehow, despite his close association with both Brown and Roe, to steer clear of involvement in this affair. In a stiff letter to Brown, Shaw states that he fully appreciates Stirling's position in not wishing to interfere, adding that 'had all His Majesty's servants in this colony pursued the same line of manly and upright conduct, much asperity and ill feeling might have been subdued and the ends of true justice effectively attained.'[4]

As happens so often in cases of genuine grievance Shaw, no doubt with some prompting from his equally indignant wife, began brooding on his previous losses and disappointments until it seemed clear to him that he had been the victim of a long sustained persecution at the hands of the local authorities. Harking back to 1830, he recalled how he and his shipmate Agett had applied for a grant north of Fremantle, which Roe had declared he could not locate but had later taken up for himself. Roe had furthermore failed to assist him in his application for a grant on the Avon, but after the ruling of the arbitrators on the Belvoir-Coulston boundary in 1831, had aided and abetted Brown in securing a further 8,000 acres by way of compensation. Shaw had been granted no recompense whatever for the loss of the same land in 1836.[5] Furthermore, Roe had been present when Hillman ran the line at the request of Brown in 1836 and had, by Shaw's implication, connived at the alteration of a boundary peg.

It was no help to Shaw's case that his submissions to Downing Street had to pass through the hands of the men concerned, allowing both Brown and Roe, usually endorsed by the Governor, to add their own carefully considered observations. Naturally they denied all charges of prejudice and animosity against Shaw, and Roe, 'much pained' to have to write in self-justification, declared that he had no notion whatever that the land he had taken up was that applied for by Shaw and Agett at a time when pressure of work had prevented the area in question being investigated by anyone other than these two men. Roe declared that any extra land acquired by Brown was the result of a private transaction with a man named Kenton, the original holder of the Coulston property. He was granted no indulgence by the government other than permission to include two grants within one set of boundaries. To the charge of Roe's having altered the position of a boundary peg in order to favour Brown's claim, 'broadly insinuated at page 37 of the Memorial and a letter from "The Reverend"

R M Lyon brought forward to substantiate the surmise', the Surveyor-General produced a counter-charge against Lyon, who, having originally made over the Belvoir block to the Shaws, had remained strongly partisan to their cause. Roe declared that while the lawsuit had been pending Lyon himself (his religious prefix set in sceptical quotes) had been detected 'making very serious alterations and additions to a letter of his own to the Surveyor-General on the subject of this very same land of W Shaw's ... that man, I would presume to infer is equally capable of altering an actual boundary on the ground.'[7]

Lyon, with other grander plans in view, had meanwhile taken the humble job of boatman plying with mail and goods between Fremantle and Upper Swan. In this way he had kept in constant touch with the Shaws and had helped them in every way possible—even, if Roe is to be believed, to the extent of attempting to fiddle the records on their behalf. George Fletcher Moore, on whom he also called at regular intervals, found him a puzzling personality.

> I do not well know what to think of him [he writes]. He was a man of war (I don't mean a wooden one), his words are those of a man of peace; he speaks at times as though he were averse to litigation, yet he is continually involved in it; professing puerile simplicity, yet arguing with the casuistry of a Jesuit; a linguist (he suddenly asked me the other day what I thought was the force of the particle 'eth' in the 1st verse of the Hebrew Bible?), a great financier who has proposed a desirable scheme of a bank which was to enrich us all—the only requisite being that the government should lend us £100,000! Yet with his varied talents, he is a mere boatman plying on our river.[8]

It was at about this juncture, when, no doubt despairing of the limited vision and lack of initiative in the western colony Lyon decided to try his luck elsewhere. Almost since the time of his arrival at Swan River he had urged the introduction of convict labour without which it was clear to him that no progress could be made. He had also endeavoured to launch a number of financial and land development schemes, none of which would seem to have been taken seriously. Nor had his letter to

Downing Street, offering to sally forth and 'subdue to the British Sceptre' the sable tribesmen of the north of the colony, earned him as much as a note of thanks. Little wonder he should have felt that his talents might be better appreciated elsewhere. He would seem to have sailed to Mauritius where he took a post of Professor of Latin and Greek, but turned up in South Australia in 1838 under the name of the Rev R L Milne. The following year he was operating in New South Wales as Captain Robert Milne. In November 1839 there is mention in the *Perth Gazette* of 'an old adventurer of the colony ... a most singular man who in his time played many parts and appeared to have a partiality for distinguishing himself in new colonies.' It was observed that a Sydney paper had recently drawn its readers' attention to a notice from the Inspector of the Bank of Australia disclaiming all knowledge of an institution called 'The Australian Agricultural Bank', to be established in Adelaide under the management of the Rev R L Milne from Mauritius, who was also seeking to purchase shares in cattle and sheep. 'There seems little doubt,' the report concluded, 'that the whole is but a deep laid scheme to obtain possession of the property of settlers. The Rev Milne we suspect is an adventurer.'[9]

Some diligent researcher may some day trace the further exploits of this extraordinary man. As far as this chronicle is concerned, however, he passed at this stage from the local scene, leaving as his monument a fairly mountainous correspondence in the colonial newspapers and official records, and some of the best information available on the languages and customs of the local Aborigines. One of his papers on this subject was published by the Aboriginal Protection Society in London in 1841.

Will Shaw, immediately after his bitter disappointment over the border dispute, applied for the necessary government permission to go to Van Diemen's Land. He also asked for a certificate allowing him to take up the amount of land in that colony to which he considered himself entitled from the sale of his army commission.[10] From one who had hitherto had little good to say of those deserting the settlement, this indicates the extent of his disillusionment with local justice. In how far he seriously considered making such a radical move it is impossible to say, but in any case his latter request was refused on the grounds that his service remission had been granted specifically for the Swan River settlement, and that his remaining there was the government's only security against his crown debts. He was, however, granted formal leave of absence and this he decided to take, perhaps hoping to ascertain the prospects in the eastern colonies for such time as he could free himself of his debts and shake the sand of the Swan River from his feet for good and all.

In order to meet his expenses, he approached the affluent merchant George Leake, to whom so many settlers were under mortgage and borrowed £151 on the security of 5,096 acres of his Avon block.[11] The remaining 2,000 acres of this property he, at the same time, signed over to his son Nat 'in consideration of natural Love and Affection and a Peppercorn'.[12] This last move may have been in order to break up the land on which he had been unable to fulfil his location duties, while still keeping it in the family. At all events there is no indication of Nat's ever working this block, and during his father's absence he remained with his mother at Baskerville.

Before leaving, Will Shaw had been required to advertise his intended departure in the *Perth Gazette*, a precautionary measure adopted in the colony to prevent settlers skipping the country without having finalized their affairs. At the same time he advertised for tenants to take over the Belvoir estate for three years, an indication of his losing battle to maintain the two properties. The estate was promptly leased to one John Eakins and two other men, to whom Shaw was to supply a team and who were to give him half the produce of the land by way of rent.

It is a pity we have no record of his impressions of Van Diemen's Land, where he no doubt visited his friends of early Swan River days, the Viveashs and Hentys. We know no more than that he was back within four months, whereupon he immediately evicted his Belvoir tenants for having failed to carry out the terms of their lease. Whether or not he had found the distant pastures any greener than those in the God-forsaken west, the trip itself seems to have revived his spirits and given him fresh heart to fight his battles with the land and the local government.

Chapter 15

1835–1842

The Organizing Hand of Governor Hutt

Governor Stirling succeeded by Governor Hutt. Will
Shaw presents his case once more to no avail. Governor
Hutt's orderly hand. Restrictions on undeveloped
blocks. Schemes to introduce competent labour.

Moore had been saddened to find that Governor Stirling had
become, from the time of his return, 'so cautious and silent',
and that he did not confound the prophets of doom with such
robust confidence as in former years. Moore himself, an indefatigable optimist, was ever at pains to depict the brighter
side of the colonial picture and was impatient with those who
compared progress in the Swan River settlement with that of
new provinces in America. In the latter country, he pointed
out, each new settlement was 'but a hiving off of a vigorous
and full-grown swarm,' whereas:

Here is an isolated colony in an uninhabited wilderness,
with an unknown climate, new soil unaccustomed to production, remote from friends, and to which assistance is
dealt with a niggardly hand, where all provisions, stock and
necessities have to be procured from other, distant, jealous
and unfriendly people, and procured by means of merchants
who thrive in proportion to their exactions.[1]

The 'jealous and unfriendly people' here referred to included not only rival interests in South Africa but fellow
countrymen in NSW and Van Diemen's Land, with whom
the Swan River colonists felt little or no affinity. In those early
years few settlers in the west would have admitted to envy of
the progress made possible on the other side of the continent

by reason of convict labour. While ceaselessly bemoaning the distance between themselves and the home country, they did not express much regret at the month's sea voyage of 2,400 miles that separated them from Sydney, and of the desert waste between that rendered land communication then impossible. From the beginning the western settlers, for all their disadvantages, had a sense of superiority to the 't'othersiders' and their riff-raff origins. Nor did they fail to point out that in 1836, while people in the east were talking of the 'failure' of the western colony, that same 'failed' area had sent a shipload of wheat to tide NSW over the effects of a crippling drought!

Local prospects certainly brightened in mid-1837 when a crew of whalers, mostly American, blew in to Fremantle on a fresh sea breeze of enterprise that was expected soon to provide an important local export. But by this time Stirling had made up his mind that he could not wait for that future prosperity which, although he had not lost faith in it, he now saw was to be achieved only by a long and fluctuating process. Nor did he any longer think the settlement likely to provide, as he had once hoped, an ideal outlet for Britain's landed gentry. He was now forty-eight and the father of seven children. His salary, though doubled during his sojourn in England, was still only £800 a year and he saw no immediate prospect of his colonial investments bearing fruit. It was not even as if the settlers seemed any longer dependent on him or showed much trust in his judgement. Many, backed by his detractors from outside, criticized his rulings on matters of land disposal and taxes, to which he saw no practical alternative. A local paper, the *Swan River Guardian*, went so far as to declare him corrupted by the fawning and flattery of his official coterie. Some claimed to find him more inclined than ever to 'wild visionary projects' for which men of sound judgement had often criticized him. They scorned his latest enthusiasm for the production of cotton in the wild, semi-tropical north—an enterprise that he declared would free Britain from its association with the slave labour of the United States—as if the colonists did not have enough problems to solve on their own doorsteps! Ambitious both for his family and himself, he must therefore have felt little remorse in deciding to return to his naval career.

The news of his resignation, announced only towards the end of 1838, was received with mixed feelings in the colony. The settlers had been proud of his distinguished bearing, and of the standards he and his charming and outgoing young wife had set for both home life and public functions in their struggling outpost. Many remembered having gained strength from his ever-helpful optimism, but felt that what the colony now needed was a leader of fresh and practical vision.

The announcement that his successor was a known supporter of Western Australia's chief detractors—the Wakefieldian theorists—and also that he was unmarried, came as something of a disappointment to the settlers. The man in question was John Hutt, whose brother William, member for Hull, was one of E W Wakefield's closest associates. Hutt had, in fact, applied for Governorship of South Australia which was just then embarking on a 'systematic' colonization scheme that, while rejecting convict labour and its attendant evils, also aimed to avoid the economic and human disasters seen by its Founding Fathers as deriving from free grants and dispersed settlement in the west. In this he had been beaten to the post by Lieutenant-Colonel Gawler, but he inherited instead the position of Governor Stirling along with some 2,000 settlers and the results of every policy listed as mistaken in the Wakefieldian catechism. He arrived in January, 1839, and the Stirlings, leaving a relative in charge of their colonial estate, departed a few days later.

George Moore, that conscientious chronicler, records the occasion in heartfelt terms:

A melancholy scene attended the leavetaking of our first Governor, Sir James Stirling, and his gracious lady. An admirable farewell address was presented as from the settlers at large and read by the Rev Wittenoom. His Excellency had prepared a speech in reply but was so deeply affected that he felt compelled to request Mr Brown to deliver it on his behalf. All that could leave their homes came from Perth to see Their Excellencies to the water's edge.[2]

There were tears shed on the Fremantle wharf as well as on the deck of the departing ship, but there was also a sense of excited anticipation in the atmosphere, for rumour already had

Daguerrotype of Eliza Shaw, taken at Perth in 1858 when Eliza was 62 years old. A note on the original in Eliza's handwriting says 'With her mothers best love – this likeness . . . is given to dear Ellen Logue from Elizabeth Shaw, in remembrance'

Captain William Shaw aged about 30 years, in the uniform of the 31st Regiment of Foot (Huntingdonshires) with which he served at the battle of Waterloo.

Scene on a typical emigrant ship

Interior of an early settler's farmhouse

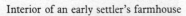

Aborigines raiding a settler camp

Aboriginal elders of the Bibbulum Tribe

A ball held at Government House, Perth, in the early settler days did much to improve the colony's morale

The belvoir homestead on the Upper Swan, sketched by Eliza Shaw in 1831

Lucy Ellen Shaw,
third daughter of
Will and Eliza, was
born at Belvoir in
1832 and married
Major Logue in
1856

George Shaw,
fourth son of Will
& Eliza, aged about
40.

Old Government House, Perth

Eliza Shaw, aged
80 years

Will and Eliza's
youngest son
Robert Cassan Shaw

Hester Frances
(Fanny) ninth and
last child of Will
and Eliza Shaw

Mrs John Nicol Drummond in her latter years. She was born Mary Shaw, second daughter of Will and Eliza

Last entry in the Journal of Eliza Shaw, 1876

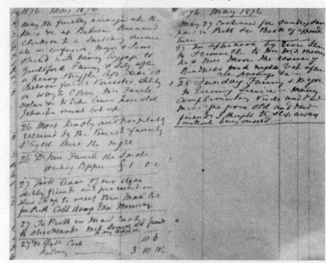

it that Hutt, despite his unfortunate affiliations, was a man of sound judgement and incorruptible integrity who could be relied upon for a fair hearing on all counts. As the accession of a fair young Queen to the throne of England had augured a new era for Empire, so, it was hoped, might the arrival of a new Governor herald brighter prospects for Swan River settlement.

Hutt made a good first impression by appointing to the Legislative Council four non-officials—namely William Brockman, William Tanner, George Leake and Thomas Peel. He also made it known that he was available for private interviews with all settlers who had problems to discuss with him.

But those who imagined that they would receive more liberal treatment than from their previous Governor were soon sadly disillusioned. Hutt, who has been described as a 'radical idealist', was a man of austere and orderly mind who had arrived in the colony already convinced that the problems of the settlement were largely due to the lack of system with which it had been formed.

Stirling, a landholder himself, had temporized as far as possible regarding the surrender of unimproved holdings, though he had warned the colonists that the time limit on their still-virgin blocks in scattered areas expired in 1840. Hutt began the process of 'tidying up' within a few days of his arrival, explaining it to the disgruntled settlers as a duty conferred on him by Her Majesty's Government, to sort out the muddled state of affairs in the Lands Department and deal with all the loosely held and widely scattered holdings on which no improvements had been made. As a compromise, however, he devised a plan whereby settlers were allowed to retain a quarter of such blocks, and in return for confiscated land were to be given 1s 6d an acre with which to purchase crown land elsewhere.

The general practice of temporarily occupying unclaimed land—commonly termed 'squatting'—that had been taken for granted in the first free-for-all days of outer settlement, was also to come under stern review. The frontier settlers were to protest in vain against the suggestion of their insatiable land hunger, stating that they were hungry, not for land itself, but for good pasture and permanent water. Being obliged to take in much useless country comprising sandy and often poison-infested areas in the blocks assigned to them, they asked in a memorial to the Governor, of March 1842, what they were to do in the summer months when their leased acres had been eaten or burned out? The imposed measure, they insisted, would merely discourage the increase of sheep and also the outlay of capital in the colony.[3] The Governor eventually introduced a system of pastoral licences in payment of a fee for the use of unappropriated land, and although many settlers either neglected or refused to make the stipulated application and continued operating as before, none could escape the tightening up of regulations on the fulfilment of location duties.

This further highlighted the urgent need for competent labour, for as the settlers' legal obligations increased so did their need for more hands to put up fences, yards and shacks, to clear for the plough, to sow and reap, husband the stock and attend the multifarious other tasks related to farming and marketing. Adverse reports about the settlement continued to curb the natural flow of immigration, and the resulting stasis was one of Hutt's immediate problems.

Before leaving England he had become a director, along with Wakefield, of an organization known as The Western Australian Company, which planned a settlement at Port Leschenault, about 100 miles south of Fremantle, to be known as Australind. It was anticipated that about 1,000 immigrants a year would come out under this scheme and the first contingent arrived in 1841. Although it was to prove yet another unfulfilled dream, it did bring in nearly 500 people, among them members of some of the colony's most distinguished families, before the grand project faded out in 1844.[4]

A plan to introduce Indian servants, urged by a number of settlers, was officially approved by the local authorities but declined by the Indian Government, leaving to speculation how this and other schemes for the introduction of Asian labour might, had they succeeded, have affected the history of the colony.

Another bait for immigrants was an agent stationed in London to encourage settlers to take advantage of bounty regulations operated by a Land and Emigration Commission.

According to official statements issued in February 1842, labourers of specified categories, either single or with small families, could apply to the Government Emigration Office in Westminster for free passages to NSW, Van Diemen's Land, New Zealand or Western Australia. Preference was given to shepherds and farm labourers, carpenters and builders of all kinds, blacksmiths, wheelwrights, harness makers, tailors and shoemakers, seamstresses and domestic servants. The generous terms of the public announcement indicated not only the demand for workers following the cessation of transportation in the eastern colonies, but the eagerness of the Home Government to be rid of as much surplus population as possible. Although it was stipulated that residents of workhouses or recipients of any kind of parish relief were not considered eligible, history was to show that this regulation was too often overlooked or somehow circumvented, resulting in an embarrassing proportion of the helpless, hopeless and totally unskilled. Nonetheless, before it ground to a stop in the Australia-wide economic recession of the mid-forties, it resulted for Western Australia in the introduction of about 450 emigrants, many of whom were to prove useful members of the community.

Will Shaw had been convinced that Stirling, for all his tact and sympathy, had been too heavily under the influence of Peter Brown and John Septimus Roe ever to make a favourable ruling on behalf of one who had fallen out with them. He had therefore been one of the first to approach the new Governor to set forth anew the case he had so far pleaded in vain.

Hutt made careful note of his claims, relating them no doubt to former correspondence on the subject and calling upon the experience of the Colonial Secretary and Surveyor-General. Receiving at last what he considered to be an unsatisfactory and evasive reply, Shaw once more patiently listed his wrongs in a wordy memorial that he asked to be forwarded to the Secretary of State for Colonies. He began at the beginning of his colonial adventure, reiterating that it was only through an act of God that the *Egyptian* had failed to arrive before the end of 1829, but that after a decade of 'mental sufferings, injured constitutions, bodily labour, little or no protection either to life or property the law being a complete dead letter, (at one period some starvation), disappointments innumerable, with exile in the Deserts of Swan River', he continued to get no more than evasive answers concerning the balance of 10,376¾ acres still due to him as his 'service or remission grant'. 'Fair promises but no redress' were his lot despite his investment of £1,385 0s 0d, and this not including his considerable outlay in rum and brandy which was required as part payment for indentured labour, and a further sum of £549 16s 4d which he had been forced to invest in 'live and dead stock' after arrival. On the other hand, one James Kenton, who had come out on the *Parmelia* and almost at once opened a hostelry in Perth, had obtained a grant of 4,000 acres (now part of Brown's estate) 'upon little more than a common chest of carpenter's tools'.[5]

This last statement would seem to have been based on hearsay. Shaw had applied to the Colonial Secretary to be furnished with a list of property imported by Kenton, hoping to forward it as proof to the Secretary of State of the local government's unjust distribution of land. This request was firmly refused on the grounds that it was impossible to furnish him with any document with which he was not primarily concerned.

Shaw again drew attention to the refusal of the local government either to deduct from his crown debts damages sustained by native depredations—themselves a proof of the poor protection granted the settlers—and to the fact that he had so far been refused a position of Inspector of Police which would have helped him pay his debts.

Hutt replied that Shaw's memorial would be transmitted as so urgently requested, but that he had no prospect of satisfaction from the Secretary of State since this dignitary had previously declared that the decision of the Colonial Board of Council was to be considered as final.

Shaw lost no time in pointing out that the Home Government's use of the word 'final' applied only in so far as the local Board had discharged its duties fairly and honestly and had not unjustly favoured certain settlers above others.[6] This led him to reiterate the full details of his case against Brown and to request that they be included with his other submissions to England.

Hutt agreed to do so but reminded him of Lord Glenelg's previous statement that it was neither in his 'power nor his province' to review the decision of the local court and that he saw no reason to doubt its propriety. Shaw's proper means of redress, Hutt said, had surely lain with the Governor in Council to whom he should have appealed at the time of the case. Shaw's answer was that this would have got him nowhere since, as admitted by Stirling himself, it would only have meant his again appearing before 'the very parties most interested in the decision and who had already appeared in so strong a phalanx against me ...'[7]

Shaw had, by this time, if not before, lost all sense of proportion regarding his accumulated wrongs. He now informed the Governor that if he was to have no satisfaction from the Secretary of State he would put his case before the 'British Public and Parliament', since there could not be 'on record in the British Jurisprudence such a glaring instance of injustice and oppression in even attempting to set aside a Bond and Agreement of the character and spirit under which this survey was executed'.[8]

This would seem to have put an end to Hutt's patience in the matter, for a note appended in his bold, even hand instructs Brown that the local government must positively decline again troubling His Majesty's Government with any more of Shaw's diatribes.

Shaw himself, however, still continued to pin his faith to the ideals of British justice and his right of appeal to the Crown, for which he had gladly borne arms in victorious combat and through which his wrongs would surely be redressed and his debts paid. With little apparent concept of the correspondence of Empire that poured day by day into the Colonial Office, he wrote always as though completely confident of the justice of his cause vibrating through the corridors of power to the foot of the throne itself.

Will Tanner, who had returned from England on the *Britomart* in 1838, had agreed to the Shaws retaining the tenancy of Baskerville and had taken up residence on one of his several other Upper Swan properties. He lent a fresh and attentive ear to their problems and agreed that the verdict in the land dispute had showed some bias in favour of the Colonial Secretary. Having failed to get satisfaction from either Hutt or the Home Government, Shaw prevailed upon his good friend to give his own written testimony of the survey of 1831 in which he had acted as one of the arbitrators. In this Tanner reaffirmed that it had been Brown, not Shaw, who had pressed to have the job done with the instruments to hand, on the reasoning that it would be as 'fair for one as for the other'. He also attested that none of those associated with the survey had regarded the line arrived at as a temporary one.[9]

Armed with this 'new evidence', Shaw again approached the Governor through the Colonial Secretary requesting that his memorial and documents be forwarded to the Secretary of State. In so doing he did not fail to remind the Governor of his Secretary's having been granted 8,000 acres of additional land when the survey went against him in 1831, adding that had Mr Tanner been in the colony at the time 'several parties would have been careful how they had instituted the proceedings against me by which I have been so great a sufferer'.[10]

Wearily Hutt replied that since the Secretary of State had so adamantly refused to interfere with the decision of the local court, it was useless forwarding any additional papers no matter what new evidence was brought forward. When Shaw came to Perth to present his inevitable reply, Hutt summoned him to a personal interview. During this he pointed out that had the British Government not upheld the decisions of colonial courts—except in cases where the royal prerogative of mercy was evoked—it would indeed have been guilty of the sort of interference with local affairs to which the colonists, including Shaw himself, so strenuously objected.

The interview seems temporarily to have mollified Shaw, though he still refused to accept the fact that he could expect no redress from the British Government. As firmly as he believed in a personal God, he had always believed in his country's concern for the sons who had fought for her. That she would send them forth to frustrate her enemies or otherwise expand her Empire, and then so cynically abandon them to injustice and ruin, he found it as yet impossible to concede. He did at least, however, pay some attention to Tanner's advice that he try to set old scores aside and concentrate on developing the good land to which he held the undisputed right.

Chapter 16

1839–1844

Nat Shaw Goes His Own Way

Will Shaw secures Toodyay property. Nat Shaw takes over. Toodyay personalities, S P Phillips, James Drummond, Government Botanist and son John Nicol, Police Inspector. Nat severely injured by Aboriginal assistants. The culprits arrested by J N Drummond and sent to Rottnest Island prison. Will Shaw urges more protection. Nat applies unsuccessfully for position of Police Inspector and takes on contract work in the Williams district.

By 1839 Will Shaw had become disillusioned with the immediate potential of his still untouched 7,096-acre grant on the Avon river near York, and had borrowed money to purchase a 1,000-acre block [Location 20] in the fertile Toodyay valley. At the same time he applied for the position of police inspector, and had he obtained this post seems to have intended moving the family headquarters from Belvoir to the Toodyay property. As it happened the position was granted to John Nicol Drummond, so it was decided that while Will Shaw and other members of his family carried on the Swan block, Nat should make a start in the Toodyay area. The proposition no doubt attracted Nat for there was talk of its soon becoming a centre for racing and horse-breeding. His greatest interest had always lain in this direction, and he had been involved for some years in the small race meetings encouraged by the Agricultural Society. He was of light build, an excellent rider and skilled in the handling and breaking of horses.

Before leaving home he had placed in his mother's care a box containing some cherished mementoes of his brief boyhood—a few curios he had brought from the Cape of Good

Hope, a collection of birds' eggs, some Aboriginal artifacts and a bundle of letters from his friend Johnnie Gamble of Thrussington, with whom he had probably long since ceased to correspond. Although Eliza used what she referred to as 'Nat's strong deal box' for her own treasured letters and business documents, it is doubtful whether the owner ever opened it again. He was a man now, anxious to make his way in the tough young colony by whatever means lay to his hand. He had energy and initiative and was at home in the bush—never afraid of solitude, indifferent to discomfort and able to live off the land like an Aboriginal. He walked with the quick, springing step of a horseman, though unable at times to disguise the slight limp he had sustained in a fall from a horse. He had several knotted ribs from the same cause and was subject, after being tossed off on his head, to occasional migraine headaches.

He left Belvoir in a horse-drawn dray in which he had thrown his working clothes, a few blankets, some basic cooking gear and a collection of tools. On arrival he selected a building site, cut timber for a shack, sank a well and roughed up some troughing for the sheep that were soon to be brought from the Swan. The job suited him well enough for, although it earned him no more than pocket money and his keep, he was able, from time to time, to take on the comparatively lucrative job of horse-breaking for Mr Samuel Pole Phillips whose big property, Culham, named after his family estate in Oxfordshire, adjoined Nat's southern border.

Phillips, a moneyed man, had gone into partnership with Edward Hamersley of Pyrton with whom he was connected by marriage.[1] At the time they took up Culham, Hamersley was planning to return to England to marry and Phillips had agreed to manage their Toodyay property meanwhile.[2] The arrangement suited Phillips very well and he proceeded to create a life in the Toodyay valley that was as close as possible to that of an English squire. Like many of the colony's early pioneers, he was a man of considerable scholarship and had almost completed his studies for the ministry when he decided to join his friend in the Swan River settlement. He appreciated Nat for his knowledge of local conditions and the handling of horseflesh, and appointed him his jockey-in-chief at Avon race meetings.

These occasions were already an institution with the settlers who had begun moving into the district several years before, among them a number of people whom Nat had known well around the Swan. The Government Botanist, James Drummond, with his wife, four sons—Thomas, James Jnr, John Nicol and Johnston—and younger daughter Euphemia, had taken up the 2,900-acre Hawthornden property in 1838.

Then there was Captain Francis Whitfield, a retired army officer and his family who had arrived in the colony in 1830. Whitfield had been appointed Resident Magistrate at Guildford and in 1838 had been transferred to Toodyay, where he and his family had started farming on their 4,059-acre property, Knockdominie.

Francis Whitfield Jnr, the eldest son, had a special reason for seeking Nat's company as he had been courting his sister Elizabeth before leaving the Upper Swan, and if the Shaw parents had hoped that her admirer's removal to Toodyay would put an end to the romance they were sadly mistaken. For nearly five years, almost every traveller between Toodyay and Guildford was entrusted with letters from one to the other, during which time Francis was an eager volunteer for taking down the annual clip to Guildford, from whence it was taken by barge to Fremantle or kept by local merchants in exchange for stores. The arduous journey of a week or more with heavily loaded bullock teams was no burden to a young man on the way to visit his beloved.

The courtship might not have been so long drawn-out had the Whitfield fortunes not met with a sad setback when they had been in the new district little more than a year. The cause of the trouble was not, in this case, the hot blood of youth, but the indiscretion of the unfortunate magistrate himself, whose affair with a servant girl had so tragic an outcome that he was forced to tender his resignation. He was thereafter not only ostracized by society but deserted by his family, his sons George and Francis going into partnership on a nearby property.

The position of magistrate was given over to Captain John Scully, whose 2,000-acre property at Bolgart lay only a few miles to the north of the Shaw block. Nat enjoyed the company of this robust Irishman, whose place was open house to convivial neighbours, passing travellers or members of the mounted constabulary, of which John Nicol Drummond was then in charge. Drummond had been chosen for this position because of his reputed influence with the tribespeople and his knowledge of their customs and languages. Born in County Cork and thirteen years old when he arrived in the settlement, he had rapidly become something of a local prototype of the bold border raiders of his Scottish ancestry. He developed his own loyalties, established his own laws and his own code of ethics. He was not only a splendid rider and a crack shot, but had learned from the Aborigines every facet of the bush law by which they lived. Rumour had it that he also shared with them the women to whom he was entitled according to the relationships bestowed on him by the south-western tribes. He was nonetheless appreciated by the settlers, especially the younger generation and, despite the fact that he sometimes admitted to having shot a native 'in the course of duty', was much respected by the Aborigines. As time passed, however, it became obvious to the authorities that although sober and hard-working he was quite impossible as a servant of the crown. His habit of cutting red tape, acting without official instructions and failing to fill in forms irritated them beyond measure.

Drummond himself saw this as the only way of handling the situation, for the Toodyay Aborigines were then behaving in much the same way as those of the Swan and Canning districts in earlier years. While firing the bush to aid their hunting they were destroying crops and, when reprimanded, took to spearing stock, stealing and threatening the settlers' lives. Old James Drummond had encouraged his children to view the Aborigines with a mixture of human understanding and scientific objectivity, and his son James Jnr, who managed the family farm, had set the example of employing a number as shepherds and general farm labourers. While maintaining a firm hand with native miscreants, he had also shown disapproval of unjust or unsympathetic treatment of the Aborigines on the part of the whites, and had established a custom of holding an annual feast to which all the local tribespeople were invited. Others followed his example and by the end of the decade, with the help of Benedictine missionaries, the unpredictable savages of the Toodyay valley and the Victoria Plains were well on the way to as reasonable an integration as had been achieved anywhere in Australia. Persuaded that infanticide was against the new law of the land, they were also on their way to becoming the drifting, part-white fringe dwellers of little consequence whose bitter frustration would be visited on the puzzled white community of another century.

John Drummond was the same age as Nat Shaw and had become friendly with him before his family left the Upper Swan. He therefore welcomed him to the district and procured for him three native helpers—Pengally, Dyuleba and Bob— who camped on the block with their families and were often, for considerable periods, the only company he had. Nat supplied rations and other perquisites in return for their services, and no doubt accepted the occasional offer of a woman as was within the tribal tradition of hospitality. Pengally, his most reliable helper, had the reputation of being something of a witchdoctor or healer, and when Nat was suffering from one of his recurrent headaches would treat him to a form of head massage known as *Booyleing*, which, if not magical as claimed, was apparently soothing.

Nat had been on the Toodyay property for about two years when one day, in June 1841, a member of John Drummond's force brought along a native who had been arrested on a charge of theft. As Captain Scully was in Guildford at the time, and Sam Phillips of Culham was also from home, Nat agreed to hold the offender in a shed pending the magistrate's return. The native was still in his custody when Nat was smitten with migraine and the obliging Pengally, possibly with no malice aforethought, proceeded to minister to him, making occasional retreats into the forest, in order, as he explained, to recharge his magical powers. On one of these brief excursions he was persuaded by the other two natives to assist in the release of the prisoner, who was related to the man named Bob. Pengally maintained, in the confused evidence that later emerged, that Bob had intended merely striking the white man on the mouth but that the blow was misdirected and the axe (no less!) descended across the middle of his face.

Mr Francis Armstrong, acting as interpreter at the subsequent trial, explained that the Aborigines were under the curious impression that a white man could be rendered temporarily powerless by a blow on the mouth and that the word *boom-a*, by which the accused described their intention, could be variously translated as 'to strike', 'to stun', or 'to kill' outright.[3] In many parts of Australia Aborigines still use the word 'kill' as meaning to hit, maim or wound. To deal a fatal blow is to 'kill dead-fella'.

Whatever the intention, the result for Nat was a severed cartilage, lacerated cheeks and a fractured jaw, but despite his terrible injury he managed somehow to stagger to his feet and holding his jaw in his hands to cover the ten miles of bush track to Scully's residence. In the meantime, Bob and his accomplices released their countryman and ransacked their master's store, getting off with what provisions they could carry—and a brace of pistols.

The story of this outrage grew in magnitude with every mile it travelled, until it was avowed that not only had Nat Shaw been dealt a death blow but that the natives concerned were now rallying their countrymen in great numbers and were pillaging arms and ammunition from isolated settlements with intent to wipe out the entire white population of the Avon Valley. The *Perth Gazette*, with sensible restraint for which it congratulated itself in a subsequent issue,[4] refrained from publishing the rumours until it was ascertained that only the three natives concerned had been arrested and were safely under lock and key. Truth to tell, the Aborigines of the different tribal groups felt no more loyalty to each other—and sometimes considerably less—than to the white families to whom they had become attached. In fact, during this time natives working around the scattered homesteads refused even to go for their customary bush walkabouts for fear of incurring suspicion of being implicated in the crime. It was, moreover, an Aboriginal named Boo-on, an associate of John Nicol Drummond, who led the offenders into a trap under pretence of assisting them to fool the police. Persuaded by Boo-on to camp at a locality agreed upon with their pursuers, they were surprised and captured by a party including John Drummond, Sam Phillips, Boo-on and two other natives. Brought to Perth by Drummond, they were tried by Judge Mackie for wounding with intent to murder, and all three sentenced to death. The penalty, probably at the instigation of Governor Hutt, was commuted to life imprisonment on Rottnest Island, from where there is no record of their ever having returned to roam the forests of their forefathers.

Governor Hutt had seen the establishment of an Aboriginal penal reserve on Rottnest Island, about twelve miles from the coast at Fremantle, as a humane alternative to the close confinement and chaining of prisoners on the mainland. It was to be a place where the natives would be 'instructed in useful knowledge and trained in the habits of civilization'. This dream was never realized, since exile from their tribal country was literally a fate worse than death for an Aboriginal. Hundreds were to die there from epidemic diseases or sheer homesickness, and none who survived their sentences returned with any desire to emulate the culture of a people capable of conceiving so cruel a punishment.

On the whole the Aborigines accepted capital punishment much more philosophically than exile. Execution was a fate they understood from their own law, even though the white man's reasons for such a sentence were often different from their own. They believed the spirits of men returned to earth in the form of birds, beasts, fish or insects, and sometimes as white men. Not only Governor Stirling but many settlers were later 'recognized' as the reincarnations of departed relatives. Now that the white man seemed clearly to have taken over, and had proved himself superior in technical advancement and the possession of hitherto unheard-of amenities, it seemed that death, with the prospect of returning as a member of this fortunate fraternity, could have definite compensations. A case in point is a report about this time of the execution of an Aboriginal named Mendie for the murder of a white man named Burkenshaw Cox at Canning River. The prisoner being taken in a cart to the place of execution assumed a degree of cheerfulness which surprised all, induced, apparently, by a firm belief that he would after death reappear in this world as a white man. He remained quite indifferent to the proceedings to the end.

Will Shaw, on hearing of the attack on his son, had hurried to Toodyay where he conferred with the leading Avon settlers, including Scully and Phillips. All were agreed that the incident should be presented to the Governor as further evidence for the need of military protection for the newly settled area, stressing that relatives of the convicted men had vowed to kill Nat should he ever return to the Toodyay property, and that they would no doubt take revenge on other settlers if immediate steps were not taken to 'awe them into subjection'.[5]

This letter, dispatched after Will Shaw's return to Belvoir with his injured son, brought forth a reply from the Governor to the effect that the population of the area was too sparse to justify the establishment of a military detachment. He expressed confidence in John Nicol Drummond's small force efficiently dealing with any further problems that might arise thereabouts.

Whether Nat had grown disheartened with his lonely battle or feared the threatened Aboriginal reprisal, he was never to return to the Toodyay property. We find him, however, after a two months' period of recuperation, writing from Belvoir to apply for the position of Inspector of Police and Aboriginal Protector, operating from Bejoording, only about ten miles north of his Toodyay block. In so doing he stressed that his knowledge of the country, habits and customs of the natives, and the references he would most surely obtain from influential settlers, rendered him especially suitable for this position.[6] Governor Hutt evidently thought otherwise, for he observed in a terse footnote to the application that 'after what has so unhappily occurred between Mr Shaw and the Toodyay natives that gentleman is surely the last person who should be selected for the post.'[7]

When next we hear of him, Nat had taken on a contract carrying job for the government which led him on a far-ranging trail between a number of outpost settlements, though he gave his address over this period as 'The Williams'—a small township on a river of that name about 100 miles south of Toodyay. He also secured the mail contract between Perth and Albany, but this he later let out to a man named John Mitchell whom he equipped with a good horse and kept in provisions. In the summer of 1844 this man, while conveying the mail from Williams to Albany, somehow missed the ill-defined track, and was lost for five days, narrowly escaping death. In a letter to the Governor explaining the delay in the mail delivery and evidently fearful of losing his contract, Nat Shaw undertook to assist in re-marking the road by blazing trees along the way. 'As it is,' he wrote, 'it is quite unsafe for travellers ... Not long ago a man of Mr Waylen's was lost ten days and at last made the road near Kojonup, near dead ...'[8] The Governor added a footnote to the letter that no blame was attached to Mr Shaw in this matter and that the mails had hitherto been carried with great regularity.

Nat's real love continued to be horse-training and racing, and it was his dream to build up enough capital to start on his own in the business of breeding remounts for the Indian army as 'Squire' Phillips and others planned to do. His prospects, however, were not very bright, for free land grants were long since a thing of the past and the meagre return of his grinding toil was no substitute for the inherited wealth or supplemented incomes of the more fortunately placed. He was never really at ease in those circles to which he belonged by birth but not by education, and he was doomed to carry, for the rest of his life, along with a lame leg, the shocking mutilation of an axe wound across his face, a crooked jaw and a broken nose. In a country where white women were at a premium, there was now little chance of his ever winning a wife even were fortune to favour him in other respects. There is indeed no evidence of his encountering any great luck in the few, hard-working, lone-wandering years that were left to him.

Chapter 17

1841–1843

Colonial Tapestry

Will Shaw's complicated finances. His hopes for wine
industry. E W Landor writes of the local situation.
Community life of Upper Swan district. Shaw friends,
W Tanner, S Viveash and families. Landor describes
a colonial family. First Upper Swan school at Henley
Park. Wedding of Elizabeth Shaw and Francis Whitfield. Their departure for farm near Toodyay.

Will Shaw's financial problems, far from being simplified, were
becoming more involved year by year. Maintaining that the
Crown owed him both land and money, he had consistently
refused to pay interest on his mortgage to the government.
Will Tanner, however, must have received his due for he
agreed to extend his arrangement of 1834 for an indefinite
period that was not to be terminated within his lifetime.
Whether Eliza had, in the meantime, received her father's little
legacy, the sum originally loaned by Tanner, is nowhere stated.

Shaw had apparently repaid the money borrowed from
George Leake in 1836 on the security of his Avon acres, but
he had since raised a further £520 12s 8d from Leake and
Shenton and another £160 from Tanner after his return from
England in 1838—both sums on the security of the Avon
property. From part of this money he had purchased the
1,000 acres of freehold in the Toodyay valley which Nat had
at once started to develop.

In 1840 he had borrowed £600 at interest from Mrs Will
Brockman's brother, Edward Hamersley of Pyrton, on the
security of his new block and his other Avon holdings.[1] He
then immediately returned Tanner his second loan, but failed
to pay interest to Hamersley who, after sueing him in vain for

£54 4s 11d in 1842 served notice of foreclosure failing payment of the £600 loan, plus legal costs.[2] As Shaw was unable to meet this sum Hamersley presumably foreclosed, taking over the 5,096-acre Avon block and continuing to bill Shaw for the unpaid interest. He was also, over this period, being sued by Leake and Shenton for £120 1s 2d, and by Alfred Waylen the original owner of the Culham block, for an unspecified sum.

Needless to say this meant that Shaw spent a great deal of valuable time plying up and down the river to attend court in Perth and trying to persuade his various creditors to bear with him until his ship came home. (In this he was apparently successful where Leake, Shenton and Waylen were concerned as they were not paid off until 1856.) Shaw believed that, given his just due, this happy day should not be long delayed, for like several others in the district he had embarked on the manufacture of wine which found a ready sale on the local market. Whatever the struggling settlers were unable to afford, alcohol was not one of them and since he had acquired two bounty emigrants to help extend his area under vines he had every hope of an expanding industry. Belvoir, with the adjoining property still under lease, would seem from some accounts to have been a fairly well developed mixed farm with paddocks given over to grazing, wheat, fodder crops and vegetables. There is no doubt however that the situation in which the Shaws found themselves during this period was often little short of desperate. The more Will turned to alcohol for consolation the worse the outlook became for his wife and family. A tragic glimpse of their predicament is provided by a letter from a young man who came out in January 1843, writing to his father in Manchester:

... I was very much disappointed on my arrival to find such a place and so dull, every one, almost, complaining ... So far as I have been it's sand, sand, sand almost middle leg deep ... very little grass and that burnt in a day or two when the heat sets in ... I'm told there is better land over the Hills ... I'll believe it when I see it, have been so deceived respecting what I have seen ...

On landing I hastened up the Country about 20 miles to see Captain Shaw, Mrs Smallwood's brother, who had been

161

sold up a short time before under an execution. Mrs Smallwood was expecting he was doing so well and even that he would be sending some of his daughters to England to finish their education, but I believe they are greatly in debt here. About the time of their sale his wife attempted her life as her neck bears ample testimony. I cannot say exactly how this state of affairs has happened, but I believe it is mainly owing to indulgence on his part and cultivating and clearing some ground, which, when the Surveyor came over it proved not to be upon his Estate, and was far the best near it which of course was a serious expense to him . . .[3]

A young barrister named Edward Landor who arrived in 1841 and some years later published an account of the colony,[4] described Will Shaw as a pioneer sheepfarmer, 'laborious and indefatigable in the prosecution of his agricultural pursuits'. The friendship he formed with the Shaw family at this time was to last throughout the years. He was interested to hear from them of their battle to make ends meet and the injustices they had suffered since their arrival. Indeed, in Landor's berating of Secretaries of State as 'instruments of broken promises and betrayed faith,' one hears an echo of the Shaws' own frustration.

The inhabitants, disappointed and deceived, have no trust in their rulers . . . from whose decree there is no appeal and from whose oppression no redress. The best informed among English statesmen know nothing of colonies, but their hardihood in legislating for them is equal to their ignorance.

He bitterly attacked the Home Government for its alternating attitudes of tyranny and neglect, for its failure to provide money for roads (had not 'the first act of Roman sway' ever been to lay down good lines of communication through the conquered country?), for its dismissal of many colonial dispatches as being deemed too old on arrival to be of any importance, and for the vetoing by a noble Duke in the House of Lords of a bill for convict labour on the grounds of its being an evil system.

In what respect, [he asks] has she [England] ever proved

herself a good parent to any of her colonies? ... She has permitted them to exist and bound them down to serf-like dependence and so she keeps them—feeble, helpless and hopeless.

Further to stress his point, Landor quotes Lord Stanley, who had succeeded Lord Glenelg as Secretary of State for Colonies: 'If you don't keep our Colonies in a state of dependence, of what use are they?' Landor may also have had in mind Shaw's case, among other similar instances, in observing that although a generally good and kindly feeling prevailed in local society, where individual interests were concerned men could be completely unscrupulous and would sneer at the idea of disinterested behaviour. This led him to deplore the lack of solid English clergy of whom there were only six—widely scattered and no bishop among them—in the colony.

The tendency of colonization, [Landor concludes] is to deteriorate. The young have no guides but self-interest, relieved by a few touches of good-nature ... Boys, the sons of educated men, are clearly made to supply the place of labourers and servants. Hardy and manly, they are naturally rough and uncouth in manner, and unhappily possess no mental stores beyond those early principles of gain which have grown with their growth ... the malleable intellect of youth is annealed by the Demon of gain upon the anvil of self-interest.

The same writer also has some caustic remarks to make about a certain type of migrant.

A great deal of discontent and repining generally prevails in a colony. People who have lived miserably in England, who have long doubtfully hovered between suicide and highway robbery, determine at length to adopt the still more melancholy alternative of emigration. After bequeathing a few tender sighs to the country which they have hitherto regarded rather as a step-mother than a parent; and having pathetically solicited the sympathy of those who more readily bestow upon them a few pounds than a few tears, in the pious hope of never seeing them more, our emigrants betake themselves to the favoured land of their adoption, in the full and confident belief that they have nothing now to do, but live 'like gentlemen', though without the means, or any other qualifications of that class. Their Faith is of that affecting and unlimited description, as to lead them to suppose that He who beneficently feeds the ravens will not neglect the rooks or the drones.

In a very short time, however, they find that they are no better off in the new than they were in the old country. The gum-trees do not produce bread, nor the banksias shoulders of mutton; and, consequently, their hopes have been miserably disappointed, and they loudly proclaim their wants and sorrows in the streets. There are unfortunately in all colonies —those *refugia peccatorum*—many emigrants of this class, idle and worthless, who have never done well, and never will succeed in any part of the world.

A colonial life is not for these men, and we recommend them to pass on to some other region as quickly as possible.[5]

The story of every colonial family of these times is crisscrossed by the same local happenings and community enterprises, and individual histories can be seen in perspective only against the common background of current events and growing traditions. Much general interest revolved around the Agricultural Society, of which Guildford was the main centre, its annual fair drawing people from all over the settlement. On such occasions prizes were given for all manner of local products, and competitions were arranged for the encouragement and display of local skills. One novel form of entertainment was a ploughing match in which two men contested the turning of an acre of ground, the owner of the outfit producing the straightest furrows being entitled to the loser's bullocks complete with yokes and chains.

It is clear from all accounts that, despite hard times, social activities were never permitted to decline. Besides private parties, musical evenings and gatherings after Sunday services, there were now organized regional race meetings and big, unscheduled rallies to the scenes of summer bushfires, women and girls in the background plying the weary men with cakes and tea.

In a generally hospitable community the Tanners were

always well to the fore, their parties enlivened by a number of fascinating novelties they had brought with them from England. These included a modern wonder known as a Magic Lantern that projected a breathtaking range of images, from Biblical and classical subjects to rather less edifying political cartoons. They had also among their treasures 'a mechanical device for displaying the movements of heavenly bodies' named after its inventor, the Earl of Orrery.[6]

With the Tanners on their return from England in 1838 had come their relatives Dr and Mrs Sam Viveash, who soon took an important place in the community. After a few years in the York area they made their home at Wexcombe, previously one of the Tanners' Swan properties, which became another focal point of hospitality.[7] Dr Viveash had evidently intended settling into the more or less placid life of a gentleman farmer, but the lamentable shortage of doctors in the colony soon forced him back into practice for 'an interim period'. This was to continue, along with magisterial duties, almost to the end of his long life, during which he and his good wife figure in most contemporary records at social functions, at sick-bed and child-bed, and on the scenes of local accidents and epidemics.

The Shaws' home also remained a popular rendezvous, for through all their difficulties they presented a cheerful family front and the two lively grown girls, Elizabeth and Mary, were a great attraction. Edward Landor's description of an unnamed Swan River family may well have applied to them at this time:

How cheerful looks that large room with its glorious fire of jarrah wood and blackboys, and how lightly those young girls move about arranging a tea-table and preparing the evening meal. The kind-hearted mother, relieved of all duties but that of superintendence, sits by the fire chattering cheerfully with the guest, whose eyes nevertheless wander about the room after a certain light and dancing shape. The host, full of hospitality and noble courtesy, discourses not only of the crops and colonial politics, but of literature and the last news from England, for like many other colonists he receives the English papers and patronizes the Quarterly Review ...

There is no beating about the bush for a bed, or an invitation to supper. Of the latter he is certain and indifferent about the former, for having slept the last night under a tree, he feels sure of making himself comfortable on the sofa. And then the girls who have no affectation or nonsense about them, crowd around and ply him with questions about their young friends in other parts of the colony, and whether he was at the last ball at Government House and what was most worn on that occasion ...

During the evening the girls sing, and happily they sing well ... Suddenly horses at a gallop are heard to enter the yard and two young fellows, fresh from the capital, come dashing into the room ... Here is authority of undoubted value for everything relating to the ball ... This naturally inspires the young people with a desire to dance, so the table is pushed aside, and mamma takes her place at the piano and bursts off with the Annen Polka.

It may seem strange to you dear reader, who have an idea that colonists are merely wild beasts, that such things could be ... But they are not entirely insensible to the good opinion of great people; for when they learned that the Polka was thought vulgar at Buckingham Palace, they had serious intentions of denying it admittance into the ball-rooms of Perth; and I sincerely believe that it would have pined away and died but for a confidently entertained hope that Her Majesty would never hear of the offences of the people of Perth ...[8]

But whether or not Landor was in fact writing of the Shaws, behind this idyll of colonial life was inevitably the story of hard toil and determined effort to adapt the standards and culture of the old world to the new environment. All the young Shaws, with the exception of little Fanny, born in June 1838, were contributing to the upkeep of the estate, for hands were never sufficient to coax a living from their unpredictable land. There were sheep to be shorn, pigs and poultry to be fed, cows to be milked. The wheat must be sown, harvested, threshed, winnowed, bagged and marketed. There was the pruning of vines, the picking and crushing of grapes, the cleaning and filling of the wine casks. Inside there was the constant work of cooking and bread-making. There was butter to churn, bacon and meat to be cured or spiced, as well as the making of jams, pickles, preserves and dried fruit. Like most of their fellow settlers the Shaws also made their own soap and candles, hand-sewed serviceable clothing from galatea, strong calico, moleskin and blue drill, and often shoes from canvas or kangaroo skins.

Somehow or other the children were also acquiring an education of sorts. Mary had two or three years broken schooling in Perth, while George, Lucy Ellen and Robert Casson attended a little brushwood school put up in 1839 at the instigation of Captain Irwin on a corner of his Henley Park property. This establishment was in charge of the Rev Mitchell, whose own children were pupils along with those of various Upper Swan settlers. These included the young Irwins, the Barrett-Lennards of St Leonards, young Edmund Brockman of Herne Hill, the two Tanner boys, several Minchins and Sam Moore's son Will. A childhood memory handed down by Edmund Brockman is of their bare-footed progress —shoes being still scarce even in the 1840s—to and from the school at Henley Park. In the summer months when the bush tracks grew fiery hot they would bound along like kangaroos from one patch of shade to the next.[9] Some of the pupils would cross the river by way of a make-shift bridge made from fallen logs—others in rough-hewn canoes. Each child carried a packet of lunch, a slate and the precious home-work exercise that sometimes got immersed or splashed when crossing the river—an accident for which no allowances were made! In the winter months between May and October, when the river was running strongly from bank to bank the children on the south side had to walk to Oakover to cross by the little bridge which Sam Moore had erected, and which served the community well until washed away in the flood of 1851.

As time went on, the school was moved from one locality to another to serve the needs of the families concerned or the convenience of whosoever could be found to undertake the role of teacher.

In the summer of 1843, Francis Whitfield, down once more with the teams from Toodyay, made formal request to Will Shaw for the hand of his eldest daughter. It was little use Will's asking whether he could keep her in the comfort to which she was accustomed, for Elizabeth had been doing a man's as well as a woman's work for a number of years. It was agreed however that they would not be married before July, giving time for the making of wedding dress complete with crinoline, and for the organization of a reception befitting the daughter of one of the 'first families'.

The marriage, at which the Rev Mitchell officiated, took place in the little Upper Swan church on the river bank, and however Eliza may have felt about the loss of the daughter who had been her closest companion and firmest support, she saw that it was the occasion of a happy and memorable gathering of pioneer families. One can picture the mixed feelings of the bride as she and her young husband started off from Baskerville in their horse and cart, waved out of sight by her two younger brothers, by the lovely eighteen-year-old Mary, Lucy Ellen and the five-year-old Fanny. They had all talked gaily of a frequent interchange of visits, but it was a long, hard journey to the settlement over the range. In winter months the traveller must often fight his way through blinding rain, the winding wagon tracks deep sunk in bog, criss-crossed by running creeks; in summer through merciless heat, the mud dried to choking dust.

The young couple were later to take over a 4,059-acre property known as Wicklow Hills, that was originally part of the Whitfield's Knockdominie holding, but it was to a small farm called Nunyle that Francis took his bride. The house on this property was a small mud-brick and timber shack with a roof of blackboy thatch and an outside cooking place. Elizabeth's lot was therefore to be the 'love in a cottage' that her mother had once written of as romantic only in fiction, and certainly not for one of her own!

Chapter 18

1842-1845

Problems on Many Fronts

Will Shaw protests against law prohibiting distillation.
His correspondence with Governor Hutt. Hutt's pre-
occupation with labour problem. Transportation of
delinquent boys from Parkhurst prison. Slump in the
1840s. Hutt's Aboriginal policy. Birth of first child to
Elizabeth and Francis Whitfield. John Nicol Drummond avenges the spearing of his brother Johnston.
Drummond suspended from force. Goes bush with
Aborigines.

During this time Will Shaw, while continuing at regular
intervals to remind the Governor of his unfulfilled land claims
and to 'solicit any information that His Excellency ... may
have received in Lord Stanley's Despatches',[1] had embarked
on the fighting of another cause. This was the right to the
distillation of spirits from the refuse of the fruit used in the
making of wine, in which a number of Upper Swan settlers
were by that time fairly profitably engaged.

From his long and detailed correspondence on the subject,[2]
Shaw shows himself to have become an enthusiastic viticul-
turist and something of a visionary, foreseeing the potential of
the south-western colony as one of the most ideal wine-producing areas in the world. He claimed that his Belvoir property
was growing grapes capable of yielding 'a first rate quality of
wine ...' one variety of which he was particularly proud being
a 'fine type of hock—"Vin-de-Grave" of a Rhenish flavour ...
with a pleasant fruity aroma bearing not the least affinity to
those wines produced at the Cape'. A sample of this speciality
he intended 'to have the honour of shortly submitting to His
Excellency's opinion and taste and for his consideration

whether so valuable an export as well as an article for Home Consumption should be neglected on account of the expense of its cultivation'. He explained his point as follows:

Wines made in these Latitudes cannot be insured to keep passing the Line without having been fed by a certain proportion of brandy which at present the producer is obliged to obtain from the market at great expense so that the cultivator's profit is absolutely thrown away because the law here prohibits distillation ... therefore ... please inform me if His Excellency in Council will allow me to distil (under such restrictions as may be for both public and private benefits), the refuse of the vineyards which will at once remove existing obstacles to the further cultivation of the vine, any impediments to which I consider to be highly detrimental to the Colony's interest, for if properly fostered and encouraged, its wines will be found one of the most valuable exports and thereby add most materially to the internal wealth of the Colony, the want of which we now feel so much.[3]

To this communication Governor Hutt appended a note, making no reference to Shaw's offer of a free sample of his wares but declaring it to be 'quite impossible for the government to grant the permission Mr Shaw seeks in the very teeth of an Act of Council. There is no doubt, however, as soon as it can be clearly shown that the manufacture of wine is likely to be established to form an exportable investment for capital in the colony that some modification of the law prohibiting distillation must be allowed.'[4]

Shaw replied regretting that His Excellency should entertain an opinion so highly detrimental to the interests of the colony, while in the cider-producing counties of England spirits known as 'still waters' were permitted to be manufactured from the refuse of apples and pears to be fed to cattle, from which it appeared 'that quadrupeds at home [were] much better provided for than bipeds ... in this Colony'. He was convinced that 'no one but a blind visionary' could for a moment entertain the idea of the colony's ever exporting grain, whereas the possibilities for the export of top quality wine were boundless.[5]

I am satisfied, [he wrote] that the colonial soil and climate are equal, if not superior, to any in Spain, Portugal or the South of France or the vintages of Italy where they have frequently to contend with falls of rain during the fruit harvest of which we yet know nothing ... Moreover vineyards may be pruned at less expense here than in any part of the world I have yet seen and we at the moment hold a nucleus of the choicest vines known in any country. My lot being cast to rise or fall with the colony I hope the Governor will not consider me out of order in attempting to advance and advocate the true interest of the colony![6]

Governor Hutt pointed out that the liquor regulations were not a matter of his own opinion but were subject to the order of Her Majesty's Government. Until some more decisive proof of the wine-growing capacity of the colony was brought to his knowledge, he did not consider himself entitled to apply to the Home Government to rescind the law prohibiting distillation.[7] Shaw was not of course prepared to leave the matter at that, and backed up his argument by a letter he had received from James Drummond agreeing with his opinion of the colony as of great wine-producing potential.

It is clear that Shaw had come up against a stone wall in this argument, for as James Backhouse, naturalist and Quaker missionary, pointed out in his colonial narrative[8] 'the whole revenue of (WA) Government, amounting to about £7,000 a year is derived from spirits in the form of duty on imports.' Even if this statement was somewhat exaggerated, it was certainly important enough to the government at this time that the import of spirits was not discouraged by the wholesale production of a cheaper local product. Hutt was no doubt also anxious to control the indiscriminate manufacture of cheap raw spirits—otherwise 'moonshine'—that if made too readily available to the 'lower orders' and Aborigines could spell the ruination of the colony.

One suspects, however, that Hutt was well enough aware of the fact that the local wine growers, in spite of the letter of the law, were discreetly distilling spirits to fortify their wines in any case. It probably embarrassed him that Shaw must keep bringing the matter to his notice instead of going quietly about his business and fortifying his wines, if such was necessary, as prudently as possible.

Of much greater concern to Hutt than almost any other local problem continued to be the settlement's chronic lack of an adequate working force. This was largely due, as he saw it, to the unplanned nature of its development, sprawling as it now did over an inconveniently vast area, the widely scattered settlements all urgently requiring road communication and other public facilities. The trickle of immigrants still coming in could by no means meet the demand for government employees, farm workers, domestic servants and artisans needed to maintain even minimal progress. Since the idea of labour from India had been ruled out by the Indian Government, and the importation of Chinese coolies had been vetoed from London,[9] where was he now to turn? Surely he should not resort to the degradation of convict labour, for which each year more settlers were beginning to agitate? In 1842 he hit upon what he hoped might prove a workable compromise, namely the importation, from Parkhurst prison on the Isle of Wight, of delinquents who were to be pardoned on arrival and indentured as farm labourers. This resulted in the arrival of about 200 boys, a few to make their way successfully in their new environment, others to become an additional problem to employers and government, one indeed—a boy of fifteen named John Galvin—to make his niche in local history of being the first white person to be executed in the colony. Convicted of murder he was hanged in his chains outside the Round House Gaol, at Fremantle in April 1844.[10]

Coincidentally, one of these 'juvenile immigrants' was named Nathaniel Shaw. Born in 1833, he was indentured to a Mr Lockyer in the York area whereabouts he subsequently became a respected small farmer. He married in 1860 and produced a family. The discovery of his name in a contemporary document led to some speculation as to whether one of the Shaws of Belvoir had begotten an unacknowledged offspring. This intriguing problem was cleared up by the discovery of the second Nat Shaw's indisputable Parkhurst origins.

By 1843 the brief boom created by the encouragement of further capital and labour was over, and the colony had begun to slump into the worst depression of its short but chequered history. Wool was down, and the sudden raising of land prices throughout Australia to £1 an acre in 1842 was soon seen to have had a particularly adverse effect on the western colony, where the variable quality of the land called for such large holdings. Many already in the settlement, or intending to migrate from England, turned to the surer prospects of better developed colonies and the old lament on the theme of labour and capital shortages was louder than ever before.

Hutt was generally blamed, but stood his ground at the expense of local popularity and approval from the Home Office, pointing out that a majority in the eastern colonies were now in worse case than farmers in the west.

Like many settlers he deplored the colony's lack of religious guidance and education, and found ways and means of granting town allotments and providing subsidies not only for the Anglican community, but to Roman Catholic, Methodist and Independent factions. This met with the disapproval of many who saw it as a denial of the rightful place in the new land of the Established Church of England.

No one in the Swan area, however, seems to have taken issue with Hutt's Aboriginal policies, for the settlers, no longer greatly harassed by the local tribespeople, now felt it reasonable enough that they be accorded British justice and that individual whites should be forbidden to take reprisals into their own hands. Hutt himself had been inclined to think that the natives should be encouraged to maintain their own code within reasonable limits and be judged, where possible, according to their own laws, but in this his opinion gave way to that of Lieutenant George Grey who had come out in 1837 with a mandate from the Secretary of State to explore the north-west coast of New Holland. Stirling had been no more enchanted with the Swan River area than Grey with the country inland from the Glenelg, where he made contact with the Aborigines—children of the sacred Wandjina whose many images he so faithfully copied from the rock faces of their tumbled hills. Grey, despite having been wounded by a tribesman's spear, had warmed to these people and found himself differing vehemently from those who belittled their mental capacity. He believed moreover that he had hit upon a solution to the problem of their integration. They should, he insisted, be taught at once that British laws were to supersede their own so that any natives who were 'suffering under their own customs' might have the power of appeal to those of Great Britain! Settlers undertaking to civilize and train an Aboriginal in useful pursuits were to be subsidised, and natives who obtained marriage certificates and registered the births of their offspring should be rewarded accordingly.[11]

Hutt incorporated much of Grey's thinking into his schemes for Aboriginal education and protection. As far as the Swan River tribes were concerned, however, it was already too late, for their numbers were rapidly declining, not from bullets or poisoned food as in other colonies, but from epidemics of measles, whooping-cough and influenza against which they had developed no immunity. People could therefore talk with tolerance and act with loving kindness towards the pathetic remnants of a race that had once challenged the march of progress.

It was only in the frontier settlements, pushing ever farther out, that colonists would scorn a policy that aimed to protect a feckless people while rendering enterprise powerless to protect itself. John Drummond himself did not talk entirely in these terms, but in July 1845 when his younger brother Johnston was murdered by an Aboriginal named Kabinger he had not hesitated to take the law into his own hands. The story as it has come down to us is that Johnston, a keen young naturalist, had gone bush with three natives to collect specimens. There was nothing unusual, where the Drummond boys were concerned, in the fact that one of the party had been the wife of Kabinger who was often with Johnston on his expeditions. This time, after an argument with Kabinger, Johnston had gone off without consulting him. The native had followed and, finding Johnston asleep with his woman in a bush camp, had put a spear through his heart.

When John Nicol heard of his brother's death, he procured a warrant for the arrest of the murderer and set out, with one of his brothers and another policeman, to track him down. John Nicol eventually caught up with Kabinger, and after a sharp encounter shot him dead.[12]

Feelings in the outpost settlement always ran high after any violent action of an Aboriginal against a white, and even normally tolerant people were apt to express themselves with unreasonable vehemence. One of the Drummonds' neighbours referred in his diary to 'the odious detestable niggers' who had cut off so fine a young man in his prime. 'I wish,' he added, 'that a good many of them were exterminated. They are not half severe enough with them when they do anything wrong.'[13]

The majority of settlers supported John Drummond wholeheartedly in the forthright action he had taken to avenge his brother. Governor Hutt, however, was not of this persuasion. Having previously reprimanded Drummond for defying official instructions, he now saw fit to suspend him from the police force and to demand that he face a court of enquiry. To avoid this latter inconvenience, John Nicol went bush with the tribespeople, who had evidently seen nothing reprehensible in his action against Kabinger. Disguising himself most successfully as an Aboriginal he remained in hiding until, at the earnest request of the Avon settlers who complained that the local natives were again getting out of hand, he was reinstated at the reduced rank of District Police Constable of the Avon district.

For the rest of his life John Nicol would continue to surprise and shock the settlers, to whom his services were indispensable. Now he had taken it into his head to court Mary Shaw, who was at that time staying at Nunyle with the young Whitfields. Elizabeth had gone home, a year after her marriage, for the birth of her first baby and since she had not made a quick recovery her sister had elected to stay with her for two or three months. It is believed that Mary was for some time quite indifferent to the attentions of this eccentric suitor, who however often rebuffed, would return with the confidence of a man accustomed to winning his argument.

Chapter 19

1845–June 1850

At Last a Convict Colony

Eliza Shaw at home in the colony. Guildford progresses. Governor Hutt replaced by Captain Andrew Clarke. Strong stand for Anglicanism. Arrival of Spanish Benedictine missionaries. Death of Clarke and P Brown. Irwin again Lieutenant-Governor. Marriage of George Fletcher Moore. Irwin tries to introduce Chinese labour. Originates State School System in WA. Visit of Bishop Augustus Short. Arrival of Governor Fitzgerald. A C Gregory reports on pastoral and mining prospects in north west. Governor Fitzgerald investigates. Is wounded by Aborigines. First mining company formed and prospectors set out for north. J N Drummond averts trouble with Aborigines. Request for convict labour promptly accepted by British Government. Arrival of ship *Scindian* with first transportees.

As the years at last convinced Will Shaw of England's indifference to his injustices, he became every bit as eloquent as Landor in the expression of his disillusionment. Nonetheless, he never recovered from his homesickness and often expressed regret that they had so far lost faith in Britain's powers of recovery as to hurl themselves into the unknown of a crude new colony. When papers from home arrived, however backdated, he would devour them avidly and discourse at length on the expanding prosperity that had been ushered in with the reign of the young Queen. The throne no longer a thing of derision or shame and the industrial upsurge settling into a pattern of peace and prosperity, he began to see Britain as leading Tennyson's 'Parliament of man', his 'Federation of the world', and he yearned for nothing so much as a turn of fortune on which they could escape from their antipodean backwater into the mainstream of human activity. If only he could be granted his full quota of land, if the labour problem could be overcome—even by the introduction of convicts— if he were allowed complete freedom in the manufacture of exportable wine, or given a government post worthy of his capabilities, he was confident that he would soon be on the way to accumulating sufficient capital to return, if only for a time, to the life of an English country gentleman.

Eliza, while upholding him staunchly in his litigious campaigns, was not, in other respects, of the same mind as himself, for whereas Will was by nature a traditionalist his wife welcomed the untried. Where Will missed the white Christmases of his youth, Eliza made seasonal fun of the preparation of such climatically inappropriate fare. Where Will was nostalgic for the miraculous burgeoning of a European spring, Eliza watched through the brief Swan River winter for the first rich flowerspikes of purple hovea, the golden glow of bush wattle and hibertia, the exquisite minutiae of ground orchids and trigger plants, the sky-blue wonder of leschenaultia. Where Will longed for the sound of the cuckoo and the lark, Eliza reacted to the full rich notes of the magpie and butcher bird, the sad, sweet cadences of the western warbler and the lively chatter of wattler and parakeet. Less introspective than Will, she did not blame their colonial circumstances for the sons the Lord had given them and taken away, nor did she brood as did her man on how different might have been the lives of their surviving children, poor Nat with his gauche ways and his battered face, Elizabeth wedded to the hard and lonely life of an outpost farm, the rest of them with nothing certain in their future but the prospect of unmitigated toil.

Where Will was frustrated, Eliza was fulfilled, extended as never in England to the utmost of her initiative, freed from the conventions of her class to communicate with humble folk of like spirit. She responded warmly to the joys and sorrows of her neighbours, always at hand to help with the delivery of a child and to bestow timely gifts of home-made produce on the ailing or bereaved. The Rev Mitchell's delicate wife, after yet another miscarriage or the birth of yet another stillborn child, gave testimony in her journal of the comforting visits of Mrs Shaw.[1] Other neighbours, too, spoke warmly of her support in times of trouble. She was obviously no fairweather friend, nor was she in the background on happier occasions. Writing to her married daughters in later years, she would often recall the fun and laughter they had shared in 'those good old Baskerville days'. She sometimes admitted to missing her English friends but never to homesickness, for her home was with her family on the Swan and her home town was Guildford, the nearby trading-post that she had seen grow from a few mud-brick cottages to a thriving agricultural centre of the frontier towns that dotted the winding, northerly course of the Avon River.

She took a personal pride in its every indication of increasing progress; in the weekly mail service that now plied up-river from Perth; in its growing number of shops, taverns, hostels and warehouses, in the wharves along the river front to which came a steady procession of teamsters with their wagon-loads of wool, wheat, fodder, sandalwood, skins, hides and tallow. She delighted in these heartening indications of the colony's industrial progress—all to be transported by lighter to Fremantle for markets overseas.

Other signs of progress that encouraged her were the flour mill and steam-operated saw set up in Guildford by Sam Moore in 1844, which provided a constant source of excitement owing to the frequent bursting of boilers, the breaking of spindles and occasional fires—lit, it was suspected, at the instigation of rival business interests. Rumours were spread that steam power was a new-fangled eccentricity soon to be abandoned in favour of older methods, but the arrival in 1845 of Her Majesty's ship *Driver*, capable of travelling under steam power alone, strengthened the case for the progressives. Will Shaw, with his younger sons George and Bob, were among the many who flocked to Fremantle to inspect the wonder ship, and hear her captain expound upon a new age of ocean travel that would soon place the colonists within weeks, rather than months, of the home country.

Conversation of these times was much as ever—on the recurring themes of land and labour problems and the shortsighted policies of successive Governors. The replacement in 1846 of Governor Hutt by a Protestant Irishman named Captain Andrew Clarke was generally welcomed, for although in retrospect the colonists would see Hutt as a just and diligent administrator, he had been too austere and studious to encourage friendship or to brighten the social scene as had the colony's first Governor.

Clarke was a friend of Captain Irwin, who had in fact recommended him for the position, hoping that, among other things, he would show a less dangerously liberal attitude than Governor Hutt. No doubt under Irwin's prompting, Clarke's reputation had gone before him as a man likely to hasten the settlement's return to prosperity, to change the unpopular land system and return to Government House some of its former style and hospitality. He brought with him not only a capable wife and a charming step-daughter, but a fresh wind of confidence reinforced by a rise of the colonial economic graph. The price of wool improved while the colonial revenue was increased by the export of horses to India, whale oil and timber to Great Britain and sandalwood to burn in the temples of China.

To add to the general wave of optimism there was a brief flutter in the middle of 1846—much publicized in the local press—of small discoveries of coal on the Moore and Irwin rivers. The excitement soon petered out but it did no damage to Clarke's reputation as the harbinger of brighter times. In fact the improved prospects were largely the delayed outcome of Hutt's policies or of the settlers' own enterprise, linked with the unpredictable fluctuations of world prices and markets.

Clarke was genuinely responsible, however, to Irwin's especial satisfaction, for a reversal of Hutt's liberal policy towards other than solid Anglican denominations. He at once refused an application for State aid from the Roman Catholic Bishop Brady, who had arrived in 1843 and had since brought out twenty-seven members of religious orders, including French and Spanish priests and a small band of Irish nuns. The Sisters, members of the Mercy order, set up a small private school in Perth, and three small contingents of Priests and Brothers were dispatched to contact Aboriginal tribes around Port Victoria in the far north, the Albany district in the extreme south and the Victoria Plains immediately north of Toodyay. The Albany and Port Victoria ventures were doomed to failure, but the Mercy and Benedictine establishments, then equally penniless, were to become important and lasting institutions. The Spanish Priests, due largely to the charm and tact of the cultured Dom Rosendo Salvado, soon won the approval and support of the settlers and by 1847 had laid the foundations of New Norcia Mission on the banks of the Moore River. It was to become one of the very few examples anywhere on the continent of a successful attempt to educate and train the Aborigines along European lines.

But Clarke was not to be a witness to this quiet triumph of Romanist tenacity. He died little more than a year after his arrival, the task of Lieutenant-Governor falling again to Irwin who carried on until the arrival of a new administrator eighteen months later. Meanwhile George Fletcher Moore had claimed the heart and hand of Clarke's step-daughter, thus putting an end to his interesting status as one of the colony's most eligible bachelors. He had also on the death of Peter Brown in November, 1846, become Acting Colonial Secretary.

Brown's death was a considerable loss to the colony, for though never a robust man, he had worked tirelessly if perhaps not always disinterestedly in the administration of his adopted land. In addition to his other duties he had been clerk of the Legislative Council, and as a member of the first Perth Town Trust had played a major part in the planning of the city. In his seventeen years of service Perth had grown from a few scattered huts and tents on the river bank to a town of over 400 houses, many of them substantial dwellings with gardens and orchards which, in Landor's opinion, 'equalled those in the finest parts of England'. Footpaths had been cleared beside the sandy streets and a bridge from Heirisson Island linked the township with the Guildford side of the river. Every step of this progress Brown had watched with a justifiable sense of personal achievement and had recorded in a journal that, had it survived, would have been of tremendous historical value. His wife had planned to publish this record on her return to England, but the ship *Hindoo* on which she was travelling caught fire at sea and all the documents were destroyed. With them must surely have gone Brown's heartfelt plea to his fellow colonists that they never succumb to the enticing but corruptive expedient of convict labour.

Captain Irwin had always shared Brown's sentiments on the convict issue, but the fact remained that for all the hopeful indications of economic improvement the problem of labour shortage and its effect on the colonial revenue was still unsolved, and it was largely on this account that the western settlement lagged so sadly behind the eastern colonies. Its entire population was still under 5,000, its public buildings minimal and its few roads no more than the rough, winding tracks of the wagon wheels. Irwin believed that any measure was preferable to convict labour, even continued 'juvenile immigration' which the majority of colonists had come to see as incorporating many of the drawbacks of the former without the advantage of government finance that had supported transportation elsewhere.

Searching desperately for ways out of the dilemma, Irwin conceived the idea of chartering schooners to bring Chinese labour on three-year terms of indenture from Singapore, but the scheme was not generally favoured and was abandoned after the arrival of a single shipload of Asian workers. His next move, made in order to increase the colonial revenue, was to impose an export tax on sandalwood but this proved as unpopular as his attempt to support James Backhouse in the formation of a local temperance society!

Though many of the forthright efforts of Irwin's short term of office were generally opposed and came to nothing, he did gain support in originating the State School system in Western Australia. Having always identified himself so strongly with the Anglican observance, he had seen it as deplorable that children of good Protestant families should, for want of an alternative, be attending the little school set up by the Roman Catholic nuns and he had created a General Board of Education as a counter-measure.

That there should be a Catholic before an Anglican bishop in the colony was also a matter of great concern to him. He was delighted therefore, in 1847, when Bishop Augustus Short was appointed to administer not only the diocese of South Australia but also that of the western colony, which he visited in the following year. His welcome was all the warmer for the reason that he did not come as a stranger, as his wife was a sister of 'Squire Phillips' of Culham and his reputation as a wise and learned man had gone before him. He called on all the scattered settlements of his western diocese and while at the Upper Swan stayed with the George Fletcher Moores. The Shaws were among the families who, despite his arrival coinciding with the hay harvest, rallied to entertain him and to witness his consecration of the two little churches presided over by the Rev Mitchell at Upper and Middle Swan. The Bishop also gave fresh heart to his struggling local ministers and appreciated their different methods of approach rather more warmly than they did each other's. The Rev Wollaston, who had come out in 1841 to administer the south-western settlements, found Wittenoom 'too High Church ... argumentative and unyielding in matters of secondary importance' and Mitchell 'too Evangelical, meek and conciliatory' and his sermons 'overly long and dull'.[2] Wittenoom and Mitchell, for their parts, would seem to have doubted the practicality of Wollaston's often over-zealous denunciation of 'dissenters' and 'Romanists' in a situation where sheer survival depended so much upon mutual tolerance. They, themselves, had always enjoyed the warmest friendship with 'the *Tranby* people' and actually encouraged the whole-hearted support of their parishioners for Dom Salvado's one-man concert in aid of his un-subsidized Aboriginal mission on the Victoria Plains.

Governor Fitzgerald, a naval captain and like Clarke an Irish Protestant, who had been formerly Governor of Gambia, took over from Irwin in 1848. He found the treasury almost depleted and many of the settlers expressing themselves as thoroughly dissatisfied with an administration that had set too high a price on crown land and had failed to overcome the crippling lack of labour—two factors that discouraged the flow of better-class emigrants. Desperate to increase the colony's limited resources, he considered a report put in by a young surveyor named A C Gregory on his return from an expedition to the north of the settlement at the end of 1846. The Gregory family came out on the *Lotus* in 1829 and Augustus Charles, then ten years old, had quickly made his way up in the survey department. Like many settlers of British origin, he and his brothers soon came to practical terms with the bush environment, including its Aboriginal inhabitants, and also developed the improved pack saddles and pocket compasses that were to become part of the equipment of every Australian bushman. Governor Fitzgerald found that A C Gregory and his two younger brothers had reported optimistically on both the pastoral and mineral possibilities of the Murchison and Gascoyne districts and soon after his arrival he sailed north with several others to make a personal assessment of the area. During their inspection the party became involved in a clash with the Aborigines from which the Governor emerged with a spear wound in the leg. This, however, had no adverse effect on his opinion of the country's possibilities.

Soon after his return he announced that the government was prepared to sell rights to a lead mine on the Murchison River. In the following year, members of a small mining company went north on horseback under the leadership of A C Gregory and Will Burges, and including John Drummond and a Victoria Plains native named Karakai to help conciliate the Aborigines. They encountered a hostile group of about seventy warriors at the Greenough River, and Drummond and his native assistant were said to have been responsible for averting serious trouble.

From this time on began the movement of flocks and herds northward from the Avon Valley to the Victoria Plains and beyond as far as the Irwin, Greenough and Murchison Rivers, while the port of Geraldton and the little mining town of Geraldine, both named after Governor Fitzgerald, became established bases in the spreading settlement.

But whatever profits might be derived in the future from the pastoral and mineral resources of this new area, the Governor was still faced with the immediate and urgent problem of setting in motion the sluggish wheels of colonial development. Nothing Irwin had to say could convince him that the settlers were not justified in requesting that a limited number of well-behaved convicts from Pentonville be sent out to fulfil a desperate need in the colony, while earning their own redemption. He quickly dispatched a submission to this effect, asking at the same time that an equal number of free emigrants be sent out to balance the population.

The Home Government probably never acted with more alacrity in responding to a request from an Australian colony. Western Australia was at once declared a penal settlement and the first consignment of seventy-five convicts, in charge of fifty soldier pensioners, some of them with wives and families, arrived at Fremantle in the ship *Scindian* in June 1850. In fact the operation had been carried out with such dispatch that this first shipment of bonded labourers arrived before the advice that they were even on the way.

For better or worse a new era had dawned for Stirling's
'Hesperia'! To a simple social structure comprising landed
gentry, merchants, yeomen farmers and servants had been
added a fifth and less respectable category—the 'bond class'.
Transportation was to provide the free labour on which New
South Wales and Tasmania had prospered in their formative
years, but the much-abused system by which convicts were
assigned to work out their sentences with private employers
was never adopted in the western colony. From depots set up
at Guildford, York, Toodyay and Bunbury, settlers were able
to hire men convicted on lesser charges who, on arrival, had
been granted tickets-of-leave for paid employment conditional
on good behaviour. At the same time gangs were set to work
clearing roads through scrub and heavy timber to link the
scattered outposts of settlement, constructing bridges and
public buildings, while from other parts of the continent rose
a clamour of criticism against this shameless revival of a de-
based and inhuman system. Loudest of all were voices from
New South Wales and Van Diemen's Land, where transportation had ceased less than a decade before.

But in the first fine flush of optimism the westerners,
prepared to sacrifice reputation for survival, cared little what
was said or thought of them elsewhere. Convict labour had
brought with it not only hands enough to build a lasting city
but, with so many more mouths to feed at government expense,
an increased local market and a fine spur to enterprise within
expanding frontiers.

Chapter 20

1850–1852

Expanding Frontiers

Effects and conditions of convict labour. Flood and fire. Tragic death of Whitfield's first child. W Cowan instigates enquiry re Drummond. Pastoral partnerships formed and first settlers move to Champion Bay. J N Drummond sets up police station and acquires land in area. Marries Mary Shaw—first white woman to Champion Bay. Death of Nat Shaw at Bunbury. Eliza Shaw recalls early memories. Will Shaw joins Volunteer Force. The Rev Wollaston reports on families leaving Upper Swan. Death of Sam Moore. G F Moore and wife return to England. Positive aspects of transportation.

R M Lyon, a forthright advocate of convict labour from the early days of settlement, had long since convinced the Shaws that it would solve one important aspect of the local dilemma. Both Eliza and her husband would live to see this opinion vindicated, but to realize also that the hoped-for progress was not to be achieved without considerable price. Even Will would look back to the first two decades of settlement as a time of comparatively high standards of social and ethical behaviour—a time when one's neighbours, however unreasonable on matters of property, were without question 'gentle folk', a time when straying stock would be returned and a house might be left unlocked.

The west was never of course to be a penal settlement in the sense of New South Wales and Van Diemen's Land, where the economy was based on the employment of the convicts to which they owed their origins. Many of the abuses of the system were avoided here but the lot of the transported criminal was grim enough at best. Insubordination still brought sentences of solitary confinement and the lash, while for more serious offences the gallows provided a simple remedy. The work of the well-disciplined chain gangs quickly showed results in the construction of a gaol and administrative offices at Fremantle, a depot for military guards, a number of roads and bridges, including one across the Swan at Guildford, and a lunatic asylum. When the urgency of this last institution was brought to question, George Leake is reputed to have defended it on the grounds that anyone who had remained twenty years in the colony must be either totally impoverished or mad. Leake, by the way, was himself neither, for he had prospered well through his merchant business at Fremantle and was said to have had it in his power to ruin two-thirds of his fellow settlers by foreclosing on their mortgages. Nearer the truth regarding the need for such a substantial asylum may well have been the effects of extreme hardship and solitude on isolated settlers and shepherds, and that some of the convicts and boys who had been deported as delinquents were from all accounts mentally retarded.[1]

By an ironical twist of history this admirably designed and solidly built establishment was to be saved demolition about 120 years later, to serve the community as a centre for the arts and a maritime museum.

While these public works were in progress, convicts who had been granted tickets-of-leave were made available to private employers from hiring depots set up at Guildford and other outlying centres. These men, while under the constant surveillance of the police and required, unless granted special leave, to remain in the district in which they were released, were permitted a considerable amount of freedom. They could choose their employers and could be granted conditional pardons for good behaviour before the expiration of their sentences. These pardons entitled them to local citizenship but not freedom to return to the United Kingdom until the full sentence had expired. For the most part they were to remain in the settlement and many to marry, their descendants often quite unaware of the shadow behind their colonial origins.

The Shaws soon took advantage of the hiring depot at Guildford and acquired two ticket-of-leave men to serve as shepherds and a third as a general handyman and farm labourer. This last was the man frequently referred to by Eliza as 'poor old Johnston', who though so illiterate as to sign his name with a cross, as 'obstinate as a mule' and often intemperate, was to remain faithful to the family into his old age.

But the act of man in transporting convict labour, though a major turning point in the history of the colony, was overshadowed for many settlers by certain concurrent acts of God. Destructive floods in the winter of 1849 were followed in the next year by disastrous fires, particularly in the Avon district. Will Shaw had hastened to join the fire-fighters but was too late to save pasture on his Toodyay property, which, since Nat's departure, he had left in charge of a shepherd. Many others in the area were also badly hit, including the Drummonds and the Whitfields who were almost burned out. The latter couple had moved in the meantime from their first married home at Nunyle to a part of the Knockdominie estate known as Wicklow, where, in July 1848, they suffered the tragic loss of their eldest child, the four-year-old Mary who was burned to death when her clothes caught alight from a copper fire in an outside wash shed.

Elizabeth's sister Mary had hastened to Toodyay to join the sorrowing parents and to help with their two remaining little ones. Elizabeth Whitfield, in delicate health after the birth of her second son, was slow to recover from this agonizing blow and Mary came to her as often as possible. In this way she became again associated with the Drummond family, including John Nicol who, whenever in the vicinity, persisted in his courtship. The mining party which he had accompanied to the north in 1849, appreciating his tactful handling of the Aborigines, had been anxious for him to remain with them but the Avon settlers had in the meantime set up an earnest plea for his return. Drummond was strongly attracted to the Champion Bay area, but his interest in Mary Shaw no doubt helped to persuade him that his duty lay in the Toodyay area. He reappeared in that district some months after his departure for the north, flamboyantly firing his rifle at imaginary targets to announce his arrival. The only person, white or black, who failed to welcome him was his superior, W Cowan, formerly secretary to Governor Hutt and then Protector of Natives at York. Cowan was not only a stickler for protocol, but Drummond had no doubt also made him aware of being something of a new chum in the field.

Cowan's official complaint against his subordinate was that he insisted, whatever his orders, on going his own way, which at that time included extending his patrol from the Avon to the Swan. By 1850 things had come to a head and Cowan's complaints resulted in an official enquiry into Drummond's activities. The investigation was held *in camera*, though much of the evidence of John Drummond's eccentricity would no doubt have proved entertaining. The participants would hardly have overlooked his reaction to the engagement of his sister Euphemia to a braw and enterprising Scot named Ewan Mackintosh, who the Drummonds had employed as a shepherd on Hawthornden. Mackintosh had quickly graduated from this humble position to become a leading pastoralist in the Toodyay district but he was not, in the opinion of the Drummond boys, a fitting match for their sister. Their protests being to no avail, they made the final demonstration of their disapproval—also abortive—of burning Euphemia's wedding dress on the day fixed for the ceremony. Despite such escapades, however, John Drummond's case was enthusiastically backed by the brothers Burges and others intending to settle around Champion Bay, and whose request that he accompany them as their escort and remain as First Constable to a small police force was finally granted.

Settlers from the Swan and Avon districts formed partnerships and travelled in convoy. The party, which John Drummond accompanied and which assembled at the Drummonds' new station at Dandaragan, included the brothers Burges, Squire Phillips of Culham, James Drummond Jnr, and his ageing father who came along for the purpose of enlarging his botanical collection.

After his arrival at Champion Bay in 1850, Will Burges was appointed Resident Magistrate and in 1851 recommended that John Drummond should be stationed at a site named Smugglers' Cove (known also as Drummond's Cove). A beautiful spot, with glimpses of the sea between sheltering dunes, and surrounded by rich natural pasture, it suited John very well. He purchased fifty acres of freehold land adjoining the police reserve and proceeded, with the help of his father, to erect a modest cottage to which he planned to bring his bride. Soon afterwards he acquired 7,000 acres of leasehold and ten of freehold in an area extending from the sea front to a point south of White Peak on which he intended forming a sheep station.

In a manner that only one of his independent mind could have contrived, he was to combine the roles of police constable, pastoralist, miner and collector of wild life specimens. Not even he, however, could prevail on the local natives to desist from molesting the settlers and killing their stock. When a party of soldiers, previously stationed at Champion Bay, were transferred on account of pearling and guano prospects to Shark Bay, the natives seeing the white man's defences thus weakened had attacked the settlement from all sides. According to contemporary accounts, game was scarce in the area and the meat-hungry tribespeople were sometimes driven to cannibalism. They had therefore welcomed the introduction of sheep and cattle and were not to be dissuaded from making off with them wholesale. Lockier Burges in giving chase had been severely wounded in the head, and on several occasions John Drummond narrowly escaped being speared, by tricks of evasion that he had learned from the Aborigines themselves. It was over a year before he could persuade Magistrate Burges to release him for long enough to get married. In fact the wedding had been several times postponed before he hurried south at last in January 1852.

The Shaws had not, for some years, taken John Drummond's courtship of their daughter seriously, especially as Mary was much sought-after by a number of others whom they considered a great deal more eligible. By this time, however, they seem to have become more or less reconciled to the match. After all, John, in the acquisition of pastoral property, showed promise of settling into a more conventional way of life and however much he may have shocked the community from time to time, he was the son of respected parents who now enjoyed the status accorded to the first-footers in the colony. The couple were married by the Rev Mitchell in the little octagonal church at Middle Swan, and afterwards at Belvoir there was a hastily organized gathering of old friends.

The newly-weds set off overland next day, travelling like the young Whitfields in a horsedrawn cart, stacked high with stores and a few items of household furniture. Since John had been grudgingly granted the shortest possible leave they must have taken 'the coast track', direct to young James Drummond's outstation at Dandaragan, reluctantly bypassing their Avon district relatives at Hawthornden and Wicklow. In an article[2] on Mary Drummond that appeared after her death in 1918, it is said that 'few ladies could have withstood such an ordeal' as she faced on that 300-mile journey, much of it through thick scrub and heavy sand and undertaken in the height of summer. 'As Miss Mary Shaw,' the writer tells us, 'the late Mrs J N Drummond was a tall stately girl of great charm and lovable disposition, a great favourite at Government House and known in the early '50s as the belle of the Swan. Reference to those halcyon days, half a century later, would always arouse a gleam of pleasure in the face of the old lady.'

That her young life had in fact been so 'halcyon' is extremely doubtful, for Mary, like all the Shaw family, had worked hard inside and out from her earliest years. She had been forced to scrape and save, to make her own clothes and help with sewing for other members of the family, and the splendid Government House occasions she recalled had no doubt been few and far between. She had certainly, however, figured brightly in the social life of the Swan. Like her mother she was notably kind and outgoing, though apparently inclined to be unorthodox for her generation. It may have been the expression of some dangerously independent-sounding views, or even perhaps her defence of free spirits such as John Nicol Drummond, that had called forth a letter[3] from her friend Charlotte Chauncey, whose surveyor father, a widower, had married a daughter of the Rev Mitchell. She exhorted Mary Shaw 'to feel the necessity of a new birth unto righteousness without which no man can see the Lord.' Miss Chauncey, after thanking Mary for the gift of a bag of down for a mattress, sincerely hoped that the books she had lent her—'especially Baxter's "Saint's Rest" had proved both pleasing and profitable ...' 'As the tree falls so it lives,' she continued, 'there is no repentance in the grave or pardon for the dead. Do not therefore my dear Mary leave these things until the accepted time is past.'

Mary Drummond is sometimes said to have been the first white woman in the Champion Bay district, but Mrs Thomas Brown had gone with her husband to Glengarry some six months before. Mary's first home in that area was the little cottage built on John Drummond's fifty-acre freehold block which he had named Redcliffe. While her husband was away on his prolonged patrols, she busied herself about her house and garden, milking their two or three cows, minding their first few sheep and raising poultry. At such times her sole protector was a native constable left in charge of the nearby police base; her sole means of defence a rifle she had never properly learned to use. It is a pity that, although reputed to have been a good raconteur, with many a colourful tale to tell, none of her experiences are now remembered.

John Drummond's role, earlier defined as one of 'conciliating' the natives, was referred to in the course of time as 'dispersing' them, which can only be interpreted in terms of all such frontier circumstances. There can be no doubt that he understood the Aborigines and was generally respected by them, but when the settlers' stock continued to be preyed upon, their stores plundered and their lives threatened, his attitude must inevitably have hardened along with that of his fellow pioneer pastoralists. The Rev Wollaston, on hearing of the local troubles, was probably correct in suspecting that many natives had been disposed of 'not merely in self-defence but wantonly and lawlessly'. It is significant at all events that Governor Fitzgerald, after his personal experience with the Champion Bay warriors, had changed the title of Protector of Aborigines to that of Guardian of Aborigines and Protector of Settlers!

Mary, who had always been greatly attached to her brothers, had hoped that Nat might take up land in the Champion Bay area, which country promised to be suitable for horse-breeding. At the time of her marriage Nat had been on his way to India on the ship *Templar* with a consignment of horses bred by Mr Little who had a property near Australind, and who some years before had personally negotiated a trade in locally-bred remounts for the Indian army. This trip had no doubt provided the most colourful experience of Nat's life and may well have been seen to augur brighter prospects for his future, but instead of the expected news of his return with a consignment of Indian-bred stud horses and some account of his adventures, the Drummonds received the melancholy news of his having suffered a fatal accident. A few days out of port on his return journey he had been kicked in the head by a restive

stallion and had died shortly after reaching his destination—
the little south-western port of Bunbury. Aged thirty-six,
buried there in the pioneer cemetery, a luckless victim of
colonial enterprise.

Apart from the correspondence he had carried on with his
boyhood friend, Johnnie Gamble, the trend of which had often
so worried his parents, he had apparently never been much of
a letter-writer. Pen and paper did not figure in his scanty
travelling effects, and after he left the Toodyay property to
battle on his own account it had been mainly through the
occasional traveller that his family had heard of him—contracting for mail—blazing a new track between the Williams and
Albany—riding a cup winner at some distant race meeting—
breaking horses for settlers around the Vasse and Australind
—ploughing for the Dempsters and 'cattle-hunting' around
Northam—sailing with remounts for India. 'But what of poor
Nat?' wrote Eliza to Elizabeth Whitfield, having accounted
for every other member of the family. Over twenty years
before she had written to the Waghornes of her two drowned
sons, '... But I think you will understand me, my best of
friends, when I say that I have more satisfaction in those that
are gone than in those who are left alive. At least I know what
has become of them but the rest may be anything but a
comfort to me.'4 Perhaps she felt much the same now about
Nat. There would be no more lying awake for her during a
wet and stormy night wondering whether he slept with a roof
over his head, fearing in the heat of summer lest he had missed
the track in some waterless wilderness, grieving for his injured
leg and his battered face and wondering would he find a girl
in all the world who could love him for his own brave heart.
There cannot, judging from the evidence available, have been
much satisfaction in his short life. The romantic memories of
his English childhood had contrasted sadly with the tough
reality of his colonial lot. The new land had been niggardly in
her response to his efforts and its Aborigines had betrayed
his trust. Even the horses that were his joy had brought him
physical injury and at last his untimely end.

None of Eliza's letters covering the period of Nat's death
can now be found, but a year or two later we find her writing
brightly enough to the Whitfields impressing upon her two
little grandsons, William and Frederick, named for her own

lost boys, that 'industry must prosper and patient perseverence overcomes almost impossible odds'. They must never brood on their losses she tells them, but should be optimistic, like Uncle George, who despite the bad season, is busy sowing 'the bread stuff' in their Biljarra block on the Swan ... She describes a happy night they had spent with Dr and Mrs Viveash and how they had kept each other in fits of laughter recounting experiences of their early days at the settlement—the night Will and Nat had both got back late and had each mistaken the other for a prowling Aboriginal—and that summer when the snakes had been so bad and dear Fanny Brockman had jumped up in the middle of Christmas dinner declaring that she had been bitten under her bodice. They would never forget how Will Brockman, in anxious haste, had slit open her best frock with the carving knife only to discover that the 'reptile' was a whalebone that had snapped in protest at Fanny's second helping of plum pudding! 'Mr Harris was there,' Eliza adds, 'who you know is an inveterate old croaker and we all laughed him into an excellent humour.'[5]

Another cheerful item of news was the Governor's establishment of a Volunteer Force to be organized by the gentry in each district, units having been formed at Perth, Fremantle, Guildford, York, Geraldton, Albany, Bunbury and Vasse. It was not precisely stated whether this force was intended to protect the colony from some hypothetical foreign foe, from escaped convicts or marauding Aborigines, but it was generally thought to be 'a good thing'. For Will Shaw, dressed again as an officer of a rifle regiment and straightening the backs of a band of slouching yokels, it was something of a tonic. It gave him an excuse to recall the soldiering exploits of his younger days and, since to have stood at Waterloo held a tang of romance for the younger colonial generation, he was accorded an attentive audience.

The Rev Wollaston, on a visit to the Upper Swan in 1853, had declared himself saddened by the neglected appearance of so many places that had formerly flourished in that area. In his own words:

Respectable people of the upper class are moving away— when they can—who once thought to make this colony the permanent residence of their children. They now dread the prospect of leaving them in a penal colony ... and they are right.[6]

Always a strong opponent of convict labour, he had somewhat over-generalized in this statement, for the neglect of most of the places to which he referred was not due to transportation. What he said may well have applied to the Tanners who had gone to England at the end of 1849—never to return—but the dilapidated condition of Henley Park on which Wollaston particularly commented was due to the fact that the Irwins had some time since removed to Perth. The rundown state of Oakover was the result of the untimely death of Sam Moore in 1849, after which his widow had been obliged to sell their farming equipment and most of their stock to meet his debts. His brother's cottage at Millendon, with the mark of Yagan's spear still to be seen in the window-ledge, was deserted, but George Fletcher Moore's failure to return from a trip to England in 1852 had been due to an unfortunate misunderstanding with the Colonial Office and also to his wife's delicate state of health. She died childless some years later, after which Moore was to live on in London—in his own words 'isolated and unfriended' until his death in 1886. It was unfortunate for both the colony and Moore himself that he never returned to the settlement to which he gave so much of his versatile ability and enthusiastic energy. His journal is probably the most detailed and valuable document extant of life in the early years of the Swan settlement, the impression it gives being of a young man thoroughly identified with the colonial life and surely destined to continue playing an important part in its development. It was after all his brother Sam's sons who were to perpetuate the family name in the colony, and to be associated, to the present generation, with flourishing business enterprises.

Other aspects of the colonial picture than those stressed by Wollaston indicated an emergence from the economic doldrums that had held the settlement at ransom for so long. The production and price of wool was on the rise, mineral prospects in the Geraldton area looked promising and pearling had begun around Shark Bay. The first experimental export of wine had been shipped to England and a newly formed Horticultural Society was offering prizes for the best essays on vine-growing. Over 1,500 convicts and ticket-of-leave men were at work on bridges, buildings and a growing network of roads, and the population had risen to 12,000. Governor Fitzgerald, despite what some referred to as his 'quarterdeck manner' performed his duties with dignity and aplomb and his lady excelled as a gracious hostess and a conscientious opener of charitable functions. Not even the gloomiest local pessimist was ever again to suggest that the colony was anything but permanent. The boundaries of settlement were expanding week by week and the names of outpost towns and stations were filling in the so-recently empty map.

Chapter 21

1855–1862

The Last Years of a Pioneer

Governor Kennedy grants Will Shaw the position of magistrate. Brighter prospects. Marriage of Lucy Ellen Shaw to Major Logue of Champion Bay. Mining developments in the north west. J N Drummond retires from police force. Mary Drummond at White Peak Station. Bob Shaw farming at Moore river. His friends the de Burghs. Shortage of women in colony. 'Needlewomen' brought from Ireland. A question of paternity. Notes from Eliza Shaw's letters. Will Shaw raises mortgage from Will Burges. Governor Kennedy replaced by Governor Hampton. Death of Will Shaw.

Governor Fitzgerald had given no encouragement to Will Shaw in seeking redress for his long-standing wrongs but in Governor Kennedy, who succeeded him in 1855, he found at last a more sympathetic ear. Much water had flowed down the winding course of the Swan since his bitter fight with the Colonial Secretary and many of those he had come up against during the progress of this quarrel had either passed on, left the colony or become too absorbed in other affairs to care whether 'poor Shaw' was kept in his place or not. Brown was dead, George Moore in England and Judge Mackie ailing and about to retire from sundry public offices.

Kennedy, like the two preceding Governors, was of Protestant Irish background. He had followed a military career until appointed Inspector of Poor Laws in his troubled country, and had gained some notoriety for his forthright opposition to the eviction of starving peasants. A kindly, family man with a keen feeling for the under-dog, he conceded that Shaw may not have been done justice on several counts. It was beyond his powers to do anything about the complicated land issues but he agreed that in view of Shaw's military career, of his having served as Justice of the Peace for some twenty-five years and worked with such enthusiasm with the Volunteer Force he should be granted some official position carrying at least a small stipend. It was therefore announced by the then Colonial Secretary, Frederick Barlee, in the Government Gazette of 19 January, 1856, that William Shaw had been appointed 'Magistrate for this Colony'. In the same month he sold his 1,000-acre Toodyay block for £300 to Ewan Mackintosh[1] whose lands and flocks had continued to increase and flourish in the Toodyay valley and to whom his Drummond brothers-in-law had long since become reconciled. He also disposed of, to Lieutenant-Colonel Bruce,[2] the ten-acre grant in Fremantle that he had held since the time of his arrival in the colony.[3] On the strength of these sales and of his new appointment Shaw proceeded to pay off at least some of his debts. These included £158 to the Government for the long-standing mortgage on Belvoir, £54 to Edward Hamersley for interest outstanding on the mortgage foreclosed in 1843 and the £120 owing to Alfred Waylen since 1842.

To many among the new influx of population, Captain Shaw with his military and pioneering background had become a colourful and respected figure—a man who had suffered much and worked unremittingly for the future of the settlement and, side by side with his kindly wife, continued to give generously of his time and experience in the cause of the community. He himself was probably happier than ever before in his colonial environment. The family were by this time back in their own—now considerably extended—home at Belvoir. They continued, however, to work a large portion of the Baskerville estate, for although William Tanner had died in England in 1853, he had left his colonial affairs in the hands of Will Brockman of Herne Hill with whom the Shaws had always enjoyed an amicable relationship.

About the time of Will's new appointment his first Australian-born daughter, Lucy Ellen, was married to a son of the learned Mr Joseph Keyes Logue, teacher of a school for the sons of gentlemen in Guildford. This was the first of their daughter's marriages that had really pleased the Shaw parents and they seem even to have been resigned to the fact that the bride, like her two sisters, was to make her home in a distant outpost of settlement. Young Major Logue had taken up land in the Champion Bay district at much the same time as John Drummond, and after the wedding he and his bride left the Swan for a newly-established station named Ellendale, about fifty miles from White Peak. This was an especially joyful turn of events for Mary Drummond, now reunited with the sister who had been from babyhood her special charge and whose life was from now on to be again closely linked with her own.

By this time a broken chain of stations had been established from the Victoria Plains to as far north as the Bowes and Murchison rivers, and several pioneers had been joined by their wives. It was not therefore quite the wilderness to which John Drummond had taken his bride. There was also a keen edge of optimism in the winds that prevailed across the grassy flats and inclined the trees to such melancholy shapes. Copper had been discovered on Drummond's White Peak lease in 1852 and John had quickly secured fifty acres of freehold and mining rights. By the time the young Logues arrived, a copper mine, floated largely on English capital, had been in operation for a year or more. The Drummonds thought their fortunes were assured, but while developments were held up for want of further capital the workers made off to new discoveries, which soon gave rise to the rich Wanerenooka and Gwalla Mining Companies that were to produce £40,000 worth of ore before the price fell in 1868.

The Drummonds were, after all, to make very little out of their White Peak Mine, but mineral activities, including lead mining, activated the new exporting centres of Geraldton and Port Gregory and brought an influx of ex-convicts, ticket-of-leave men and Cornish miners into the lonely land. It was the hope of every man-Jack of them one day to chance upon the glint of gold that had attracted the attention of the world to the eastern colonies and that was enticing too much of the settlement's hard-won population. Few of these early miners would live to see the great western gold discoveries of more than thirty years to come, and none would have foreseen in his wildest dreams the mighty north-west mineral boom of the following century.

John Drummond's career in the Police Force fared little

better than his mining activities. He had been bitterly frustrated when his request for further helpers to protect an increasing number of harassed settlers resulted only in the reduction of his small force. Retrenchments of this sort had been considered necessary to cut costs, for despite the generally more buoyant state of the economy, the new Governor had, like his forerunners, been faced with a depleted Treasury. Relations between John Drummond and Magistrate Burges had meanwhile become strained and in 1857, in order to prevent serious friction, the Governor appointed Drummond to take charge of a small force in Albany. He at once resigned, a move that had been anticipated, for it was generally known that he had too much faith in the pastoral and mining future of White Peak to consider abandoning it. He and Mary thereafter built a home for themselves within sight of the white-capped hill for which their property was named.

Mary was at this time expecting her first child, a fact that evidently did not deter her from riding to visit her sister at Ellendale. In October 1857, as a result of her saddle turning, she suffered a severe fall, no doubt accounting for the fact that her baby arrived prematurely and died shortly afterwards. She and John were to have no other children of their own, but Mary's loving arms were to embrace many little ones—including the numerous offspring of Lucy Ellen and Major Logue. Her heart and home were always open to the unfortunate or the wayfarer, her days filled with homely tasks and kindnesses, and if there were not always children about her skirts, there were poddy calves and motherless lambs, ducks and fowls, cats and dogs and pet parrots. No wonder the former 'belle of the Swan', herself childless, was to earn the name of 'mother of Champion Bay'. Although she and John employed two or three trustworthy Aborigines from the Toodyay district. Mary declared she could never leave White Peak, except for visits to Ellendale or other nearby stations. Her mother, missing her sadly sometimes reproached her for becoming tied down by so many self-imposed tyrannies:

Remember dear girl what too much care does to both young and old—be sure and don't fret if your hens do not lay two eggs a day instead of one ...[4]

and at another time:

> Why not come to see us at race time? Why *not* dear Mary?
> What signifies it if you imprison yourself to look after and
> keep together the whole world and lose your own health?
> Surely John was bachelor long enough to know well how
> to order things to be done without you for a short time.[5]

Even Elizabeth Whitfield with her brood of four sons and two
little girls managed occasionally to visit Belvoir. Of all Eliza's
family only George and Fanny were now at home; Bob, aged
twenty-three years having gone off to work a thirty-acre block
beside the Bulgurra pool on the Moore River, North of
Gingin, which the Shaws had leased from one Joseph B Ridley
in 1857.[6]

From the cross-references of family correspondence we
gather that Bob was, at that time, a young man of pleasing
enough disposition, doted on by his sisters and generally
popular. He was musically inclined and had a repertoire of
songs that he sang, with little persuasion, in a pleasing tenor.
In this he was sometimes accompanied by his Aboriginal
helper Charlie, whom he regarded less as a servant than as a
companion. Charlie's parents must have at some time been
employed by the Shaws as they kept in touch with his widowed
mother who lived in the vicinity, while on Bob's visits to
Belvoir over the ensuing years it was evidently taken for
granted that Charlie slept at the house and dined with the
family. Together Bob and Charlie cleared a few acres on the
Moore River block, borrowed two working bullocks, a plough
and a bag of wheat from their neighbours Mr and Mrs Robert
de Burgh and put in a crop.

The de Burghs had bought the Moore River property of
Cowalla in January 1858 from Francis Whitfield's two brothers
George and Edward, who had moved there from Toodyay in
the drought of 1850. At much the same time they had also
purchased Caversham, a few miles down river from Belvoir,
and for many years divided their time between the two properties. Eliza found much in common with this kindly couple—
Robert de Burgh, the son of an Anglican Canon, being from
Dublin, and his wife ever ready to exchange amusing anec-
dotes, recipes and household hints. When Bob moved to the

next door block they committed themselves to keeping an eye on him—a promise to which they were to prove more than faithful, defending his actions even when his own mother was no longer able to do so. Their property was on the direct route to the northern outposts to which Bob and his offsider were soon to move, and as they were frequently up and down the track they were never long out of touch.

It is difficult to determine for how long Bob actually worked the Moore River block, but it was no doubt up to the end of 1861 when he was listed as a foundation member of the Victoria District Agricultural Society. For a while he continued to grow wheat there while taking better paying contract jobs between seasons. One of these was a government assignment to blaze a stock route from the Moore River through to Dongara from Robert Brockman's[7] property, Nambung, forty-six miles north of the Moore River, and he thereafter took on jobs for Champion Bay land holders including the Browns of Glengarry, the Sewells of Sand Springs, the Davises of Tibbradden and the Du Boulays of Minnanooka. His headquarters during this period were at White Peak with Mary and John Drummond, and he sometimes stayed at Ellendale where Lucy Ellen and Major Logue were raising a lively family.

His elder brother George meanwhile remained at Belvoir and was obviously the mainstay of the family, even though Eliza's observations indicate that he was hardly a ray of sunshine and that he was inclined, at least before his father's death, to some improvidence. This latter suggestion may not have been quite fair to George for his parents never seem to have considered that a son, no matter how hard he worked, should demand more than pocket money and his keep. It was probably for this reason that both Nat and Bob had gone off on their own as soon as possible. Neither of them had been in a position to marry even had they wanted to, or had they been able to find a suitable wife in a colony so overweighted on the male side. This disparity had been accentuated by the introduction of male convicts which the government had attempted to alleviate by importing a number of so called 'needle-women' from Ireland. Some of these, despite earnest efforts to procure a superior type, were no more than the pathetic dregs of a poverty-stricken land. Others from orphanages that had been filled to overflowing in 'the great hunger' of the 1840s had been trained in needlework, lace-making and household tasks by Catholic nuns. These had no difficulties in finding employment and husbands—a few to marry established farmers but more to find their mates among lonely shepherds and ex-convicts. This was some help, but for the majority of single men the problem of acquiring a wife was almost insuperable. The sons of gentlemen farmers hesitated to court girls of their own class unless able to provide a home and a proper standard of living, which accounts for the seeming contradiction of there being so many unmarried daughters among the local gentry. Few of the sons of these families, diffident to seek mates of their own social status, felt any less inhibited regarding the humble Irish girls who were mostly illiterate and Roman Catholic to boot. There is no doubt, however, that some of them provided the men of the colony with passing alliances.

A letter of 1861 from Frederick Barlee to the Resident Magistrate of Champion Bay[8] reveals that Bob Shaw was being sued by a girl called Mary Bray for the maintenance of her illegitimate child. He was also, apparently, like many young men of the time, sharing the favours of native girls. Some of Eliza's descendants declare that she took charge, about this period, of a half-caste boy whose mother had died but who, as his likeness to her husband became too marked to be explained away, she eventually gave into the care of a couple at Gingin. That the child was in fact Will Shaw's seems unlikely, though it may very well have been his grandson.

But if Eliza wrote of such matters to her daughters, the letters have not been preserved. Her loving, rambling epistles of the time were filled with domestic details and items of local gossip not concerning her own:

Annie F, next door was to be married to the ploughman though 'it was to be a race between the parson and the doctor by the looks of her'.

Mrs F, having taken on the farm, would no longer demean herself to take in the Shaw's washing and she and Fanny had been most sadly put about.

She had finished the strips of embroidery for dear Ellen's long drawers and would have them ready in time for the Toodyay fair.

However many of the family could come for the Guildford races they would find the gates of 'Belvoir Castle' flung open to them in welcome as usual.

The boatman from Perth had been held up by tempestuous weather that had tipped the river over its banks again. Her stock of needles was therefore very low and no good ones amongst them but she would send Elizabeth what she had.

She was being plagued with a shocking attack of nettle rash and could not bear to wear her stays or as much as a piece of string about her waist.

Elizabeth's little daughter Mary who had been staying at Belvoir for some months had been about with her visiting the neighbours and very well behaved.

John Drummond had been ill and Mary thought he should come down for advice but could not come herself as she had taken in the Logue children whose mother had been far from well and their father anxious and out of spirits.

The Guildford district was showing great advances as a result of convict labour in government projects and also because of the introduction of steam boats running up river from Fremantle.

Belvoir was doing quite nicely with its wines and Will declared that if only they had the capital to extend the acreage under vines and add to their equipment their troubles would soon be over.

It was no doubt with this in mind that in 1859 Will, having already freed himself of most of his mortgages, took out yet another on the Belvoir estate. This was for £809 6s 8d, the biggest single sum he had yet borrowed—from his one-time neighbour and staunch friend Will Burges, then of Champion Bay. Eliza, who seems to have worried more over their debts than did her husband, declared that he was evidently so accustomed to being weighed down under a burden of liability that he felt lost without it. Will's own interpretation was that the colony was at last manifestly on the move and that enterprise was therefore justified.

Settlement over the Darling Range was rapidly closing in and had now spread east for almost 100 miles. Ports had appeared on the coast between Fremantle and Albany, where settlers were consolidating their estates and the timber cutters were already exploring the southern forests. By 1861, following the promising reports of F T Gregory, the northern pastoral frontier was being extended beyond Nichol Bay. Where the Shaws were concerned this meant an increasing market for their wine and, as Will Burges knew very well, the demand by the now-prosperous settlers of the Toodyay, Victoria Plains and Champion Bay districts already exceeded the supply. Everything pointed to a new era for the Cinderella colony and to the success of such first settlers as had had the courage to hold on. Will Shaw, in his latter-day euphoria, evidently forgot that there were some amongst the early settlers, including themselves, who had had no alternative. He was sorry to say good-bye, in February 1862, to his good friend Governor Kennedy but he was prepared to see a fortunate prognosis in the appointment of the colony's sixth Governor —Dr John Hampton, who had been Comptroller-General of convicts in Tasmania and would surely bring the benefits of his experience to a situation that had tended to become lax under the kindly Irishman.

Clearly to Shaw, in his seventy-fifth year, fortune promised at least to smile on the settlement. What he had not foreseen, or did not want to face, was that the future, for better or for worse, was no longer to concern him. The *Perth Gazette*, announcing his death in May, 1862, remarked that he was one of the colony's earliest settlers, 'a veteran of the Peninsula and Waterloo and highly esteemed in his neighbourhood'. He was buried at the Upper Swan Church, near his Belvoir residence, though he had required in his will that he would like if possible, to lie beside his two beloved sons, above the river at Baskerville.

We are left with a tantalizingly incomplete picture of a complicated character. That Will Shaw was brave, enterprising and hardworking there can be no doubt. He was obviously also a romantic and sensitive man, deeply attached to traditions and old associations and by no means as adaptable to new conditions as his wife. It is also apparent on the evidence available that he was his own worst enemy, for while craving the esteem of his fellow colonists, he had done much to damage his own prestige. Eliza's thanks to the Waghornes for having supported him in situations involving 'calumny and misrepresentation of character', would have been of little significance had he not himself been brought to court on such charges in the colony. In fact there were times during his long fight with Brown and the local government when a modern psychologist might well have pronounced his behaviour to have been paranoiac. Although there were many about him more unfortunately placed, he was convinced that his case was uniquely difficult and the treatment he received so unfair as to reverberate through the halls of British justice. The wonder is that, in spite of his occasional immoderate outbursts, he kept as many good friends as he did. Perhaps it was the naivety manifest in his blatant lack of judgement that called forth a protective attitude in some of his more sophisticated associates—people such as Will Tanner, Will Burges and Sam Viveash, the Brockmans and the Moores. The recognition that came to him in his latter years had undoubtedly cheered and mellowed him and he went out leaving a better impression than had he died in earlier years. It was remembered of him that he was by nature a generous man, prepared even in the leanest times to share what he had with needy neighbours. Moreover in his latter-day term as magistrate he would seem to have acted with discretion and kindly tolerance for the frailty of his fellow colonists, while with his remaining children and grandchildren, some of whom were with him in his last hours, he appears to have left a fond and lasting memory.

When it was seen that he was near the end, Elizabeth Whitfield and her children had hurried from Toodyay and Lucy Ellen Logue with her husband from Champion Bay, leaving Mary Drummond in charge of her family. Mary, unable therefore to come herself, had sent a heartbroken letter to which Eliza replied on black-edged paper:

We miss him at breakfast and at dinner but above all in his warm, snug corner of the sofa of an evening and just towards sunset I cannot divest myself of the feeling that I hear his footsteps on the verandah ... He sleeps in such a peaceful, sequestered corner in our little churchyard, chosen for him by George for I was quite incapable of taking part in these arrangements. Well did he conduct all though his heart was bursting with sorrow. Elizabeth's grief was very deep and her poor children felt it more than you would have expected those of their age to do. It would have been a great relief to us all if dear old Bob could have been with us to help his brother ... No letter from Bob this mail. I suppose as usual he works so hard all day that he is too weary to write at night. I would not have him neglect his business for the sake of visiting home.[9]

Chapter 22

1862–1868

The World of the Widow Shaw

Unwelcome neighbours. George Shaw in charge at
Belvoir. Fanny Shaw, spinster daughter. Bob Shaw
acquires a property at Champion Bay. Eliza Shaw be-
comes post-mistress. Her links with family in England.
Death of Sir James Stirling and Thomas Peel in 1865.
The end of transportation.

When Eliza donned a widow's bonnet in her sixty-ninth year
it was certainly no symbol of retirement, for she was from this
time on at least as busy as ever before.

Besides the Belvoir property they were still leasing the
better part of Baskerville and were also agisting stock, at £1 a
year per thousand acres, on 12,000 and in some years 14,000
acres of crown land in the vicinity of Belvoir.[1]

Eliza had resigned herself to the fact that if there were a
dozen good servants in the colony, which she doubted, none
of them was likely to come her way, but in any case, as she
wrote to Elizabeth, work did her good. She complained sometimes of suffering from colds which tended to attack her
'nerves and spirits', causing her to be 'a little dull sometimes
and to conjure up fears where no fears are'. There was, however, some cause for nervousness in these times. Their old
watchdog, Boatswain, had died and never had there been more
need for him. With the influx of lower-class emigrants to
balance the convict population, the neighbourhood, she de-
clares, had become 'a nest of hornets'. Many of the newcomers
had proved quite unemployable with the result that the settlers
were molested by 'tramping vagabonds at all hours of the day
and night'. They were indeed surrounded by 'the vilest of the
vile'. One despicable fellow, who admitted having come to the

district with no more than the clothes he stood up in to live off his neighbours, had put up a public pound close to the road and was forever pouncing on their milking cows and demanding 3d a head for their release.[2]

As time went on Eliza regretted more than ever the miles that separated her from her three daughters and youngest son.

> How many, many times [she wrote] I have wished we were nearer to each other and could be of more mutual help and comfort to each other in sickness and in health. We do indeed seem cut off from everything and everybody near and dear to us and might as well be buried alive as far as family intercourse goes. If it were not for letters we should utterly sink in despair.[3]

Travellers from the north sometimes brought news of her daughters, and friends wrote praising them for their kindness and capability. Eliza cherished these letters and repeated the messages lovingly:

> Mrs Kenneth Brown speaks so highly of the kindness of Mary and Ellen to poor Mrs Davis and says I ought to be proud of two such daughters. I am proud indeed of all my daughters and my sons too. I know they are not surpassed by any for *anything* and few, very few, can come up to one of them.[4]

George, after his father's death, would seem to have assumed a mantle of greater responsibility than had been evident in previous years. One gathers, however, from his mother's remark to Elizabeth that his sobriety was not always to be counted on.

> I am sure you would be pleased to see the struggle poor old father George (with all his faults) now makes for a living. He seems to have taken quite a start and sees the necessity of *making* as well as *spending* money. He should now be given his due for looking to the main chance of getting bread and meat as well as the pure juice which cheers the heart of man, aye and woman too, if not taken in such quantity as to stir up a *storm in a tea cup*. Perhaps it is as well we did not

make too much this year as it may teach moderation, though the habit of using it like water may never be quite conquered.[5]

At other times Eliza laments that 'poor old George' has no companion of his own age group. He was not, one gathers, as generally popular and sociable as Bob and his bachelor status was not thought likely to change.

> George is a bachelor verily [his mother writes]. He is growing very fussy and sometimes sharp almost to acidity.[6]

At another time, noting the poor crop of carrots that resulted from his planting, she observes:

> Poor George will never be a clever gardener—he never gave his mind to it ... but if all were as good the world would be fuller of 'practical Christians' than it is (rough as the side of his tongue is, *as you say*.)[7]

Shortage of labour was still a real problem and apparently even rouseabouts or yardmen were hard to come by:

> Everything in the garden wanting to be done and no one to do it. Poor George is sadly perplexed. With the help of two natives he has got a few potatoes in but I fear too late to come to much. He is under engagements to deliver hay but not a hand to help him cut it for love nor money. God only knows what he is to do for a ploughman ...[8]

The job he liked and at which he excelled was the manufacture of wine. At this task he was skilled and meticulous in its every phase and it is little wonder he sometimes enjoyed his own product to excess. Over the next few years the Belvoir wines, to Eliza's considerable pride and joy, gained both in quality and reputation, with regular orders coming in not only from down the river at Perth and Fremantle but from the south-western settlements and the now fairly affluent northern farmers and graziers.

And what of Fanny, 'the baby of the family', twenty-four years old at the time of her father's death? She had acquired a basic education in the little Upper Swan schools that moved about to accommodate the majority of pupils and she was included in the social life of the established families. She went to parties 'in full toggery' at the Brockmans of Herne Hill, the Hamersleys of Pyrton, the de Burghs of Caversham, the Viveashs of Wexcombe and their relatives the Middletons of Ellensbrook. It is all the same impossible to escape the conclusion that, bound in the Victorian tradition to the role of unmarried daughter, Fanny was a devoted drudge. Eliza makes little reference to her in letters of this time except to say that she grieves sadly for her father, has been hard at work on that 'all-consuming ever-craving threshing machine', that she and Johnston have taken the dray into Guildford, presumably to market, that she has been 'up to her ears' making jams and preserves, taking honey from their hives or busy at the ironing. On one occasion she enclosed for Elizabeth some of Fanny's recipes which she said would be found economical and delicious. (Some of Eliza's own recipes, such as one for onion gruel guaranteed 'to bring out a perspiration' and relieve a fever, sounds anything but delicious.)

Bob, during this time, had been keeping his eyes open for a block of land near his sisters at Champion Bay and in March 1864 Eliza heard from Mary Drummond that he had secured an 8,000-acre lease near Ellendale. Eliza replied that although she was sure they would miss Bob's company she was pleased that he now had 'a station' near Major Logue, who with his steady habits and practical experience would be the greatest help to him. 'I know,' she writes, 'that they will never lose sight of his comfort and will often take a run up and set him to rights a bit and that the children now and then will be a great break to the monotony of his bachelor's hearth.' She was delighted also that it was such 'a pleasant visiting neighbourhood with the Browns, the Davises and Du Boulays, all musical people who know how to pass many an evening away which might otherwise be spent so as to bring headaches in the morning.'[9]

Both Mary Drummond and Ellen Logue felt strongly protective towards their youngest brother, and like the de Burghs and a few other Champion Bay friends were prepared to excuse his unpredictable ways and bouts of immoderate drinking by reason of his other attributes. He was evidently a good bushman with a genuine capacity for hard work and if he undertook to blaze a track, to sink a well or put up a yard or fence it could be guaranteed to be well done. He had besides a friendly disposition and presented a convincing version of a hard-luck life that began with a lack of parental understanding, followed by endless instances of betrayed trust—employers who had failed to pay him his just due, 'mates' who had robbed him and women who had trapped him into paying for the sins of other men.

Engaged on contracting jobs that kept him on the move along the bush tracks, he had been able better to cope with the demons of loneliness and frustration that haunted him relentlessly when he attempted to settle down. As a roving bushworker his access to alcohol had been limited, but with a place of his own he kept his store well stocked. The result was that the only positive record of his station life, apart from the registration of his holding, is a reference in the Geraldton police files to his having reported an attempt on his life.[10] Evidence gathered from his servant, George Bickerstaff, however, suggests that he had slashed his own throat, though failing next day to recall having done so.

If any of this news came his mother's way it is not recorded, and she continued to send cheery messages and pots of jam and pickles to her 'dear hard-working boy'. He seems to have got home for the annual Guildford races over this period, timing his visits so as to travel with the de Burghs from Gingin and spending as much of his time with them at Caversham as with his family at Belvoir. He professed to having a great affection for his old home and sometimes declared to his friends that he was striving to make enough money at Champion Bay to come back and help George build up the family estate. Truth to tell, however, he had usually fought with George by the time he returned north.

Eliza, during this time, had taken on the first public duty of her life. A notice in the Government Gazette of June 1865 signed by Frederick Barlee, Colonial Secretary, informs us that 'Mr Fawell of Coulston, having resigned the situation of Post Master for Upper Swan, this service will as a temporary measure be discharged at the residence of Mrs Shaw.' Although she had probably undertaken this job mainly for the convenience of her neighbours, it suited her friendly nature and love of gossip, or of keeping her 'ear to the ground' as she preferred to put it, for it meant neighbours calling to collect and dispatch their mail, many of them staying to chat over a cup of tea. She wrote to Elizabeth that she would find her old home quite 'crazy' under the circumstances, but at least she was now able to report on a wide range of births, deaths, marriages, sicknesses and misfortunes as well as the progress of local public works and the lamentable effects of 'the curse of gold' on certain people of high standing in the colony. Dear Mrs Brockman, whose daughter Margaret had died so tragically in her early twenties soon after Will Shaw, was still sick with grief and her husband looked 'hunted off his legs and very thin'. The Gull family were all abed with colds, but Mr Logue (Major's father) was about again and 'now slept soundly and well'.

Her correspondence reveals that Eliza had maintained over the years at least a tenuous link with her family in England. In 1862 she mentions her brother, Nat Cooper, writing from time to time and on one occasion sending a photograph of himself and his daughter. She also notes that her sister Caroline, born at Newcastle, Northumberland in 1796, had died of smallpox at Chelmsford, Essex, and that her other sister Sophie had married a man named Dixon and was living at Menworth House near Birmingham. In 1865 she must have written to Sophie asking for a copy of her birth certificate or some proof of her being the eldest daughter of Captain Nathan Cooper of Leicester, for her sister had sent a page from their father's Memorandums in which he had noted the birth of his daughter 'Betsy' at Newmarket on 16 November 1794 'at four o'clock in the morning'.[11]

The object of this interchange was probably to claim some money due to her, as a result of her sister Caroline's death. In this she must have proved successful, as her latter-day journal indicates that although she had not paid off the Belvoir mortgages, she had money out on mortgage to others. She also requests in her will that £1,000 of the money left her by her father be paid to her daughter Fanny.

In all the chit-chat conveyed in Eliza's letters over this time one finds no mention of the deaths of the two prime movers in the founding of the colony. James Stirling, by that time an Admiral of the Fleet and with another life-time of adventures behind him since leaving his Australian colony, died at Guildford in Surrey in April 1865. At the end of the same year Thomas Peel's death at his dilapidated Mandurah residence passed almost unnoticed, the history of his grand but disastrous settlement scheme to remain all but forgotten until the publication of his biography a century later.[12]

By this time the writing was already on the wall for the convict transportation that had brought so much new hope and so many new problems to the thirty-six-year-old settlement. Protests from the eastern colonies that had been powerless to prevent its introduction on humanitarian grounds were gaining force for the practical reason that so many unwelcome ex-convicts were arriving there from the west. The British Government gave more hearing to their case by reason of the cost involved in transportation, at a time when so much money had been poured out in the Crimean war, in the Indian mutiny of the mid-fifties, the Maori wars of the sixties and the unending troubles in Ireland.

When it was announced in 1865 that transportation was to end within three years, the majority of western settlers were not disposed to protest, though they were prepared to admit that the system had achieved much for their isolated colony. Over the eighteen-year period the population had risen from 5,886 to 22,915 and the increased shipping had been helpful to commerce, including the export of heavy timber and sandalwood. Convict labour had helped develop not only the widespread holdings of the pastoralists and agriculturalists, but the mining of lead and copper in the north. It was also seen, however, that the careful screening of transportees, guaranteed at the outset, was no longer being applied and that crime, much of it attributable to lack of women, had increased disturbingly. 'The system' had achieved its end but had also inhibited the emigration of the type of settlers that in Stirling's dream were to have imposed a pattern of behaviour modelled on the best traditions of British gentility. For all its benefits, transportation had served further to isolate the already remote colony from the rest of the world, and the Swan River settlers were embarrassed that visitors, however distinguished, were required to leave with certificates—demanded by South Africa and the eastern colonies—stating that they had never been transported as convicts to Western Australia! Moreover, the people of Perth were tired of the ten o'clock curfew and of being questioned, if abroad after that time, whether 'Bond or Free'. Despite the public works for which Governor Hampton's vigorous policy was responsible, many were reminded, by his stern disciplinarian control, of the harsh régime that had brought such disrepute to the Eastern colonies. The last transportees to arrive in the Hougoument in January 1868 brought the total convicts sent to the colony to 9,668. Enough was enough.

Chapter 23

1869–1875

Wild Grapes

Results of convict labour on growth of Perth. Eliza
Shaw visits old friends and recalls memories of early
years. Discusses current events—escape of Fenian
prisoners to USA. John Forrest's expedition inland.
Eliza Shaw visits family at Toodyay. Death of her
daughter Elizabeth Whitfield, and her son George.
Bob Shaw returns to Belvoir. Calls of condolence.
Bob Shaw's conduct causes anxiety. Eliza seeks advice
of friends. Belvoir advertised for sale.

'I dread going to Perth,' Eliza wrote to Elizabeth in April
1869, 'for I have been feeling wretched and truly miserable
and not fit to undertake even that journey, but I am literally
bare-foot and not a pair of lace-up boots to be had in any of
the Guildford stores.'

There was an occasion thirty-eight years before when,
pregnant and worn with grief over the recent loss of her two
boys, she had felt almost incapable of making this same journey
to attend the Governor's first ball. Then, as now, she was to
return refreshed and with new heart to carry on, for Perth
since her previous visit all of twelve months before, had
changed remarkably. Governor Hampton, knowing that convict labour was soon to be suspended, had made determined
efforts to complete a programme of public works that might
otherwise have taken a decade. St George's Terrace, that had
been a sandy track when Eliza first walked it on a visit to the
Stirlings' humble quarters in 1830, was now a fine broad
thoroughfare with side-walks formed from wooden blocks, and
a fine brick barracks with a battlemented central arch dominat-
ing its western end. A Government House of fitting size and

elegance and surrounded by well-kept gardens had also materialized with, next door, a Supreme Court of quite imposing architecture set in flourishing botanical gardens. Across the terrace was the Cathedral, the Deanery and at the west end of the terrace the Bishop's residence occupied by the colony's first Anglican prelate, Mathew Blagden Hale. Nearby—almost completed—was the new Perth Town Hall with clock tower and colonnades, and on the summit of Victoria Square the Roman Catholic Cathedral built by Spanish Benedictines. Between these imposing edifices were a growing number of shops, hotels and business houses and on the river side of the terrace were the homes, gardens and orchards of some of Perth's most prominent and affluent citizens.

Eliza paid a few calls and returned to Belvoir not only with her lace-up boots but with absorbing topics of conversation for many weeks to come. At the Wittenooms' town house, The Bungalow,[1] in Hay Street, she had talked old times and recent happenings with a number of Perth friends bidden to meet her by the widow of Charles Wittenoom, son of the Rev John Wittenoom who had died in 1855. Charles had married twice, the second time, a year before his death in 1866, to Sam Moore's daughter Annie, then living at the Bungalow with her little daughter Florence and two sons of her husband's first marriage. Mrs Wittenoom's mother, Mrs Sam Moore, was also at The Bungalow when Eliza called and between them there was much talk of ties uniting the old 'first families' and becoming every year more complicated. Their conversation would hardly have betrayed a snobbishness in the local gentry, for the sharing of tribulations had brought them in close touch and set them on a friendly calling basis with all classes in the community. Nonetheless their memories were never at fault in recalling the circumstances surrounding the arrival of every family in the settlement and the social status from which they were derived. Even the passage of time and the levelling of telltale accents would lead to no confusion among descendants of those 'first families' regarding which folk were of 'the quality', which of yeoman, farm-labouring, servant or convict stock and which, however prominent in the social register, were or had been 'in trade'—this last meaning anything in the nature of shopkeeping.

Like Eliza, the Wittenooms and Moores had also extended

branches to the Champion Bay area. The Rev Wittenoom's first Australian-born daughter, Mary Dircksey, had married Kenneth Brown of Glengarry ten years before and she it was who had written so warmly to Eliza of the kindness of her two far-away daughters. Details were exchanged of her tragic death in childbirth only a few months before. She had left a young family, including the eight-year-old Edith who, in 1921, was to become the first woman member of any parliament in Australia. Mrs Brown's younger sister Augusta had married Tom Burges of Bowes Station, nephew of Will Burges who had been a close friend of the Shaws for so many years.

Apart from family gossip there was talk of recent happenings of more general interest. There had been the excitement, little over a month before, of the escape to the United States of America in a whaling vessel of a number of Irish political prisoners, including a quite notorious rebel named John Boyle O'Reilly, sent out under maximum security and sentenced to hard labour.

More recently still—on 15 April, 1869—young John Forrest, who had attended Bishop Hale's school with one of the young Wittenooms, had left Perth in charge of an expedition into the unknown interior. The primary object of his undertaking was to search for the Leichhardt party, reported to have been murdered by natives at a place to which an Aboriginal informant had volunteered to lead them. Many said it was 'a wild-goose-chase' but Forrest was a qualified surveyor and would, it was generally agreed, use the expedition to good effect in discovering new country. With the rest of the colony Eliza awaited the return of the Forrest expedition with breathless interest. George brought the news from Guildford early in August that the party had returned to Perth—after a journey of nearly 2,000 miles, most of it through totally unmapped wilderness. The Aborigine's information having proved quite unreliable, they had found no trace of the Leichhardt party, and no country of any use for agriculture or pasture, though Forrest had recommended it for geological survey. Governor Weld, who succeeded Hampton towards the end of 1869, praised the explorers warmly and they were accorded a rousing welcome.

Not long after her trip to Perth, Eliza felt well enough to undertake one of her rare visits to her family at Toodyay, travelling with her son-in-law Francis Whitfield in a horse and trap. The five surviving Whitfield grandchildren, all of whom had spent considerable periods at Belvoir, now ranged in ages between nineteen and fourteen years old. Mary, the eldest, an attractive girl to whom Eliza, having had much to do with her upbringing, was especially attached, accompanied her grandmother on visits to old friends in the neighbourhood including the Drummonds of Hawthornden. The head of that family, the colony's first Government Botanist, had died in 1863 and his wife about a year later, the property passing into the hands of their son James Jnr, who had built a fine two-storey home in place of their first modest farmhouse. Old James Drummond had maintained close touch with his son John and daughter-in-law Mary at White Peak, from where they had sent him seeds to be planted in his Toodyay garden and also to be forwarded to his botanist friend Dr Joseph Hooker in England. At the time of Eliza's visit in early spring she was delighted to see the green paddocks dotted pink and white with the daisy heads of beautiful Champion Bay everlastings.

It was a happy time for her, surrounded by young people as she loved to be, and enjoying 'a good old wongi' with her beloved eldest girl—her 'green spot in a desert land'. They had shared many sorrows over the years but could always, when together, find much to laugh about in their memories of times past. The only shadow over their reunion was the weariness Elizabeth could no longer disguise in going about her endless tasks. In all the twenty-six years of her married life she had had no real holiday. Even on her occasional visits to Belvoir, the house had always been full and it had been for them both, as Eliza wrote, 'a toil of a pleasure'. At fifty she was already worn out and this visit was in fact the last time she and her mother were to be together. In April 1873 the sad tidings reached Belvoir by the newly connected telegraph line between Toodyay and Guildford, that Elizabeth had died in her sleep. She was buried with her first baby daughter Mary in the little bush cemetery at Nardie.

Of Eliza's nine children there were now only five left and of those all but two were far from home. Although she wrote to them regularly it was her letters to Elizabeth, perhaps the most cherished, that were the best preserved. She kept a daily journal, the many volumes of which she reported having stored in 'Nat's strong deal box', but only the last of these, commencing on Christmas Eve 1875, has been preserved.

Eliza was by this time in mourning once again—now for her son George who had fallen victim to a current outbreak of diphtheria. Epidemics, except for measles and influenza, usually fatal only to the Aborigines, had not been common in the colony whose people, by and large, were a hardy lot, relying for the most part in times of sickness on simple home remedies and common-sense. The scattered cemeteries, however, bear grim witness to the toll taken of young and old by that epidemic of 1875. Bob had been sent for and had come at once with 'Black Charlie' from Champion Bay, reporting having been robbed of £16 on the way. Some days later a telegram from his sister Mary Drummond informed him that the money had been found where he had dropped it on the track. It is obvious from his mother's journal that he intended taking over the management of Belvoir in his brother's place, and although he had not got on well with George over the past years Eliza accredits him with being grieved to the point of collapse. He was, she reported 'suffering night and day from high nervous affliction ... and anxiety of mind, having worked hard building a beautiful wheat stack, saying he thought his poor brother would be glad to hear it was nicely done.'[2]

Eliza and Fanny did their best to provide the usual Christmas fare for the three family members and four servants—Johnston, Hogan, Gardiner and Charlie. They sat down together to 'a nice dinner of roast mutton and plum pudding, etc, with a proper allowance of wine and all pleased and satisfied until Hogan and Michael Nolan from next door ... fell upon Johnston. When Fanny ordered them out Hogan picked up his alls and has not returned.'[3] Where was Bob meanwhile that his sister was forced to maintain order? Eliza could not yet bring herself to write explicitly of her son's condition, but on Boxing Day she reports sending Gardiner down river to fetch Mr de Burgh who slept the night in Bob's room and next morning returned with him to Caversham. 'I had a nice letter of invitation for him from Mrs de B,' Eliza explains. Her brief and guarded jottings over this period reveal that the situation at Belvoir was reaching a crisis. Now in her eighty-second year, she was trying with one desperately overworked and overwrought daughter to run the estate with a staff of three intemperate farm labourers, one faithful Aboriginal and a hopelessly alcoholic son.

George, whom she had often criticized for paying too little attention to various tasks and for his occasional over-indulgence in 'the cup that cheers', was referred to in retrospect as the staff and mainstay of her life. She looked back now in her bitter trouble and bewilderment on the 'bountiful blessings of the past' when her life, with Will and George close at hand, now seemed to have been comparatively secure and trouble-free. She was every day reminded of George's thought for others and his affection for the children of their neighbours and farm labourers. He had had little enough to leave, but he had asked on his death bed that a certain cow and calf be given to Nat Knight's infant daughter and that his favourite horse (which Eliza could ill spare) be given to the ploughman's son. He had had a special thought too for 'Black Charlie's' ailing mother to whom he had been attached from childhood. After Christmas Fanny and Charlie had ridden together to visit her and to give her a silver chain to wear as a keepsake of 'Master George'.[4]

Every day friends called to offer their condolences. The young Moores came from Oakover and their mother Mrs Sam Moore, with her daughter Mrs Charles Wittenoom, all the way from Perth. Then there were the sons of Will Brockman who had died in 1872, reviving fond memories of childhood days when they and poor George had attended Mr Mitchell's first little school across the river at Henley Park. On New Year's Day came Mrs Edward Hamersley of Pyrton, herself widowed little over a year before, with her daughter Margaret and John Forrest who were to be married the following month. Eliza was much impressed with the big, bearded young explorer, who after his expedition of 1869 had set out again to establish a land route around the coast between Perth and Adelaide, and yet again in 1874, this time crossing the unknown heart of the colony from Champion Bay to the overland telegraph in South Australia. Other visitors were the Minchins of Spring Park, the Viveashs now living down the river at Ashby, Mrs Viveash's brother Mr Middleton and his family of Ellensbrook, and their good clergyman Archdeacon Brown and his wife. In fact the names of all the old families in the district weave in and out of Eliza's often agonized account of her daily life at this time.

Somehow or another, meanwhile, work went on in the vineyards and around the farm, though there was little leadership from Bob and ill-feeling among the men. Nolan, sulky after the fight on Christmas Day, had driven all the Belvoir horses into the bush and Johnston was obliged to go in search of them. Bisdey and Nolan then refused to work with Johnston on Baskerville and Johnston, to demonstrate his feelings, 'dodged the horses through and through the vines and vineyards and into Nolan's wheat'. Sometimes Eliza describes Johnston as 'in tantrums', 'greatly disguised by liquor', 'pretending to mend fences' and generally 'getting into his old habits of shirking'. As Bob's behaviour went from bad to worse, however, Johnston seems to have taken a pull and is reported to be 'working diligently' ... wood carting and jobbing, securing posts and rails from bushfire, cleaning out the barn, butchering, cutting sedge for thatching the haystacks, attending to the pigs, and generally helping Fanny. Bisdey was at one stage dismissed for 'behaving improperly' to Fanny, but was soon back on the books, his efforts at 'winnowing being described by Fanny as "medium to worthless"'.

In desperation Eliza wrote to the Whitfield family asking whether anyone could lend a hand over the harvest. Mary, the eldest girl, had recently married a young farmer named Sam Green, a son of Dr Alfred Green who had come out as assistant surgeon on the *Warrior* in 1830 and had later taken up land at Wonnerup in the south-west. Sam Green had been educated at Bishop Hale's school along with other native-born sons, some destined to play leading roles in the colony's development. He had taken to Mary's grandmother at their first meeting, and sympathetic of her position, had responded at once to her call for help. He had even, Eliza tells us, been prepared to walk from Toodyay to Guildford but had managed to get a lift to Belvoir in a dray. He could not stay long but while there he seems to have done the work of ten men—harvesting and stacking, hooping wine casks, mending the dray, propping up the fruit trees. Eventually, Eliza insisted on lending him the horse she used in her trap to get him home, even though it meant that she was, from then on, dependent on her neighbours for transport.

During this time the Shaws were selling not only wheat and wine but often meat, at 4d to 6d a pound, and occasionally livestock. Eliza's detailed report clearly demonstrates the interdependence of the community, the Shaws and their neighbours constantly borrowing or hiring each other's labourers, threshing and winnowing machinery, teams and other items of farming equipment. Eliza's advice on farming methods was often asked and gratefully accepted by less experienced neighbours, if not by her son. Observing him one day struggling with a lopsided haystack she suggested that 'one end of the stack be cut off to the top' which advice 'gave great offence and drew forth not very pleasant sentiments'. He was no more ready to take advice on the making of wine, which despite his comparative lack of experience he now declared was the only activity in which he intended taking any part. He started superintending the cleaning of the casks but, impatient of the preliminaries, wanted the job done in a hurry, and according to his mother, in a slovenly manner. She feared that the current vintage would not come up to that of former years. His next step worried her even more, for on the grounds that they must get the grapes off before the bees destroyed them, he cut them while they were still half green. The result was a sour-tasting, excessively potent product, which, while too well appreciated by Johnston and the natives employed to clear fire-breaks in the bush blocks, Eliza feared was unsaleable. By this time her guards were down. 'There was neither anarchy nor confusion until he came,' she wrote. 'Now nothing is being done to benefit either the place or any person on it.' He was 'non-compos every day by 11 am, and by evening ! ! !' On and off he was 'seriously ill ... under severe attack, and refusing to have anyone but Fanny attend to him.' He would listen to neither 'reason, remonstration nor entreaty', and refused the advice of Dr Viveash who visited frequently and anxiously with his wife from Ashby. Poor Fanny, worn out by sleepless nights and working by day on the threshing machine in the blistering February heat, was one day found by her mother in a dead faint. With no other hands in evidence, Eliza was forced to summon Bob from his bed and with a strength begotten no doubt of remorse he 'kindly supported her to her room'. He seems however to have quickly forgotten the incident and was soon shouting for her attention.

It is sad that what ought to be so great a blessing should be the bane of the colony [Eliza writes]. My present trials are greater than I can bear to describe.

Seeking solace from her Bible she found the psalm from Isaiah, which apart from demonstrating that her problem was no modern phenomenom was of little comfort after all:

My well beloved hath a vineyard in a very fruitful hill: And he fenced it and gathered out the stones thereof, and planted it with the choicest vine, and built a tower in the midst of it, and also made a winepress therein: and he looked that it should bring forth grapes, and it brought forth wild grapes.

Isaiah, Chapter 5, verses 1 and 2.

Only the de Burghs had any influence over Bob, and from this time on he was more often at Caversham than at home. It is puzzling that these good friends, knowing his weakness as they must very well have done, could still consider him capable of managing the estate. Perhaps he displayed to them another side of his character and had convinced them that his mother's attitude was at the root of his problem. At all events, Mr de Burgh must at last have taken her to task on the matter as Eliza succinctly reports:

Gave Mr de B to distinctly understand I had not the slightest intention to put the management of my affairs in Bob's hands. He expressed himself surprised ...[5]

What the de Burghs may not clearly have understood was the complicated situation in which Eliza had been placed. The terms of her husband's will were that she should inherit all his property, land, buildings, livestock and equipment and should at her death bequeath to all their children 'share and proportion alike'. He exhorted them most earnestly to reflect before disposing of the property 'it being the only resource for the unfortunate to fall back on in the hour of need and destitution'. It was a simple enough injunction on the face of it but the information not included in the document was that the estate was under mortgage to Will Burges for £809 6s 8d and to the Tanner estate for £180. Tanner was long dead as was his executor, Will Brockman, who had left his affairs in the hands of his son Edward.

Eliza, feeling herself to be in 'insurmountable difficulties', turned from one to another of her old friends, gathering a plethora of contrary advice that served only further to confuse her. Will Burges, to whom her husband had exhorted her to turn in time of trouble, advised her to engage a competent manager and live on at Belvoir as before. Henry Brockman, her late friend Will Brockman's son, advised her to let the estate and, evidently realizing her need for ready cash, paid her £100 down for fat cattle at £4 a head. The late Sam Moore's son, W D Moore of Oakover, agreed with Brockman and sent a man named Marrs to bid for the lease at £80 a year. Not at all sure of Marrs, she wrote to young Hugh Hamersley of Pyrton asking whether he was interested. He was not but he came to confer with her and warned her of 'land sharks' who might be pressing her to sell for their own ends. One wonders to whom he was referring, since it is hardly likely that it could have been to T C Gull, a reputable merchant of Guildford and related by marriage to Hamersley. He was also an old friend of the Shaws, who had advised Eliza to call in her mortgages, authorize the sale of the estate and 'live on the proceeds'. It was Hamersley's opinion that she should rent the property.

In the meantime Eliza had written to members of her family —the Whitfields, Drummonds and Logues—asking whether they would like to purchase the estate collectively or whether any would be individually prepared to take it on. None of them was in a position to make any move in the matter so Eliza pursued the idea of leasing the estate to an outsider.

But at this stage Gull prevailed, having convinced Eliza that she actually had no option but to sell. He no doubt also saw this as his only chance of being repaid a debt outstanding from the Shaw family for some years.

Alas, how can I write that dear Belvoir is advertised for sale to save us from God only knows what. Sad and gloomy seems my future ... Would I were blessed with someone who would have taken my poor dear George's place ... Oh may I continue to trust in His Word, who has said ... 'As your day is, so your strength will be also' ... We must not murmur but hope and trust, but I fear and tremble.[6]

Chapter 24

1876–1877

The Last Journey

Belvoir withdrawn from sale. Eliza Shaw joined by
grandchildren Sam and Mary Green. Major Logue
arrives from Geraldton, Francis Whitfield and son from
Dandaragan. Packing for Champion Bay. Ship delayed
by case of K Brown. Farewell to Belvoir. Eliza and
Fanny Shaw at White Peak. Sale of Belvoir to W T
Loton. Death of Eliza Shaw at White Peak Station.

Eliza's fears were not unfounded, for Bob had rallied the fairly
formidable support of a contrary legal opinion, endorsed by
that of the de Burghs. With this backing he informed his
mother that whoever had advised her to sell was acting, not in
her interest, but in his own, hoping no doubt to seize upon a
good property at a bargain price. He insisted that according
to the terms of her husband's will she had no legal right to
sell and that if she was determined to proceed in that direction he would take her to court.

That Bob meant what he said Eliza had no doubt and the
prospect of such a public airing of their family problems threw
her into a real state of panic. She at once called on her friend
Mrs Middleton of Ellensbrook to take her into Guildford,
where she told Gull that he must at once withdraw the estate
from the market.

Not unnaturally Gull was annoyed at this display of non-
confidence in his opinion, and of losing the chance of being
repaid his money. In Eliza's own words: 'he very roughly, and
I think cruelly, in the hearing of Mrs Middleton, threatened if
I did stop the sale he would ask for his account and wash his
hands of the business altogether.'[1] Eliza flounced out of his
office and telegraphed to E W Landor who had remained on

friendly terms with the Shaws since his first trip up the river in 1841, and who was then a practising barrister in Perth. He came at once, gave what advice he could, and agreed to negotiate the withdrawal of Belvoir from the market. 'The kind and considerate way in which he met and treated me,' Eliza states, 'was a great contrast to Mr G's.'

Bob confronted her on her return to Belvoir with formal notice that he intended taking her to law, 'But providentially,' Eliza writes, 'I had made up my mind before he came to stop the sale at all hazards and to forthwith stay any more proceedings or expense in the dreadful, perplexing matter.' Given this assurance Bob proposed that she should retire to some other place of residence while he took over the entire management of the property. 'I pointed out to him my position,' Eliza says, 'and told him after much conversation, that if he could get a responsible security that would guarantee my yearly income I would come in at once to his terms. Fanny witnessed my saying so but he went off as usual sulky and under very *unkind feelings*—conduct and language disgraceful and unjust—the whole day has borne evident marks of what has been gradually increasing for years ... What I have been obliged to bear with is only known to one more besides myself—there are *things* unspeakable and even the truth must not always be brought to the front.' One wonders to what lurking skeleton Eliza here refers, since Bob's alcoholism was surely common knowledge. Some days later she writes again in the same vein: 'I dread exposure but it is now coming to that extent that my sore and great trouble of more than a year's standing, must soon come to a crisis. Alas, it has been noticed long ago. But still there are things that are unspeakable and therefore harder to bear. The loss of my best staff of life is nothing compared to the woes I feel every day from those that are left behind and the world knows nothing of.'[2]

Bob, after much fruitless argument, returned to Caversham to reappear a week later with Mr de Burgh and his son-in-law, James Morrison, who owned a property named Waterhall near Guildford.[3] Morrison also operated as a stock and station agent and auctioneer in both Guildford and Perth, and had come, he declared, in a purely friendly capacity 'to settle something about the future of *letting* Belvoir ... After a great deal of discussion ... Mr Morrison made a proposal which he and Mr de B urged me to sign and which I did, not at all believing that the family could or would agree to the proposal made, the terms of which I had no part in the making. But anything to bring this dreadful suspense and uncertainty to an end.'[4]

Eliza endeavoured at this stage to gather together the remaining members of her family to talk the matter out. She wrote to Mary and John Drummond, to Ellen and Major Logue and to Francis Whitfield, who soon after his wife's death had moved with his family to Dandaragan. As before, the first to respond was young Sam Green who arrived with his wife Mary and baby daughter Eve, declaring that they would stand by Eliza until some settlement had been made. The young people brought with them to Belvoir a welcome breath of normality. Eliza suddenly observes quite cheerily that she sees 'every appearance of a splendid season coming on,' and she proceeds to list their daily tasks as though life at Belvoir was going on as it had always done. For the first time in many months the family goes to church. Johnston is 'jobbing about very steadily—mending a fence in the horse paddock and putting in potatoes. Sam Green is looking to the stock, repairing and clearing the Biljarra fence, bunging down casks of red wine.'

Only when Bob turned up did the wind veer again to the east—'Bob from below, wrathful about some reports he had heard in Guildford'. He declared that people had been circulating lies about his treatment of his mother and sister and were holding him responsible for their financial disaster—as if, he declared, Belvoir had ever been anything else but a disaster! His conduct was 'disgraceful and defiant—almost amounting to blows and his threats were fearful to listen to'. Yet he seems to have tried, pathetically, to take a grip of affairs, his every attempt narrowly watched by his mother who had now given up any pretence of tolerance for her irresponsible son. 'Bob bunged up some casks of red but so as the air and wine oozed out. Cloth too thin. Had to bore bungs out with an auger ...'[5] 'Bob killed little beast, but it was badly bled and not too nicely cut up.'[6]

His final bid to take a hand in affairs was to announce that he had made a certain proposal to various members of the family. This Eliza dismissed in a few brisk words: 'I pointed out how utterly impossible it was. Francis [Whitfield] could not if he would. Fanny could not and I do not think that Major [Logue] would.' This was evidently the last straw for Bob. Having bade good-bye to the de Burghs he returned to Belvoir, packed up, mustered his horses and set off alone for Champion Bay, whence 'Black Charlie' had gone off a few weeks before 'on loan' to a friend.

On 18 April, 1876, Eliza records with relief the arrival of her son-in-law Major Logue who had travelled from Geraldton in the *Georgette* to lend her his 'head and hands'. Of all the family she valued his advice the most highly, and it was to him she left the final decision of what was to be done. Major set about his task in a businesslike way, first making a careful assessment of the estate, counting the stock, checking the fences, looking over the machinery and testing the wine. He then went down to Perth to consult solicitors Leitch, Sewell and Meagher who were dealing with certain aspects of Eliza's complicated affairs. Some time before his death, Will Shaw had gifted to the Logues a portion of the Belvoir property in the hope no doubt of its influencing them to return to the district. Major now made it quite clear that he relinquished on behalf of both his wife and himself any 'benefits or entanglements with the Shaw property'. He must clearly have seen that there would be little enough accruing from the estate—either leased or sold—to provide even a modest living for Eliza and Fanny. Major's proposal was a tactful compromise by which they were to go to Champion Bay for an interim period, leaving Belvoir in the capable hands of Sam and Mary Green. Eliza could then come to a decision about the estate in her own time.

Plans were made for their departure on the *Georgette*, the little coastal steamer that had recently been in the news for having pursued the whaling vessel *Catalpa* in which the last of the Fenian prisoners were making their escape to the United States.

Packing up proceeded in an orderly fashion, Eliza recording where she was storing, over her 'absence', some precious garden seeds, hops, dried peaches, raisins, currants, and soap-making ingredients. In Nat's 'heavy deal box', along with his will and other papers, she put the Belvoir wine statistics, the family Bible and Apocrypha, and various other documents including her journals dating from Will's death to the previous year. One wonders what became of this box and its precious contents. Perhaps Eliza's frank outpourings of day-to-day events were too embarrassing to the later generation of her family or otherwise deemed of too little interest to be preserved. At all events it would seem that only the last journal that she took with her from Belvoir has survived. When the packing was almost complete, Francis Whitfield and his son Frank arrived with their team from Dandaragan, but with too many problems of their own to be of more than token assistance. Forced out of his Toodyay property under a heavy load of mortgage, Francis and his motherless family were then attempting to start from scratch in a comparatively new area. They had contracted to bring a neighbour's woolclip down to Guildford and were to return a week later with stores.

During this time two wealthy merchants, Walter Padbury and his partner William Thorley Loton, had shown some interest in the purchase of Belvoir and had come up to inspect the estate. Major informed them that Eliza was not, as rumoured, obliged to sell but might be prepared to consider an offer of £1,500. This price the partners declared exorbitant and made no bones about calling attention to the poor condition of the fences and farm buildings and all that needed doing to render the estate a paying proposition. Eliza refused to come down in her price and the matter was closed—at least for the time being.

Everything was now packed and ready but the long-drawn-out trial of a well-known Champion Bay resident had delayed the departure of the *Georgette*, which was engaged to return a number of witnesses to that district. This man had been accused of having shot his wife dead at Geraldton and since he was of a prominent family whose members had been among the explorers and pioneers of northern settlement, the matter had become a main topic of conversation throughout the colony. Eliza wrote of the defendant's having been brought to Perth 'confined in an iron cage made expressly for him', adding that she feared he would be found guilty of deliberate murder. The dead woman's baby daughter was in the meantime being cared for by Mary Drummond, who was to rear her as her own daughter.

The case, involving many influential relatives and friends of the defendant, dragged on for weeks despite evidence that would no doubt have condemned a person of less account in a single session. Truth to tell, the affair was felt to be a personal tragedy by many of the older settlers who had watched the accused grow up among the bright and promising young men of the colony. The delay caused by this unhappy event was obviously taking its toll of Eliza and her patience had worn thin. Though she declared that she no longer exercised control over her estate, it is obvious that little escaped her eagle eye. She records at some length her forthright disapproval of the impetuous Bisdey having begun pruning the vines a whole month too soon! 'June 20th is the time we begin and finish on July 6th as he should well know . . . besides he was cutting the vines *upward* instead of *under*. When he was inclined to be impertinent I gave him notice that if he did not desist I would not pay him one farthing . . . pointing out that should frosts come our vines would most likely perish down to the first buds.'[7]

With Bob now elsewhere the entries run on as though nothing had happened to disrupt the Belvoir routine.

Johnston to mill and jobbing. Bisdey and boy taking honey . . . Bisdey pruning pears—prematurely . . . Sunday morning service—Major read the prayer . . . Sam Green to see Warren about the wine he got from poor George which he had tried to prevaricate out of . . . Dora Viveash married by Rev Archdeacon Brown, Middle Swan, to Charles son of Dr and Mrs Ferguson, 10 am, and afterwards to breakfast at Dr Viveash's home, Ashby . . .[8]

By the end of May, the court case still unresolved, it was announced that the *Georgette*[9] could delay no longer. Eliza in a final confusion of good-byes found no one so hard to take leave of as 'poor old Johnston' who had for weeks past gone about his 'jobbing' under a heavy cloud of gloom and was by this time in utter desolation. Between the last brief lines of her diary may be read something of her own carefully controlled emotions:

Major and Sam started with heavy luggage to Guildford. Fanny and self, after a heavy struggle, left dear old Belvoir on way to Champion Bay. Most kindly and hospitably received by the Viveash family at Ashby where we stayed the night ... Took leave of our dear friends and proceeded in their dray to meet the mail cart to Perth ... thence to the home of the Stricklands and met several old friends to say adieu. In the afternoon by river steamer to Fremantle to the W D Moores—both the essence of kindness. Many complimentary visits from old and new friends. And I had thought to slip away without being missed![10]

There Eliza's journal ends. It is only from a few last letters to her granddaughter Mary Green that we gather something of her homesickness for Belvoir and her old Upper Swan associates. She refers to the 'dear lamented home' to which she is attached by the sacred ties and memories of many years, and prays that the Almighty will some day replace with a crown the heavy cross she bears.

Sam and Mary Green had agreed to remain at Belvoir only until Eliza had reached some decision, and at this stage she intended advertising for tenants. Many people were trying to persuade her to remain at Champion Bay and both Mary Drummond and Lucy Ellen Logue proposed setting up separate quarters for Fanny and herself. Nonetheless, Eliza felt that both she and Fanny belonged to the Upper Swan and should try to rent a little house in Guildford.

'I fear Belvoir will not pay me very much this year,' she wrote from White Peak in October 1876, 'and as it is not my intention to break into the Principal, I shall have to use great economy to make what income I may have support Fanny and myself, pay house rent, wood and water. I of course must look forward to walk as I cannot ride.'[11] She was pleased that Belvoir was meanwhile still regarded as a family centre and had been the scene of Ellen Whitfield's recent wedding to Robert Williams. She recalled that the bride had been born at Belvoir in 1853 on one of the rare occasions when her mother had visited her old home. All at Champion Bay tasted and approved the wedding cake. Mary Drummond was busy, as ever, and had little time to move about, but they had lately visited several neighbours—all now living in fine style in what Eliza had once thought of as the remotest wilderness. The Sampson Sewell's place near White Peak was quite a mansion

—most elegant and comfortable—with beautifully kept grounds and gardens. Mrs Sewell, like Mary Drummond, had adopted a little girl, but 'of the bond class'. Mary's baby was 'a merry little cricket' and had brought great joy to her adoptive parents. It was only to be hoped they could keep from her the terrible story of her father's end, for he had been eventually condemned to death and executed on 10 June of that year.[12]

Many of the people to whom Eliza refers over this period were in future years to haunt the imagination of the Geraldton-born writer Randolph Stow, inspiring his earliest novels—*A Haunted Land* and *The Bystander*.

Eliza's agonized state of uncertainty regarding what best to do with Belvoir came to an end at last with the death of Will Burges towards the end of the year. He had left his estate in the control of his brother Sam who decided promptly to foreclose on a number of mortgages including the £809 6s 8d raised by Will Shaw in 1859. Will Brockman, trustee for the Tanner estate had died in 1872 and his son Ralph, who inherited his father's responsibilities was also anxious to terminate the long-standing Belvoir mortgage taken out with Will Tanner in 1834. Eliza had now no option but to close with W T Loton for £1,300. The deletion of the two mortgages from this sum meant that Eliza would realize no more than £361 on the property to which she had devoted forty-six years of her hard-working life. This sum, with the interest on whatever small principal she had by, was insufficient even to rent a house at the Upper Swan. In any case she had now decided that she could not after all bear to live in the vicinity of her old home and that she and Fanny were better off with family members at Champion Bay. When Fanny and Major Logue went to Perth to complete the transaction with Loton, she remained at White Peak 'minding' Fanny's precious cockatoo and finding some consolation in the loving company of her daughter Mary, in the prattle of the baby girl and in visits from the Logue family at Ellendale.

It was now clear to her family that her strength was ebbing away. Sitting in a sheltered corner of the verandah at White Peak, her sewing or her Bible in her hands, she would fall asleep, sometimes calling in the strong voice of command or reproach that had rung out over many years from the old home above the Swan. She continued to find comfort in her faith and in the prophets of old who had voiced the problems of her own time:

> What could have been done more to my vineyard that I have not done in it? Wherefore, when I looked that it should bring forth good grapes brought it forth wild ones?
>
> Isaiah, Chapter 5, Verse 4

The vineyards for which her husband had fought so hard would seem to have brought more problems than blessings for Eliza, but she can hardly have found her daughters wanting in consideration and care for her, poor Fanny least of all. Although no great beauty, she was a capable and warm-hearted woman and it is hard to believe that she would have lacked matrimonial chances. Rather it would seem that when her elder sisters went off to make homes of their own she had regarded it as her inescapable duty to remain with her parents. Always at her mother's side, she had seen the end of Eliza's life as fore-shadowing for herself a lonely and impecunious middle age.[13] Since coming to Champion Bay she had sadly missed her old home and beloved associates in the Upper Swan but could have seen no chance of ever returning to set up an establishment of her own. The reader may be pleased to learn that her fate was not after all to be so desolate. In 1880, at the age of forty-two, she married Captain James McLean Dempster who had come to the colony in 1829 as master of the schooner *Eagle*. He had previously married the daughter of Captain Charles Pratt, the ship's owner, and had taken over the management of Pratt's Northam property where the couple reared seven children. He was a widower of only four months' standing when he married Fanny Shaw with whom, to the time of his death ten years later he was to enjoy a happy companionship.[14]

Mary and John Nicol Drummond were to live to a ripe old age and to celebrate their Golden Jubilee in 1902. They had in the meantime retired to a little place known as Sea View near their first home overlooking Drummond's Cove. It was here, four years later, that John Drummond, by this time firmly established in local legend for his toughness and eccentricity, died at the age of ninety. His widow, devotedly cared for by her adopted daughter, Mrs Will Burges, soon afterwards came to live in Perth where, like her mother before her, she is remembered by a host of friends and relatives as an 'enquire within' on all matters pertaining to household and farm management and a mine of historical information that was unfortunately never recorded. She died, aged ninety-five, having survived her husband by about twenty years.

Major and Lucy Ellen Logue lived on at Ellendale to the end of their days. Although only two of their large family married and produced children, their descendants, like those of Francis and Elizabeth Whitfield, found fruitful links with many prominent families in the Victoria Plains and Geraldton districts. Ellendale is now owned by their grand-daughter Mrs Anne Logue Oliver and her husband Edward.

It would be satisfactory to record that Bob had at last become reconciled to his mother but there is no evidence of this, nor of his ever having developed his Champion Bay lease. He would seem, after his final return from Belvoir, to have become a 'permanent itinerant' worker operating with his faithful companion 'Black Charlie' between Dandaragan and Shark Bay. References made to him in the reminiscences of G J Gooch,[15] pioneer pastoralist of the Gascoyne district, show him to have been an experienced bush-worker, making a modest but significant contribution to the scattered community. On one occasion he is recorded as having returned with Charlie Brockman from an exploring trip along the coast, during which they had survived a waterless hundred-mile stretch. He is mentioned as having put up a good stockyard of jam timber on Wandagee station and as having trained a team of ten natives in a new method of washing wool by which they were handling 400 lbs a day. Gooch was at one time called upon to inspect a tank put up by Bob Shaw on the Manilya-Carnarvon road. He found the work well done, and since a number had died of thirst on that track the writer wondered how many would owe their lives to this amenity, always afterwards referred to as 'Shaw's Tank'. We are told that Bob Shaw travelled the lonely miles in a horse-drawn wagon which, with his few worldly goods, was demolished in the terrible Gascoyne fires of 1894, from which he was lucky to have escaped with his life.

Bob was the only one of Eliza's five sons to marry. His wife was a part-Aboriginal woman of the Shark Bay area, the up-bringing of whose children was to become largely the responsibility of their aunts, Mary Drummond and Lucy Ellen Logue. Eliza was never to see the only grandchildren to bear her husband's name—the 'heirs forever' for whom they had hoped to establish an estate in the British tradition of heritage. In any case, although one at least, the redoubtable Harold Shaw, earned a respected place among the crack shearers of the Murchison district, they would have found little in common with the established gentry of the Swan.

But with subsequent fortunes and misfortunes of the family is another tale. This story comes to an end in the spring of 1877, when the green crops of imported origin were brightly spattered with the wild flowers of the land. It was then that Eliza slipped quietly out of life, to be buried in a corner of the White Peak orchard where the Drummonds had lain their infant daughter over twenty years before. Her death, like that of many more prominent pioneers, received little comment in the otherwise verbose local press of the day. 'The widow of the late Captain William Shaw of Belvoir Upper Swan has died at White Peak Station the home of her daughter Mrs J N Drummond.' Nothing more. The eyes of an Australian-born generation were focused on new horizons. To them only the present and the future were of any significance. The people to whom they owed their new concept of freedom in a new continent would become of interest only when too much of the past had been trampled under their urgent forward surge.

Appendix 1

List of Passengers who arrived at Fremantle
on 14 February, 1830
by the *Egyptian*

Mr and Mrs Agett & 6 sons
Peter Wicks, servant
Hannah Wicks
Ann (child)
John Dawson
Amelia Blagg
Wm Shaw, Esq
Mrs Ditto
and 4 sons
Miss Eliza do
  „ Mary do
      Markram, servant
Anne Haggs   „
Mr and Mrs Boyd
Walter Jones, servant
John Franklin, „
G W S Earl, Esq
Thomas Jones, servant
E Roberts
Daniel Peppiet, servant
Mr Wm Manning
James Davy
Mr and Mrs Purkis
Miss Louisa   „

Miss Elizabeth Purkis
Miss Emma   „
Master F   „
Henry Hubbard, servant
Ellen   „
Mr Peter Shadwell
Wm Gurden
Rd Bambrick
Wm Carrol, servant
Ann   „
Mr James Chapman
Henry & George „
Miss Ann   „
Mr Lionel Lukin
Mr George Lukin
Wm Syred, servant
Elizabeth Syred and 1 child
John Pearl
Thomas Gillan
Mr Wall
Wm Pearse, servant
Mr Charles Wainwright

(CSO Records, 1830, Vol. 5,
WAA.)

Appendix 2

ORIGINAL SWAN HOLDINGS

	Grantee	Name of Property
Loc 1, Nth	Lieut H Bull	Belhus
„ 1, Sth	G Leake	
„ 2	P Brown	Coulston
„ 4	W Shaw	Belvoir
„ 5	W Tanner	Baskerville
„ 5a	G F Moore	Millendon
„ 6	„ „	„
„ A	W S and L Burges	
„ B	F C Irwin	Henley Park
„ E	A Minchin	Spring Park
„ F	W H Smithers and Haddrill	Albion Town
„ F1	„	„ „
„ G	R Edwards Jnr	
„ G1	E P Barrett Lennard	St Leonard's
„ 9	W L Brockman	Herne Hill
„ 10	Sam Moore	Oakover
„ 11	T N Yule (later Ferguson)	Strelly and
„ 11a	„	Houghton
„ H	E P Barrett Lennard	St Leonard's
„ I	Sam Moore	West Oakover
„ K	S A Partridge	Priory Park
„ K1	D Agett	
„ L	J S Roe	Sandalford
„ M	R de Burgh	Caversham
„ M1	E Hamersley	„
„ 14	W Tanner	Wexcombe
„ 14a	„	„

	Grantee	Name of Property
„ 15	R Lewis and F D North,	Spring Park
„ 30	James Drummond	
„ 31	„ „	
„ 32	„ „	
„ 33	J W Hardey,	
„ 35	H Camfield	Burrswood
Loc N & O	Hamersley family	Pyrton
„ O1 & P	Milligan and Tanner	Lockridge
„ Q2	W Tanner	
„ S	P Brown	Bassendean
„ U	J Whatley	Hones Green
„ W	W Tanner	
„ X	J Drummond	
„ Aa	W Tanner	
The	J Hardey, M & J S Clarkson	
Peninsula	G Johnson and other Tranby families	

Notes and Sources

Abbreviations

WAA — Western Australian Archives, Battye Library, Perth.

HSJ — Journals of The Royal Western Australian Historical Society (Inc).

CSO — Colonial Secretary's Office.

GFM — G F Moore, *Diary of a Settler Ten Years in Western Australia* (inc an Aboriginal Vocabulary), London, 1884

ES to W — Eliza's Shaw's letters to Waghornes.

PG — The *Perth Gazette*.

SWP — Swan River Papers.

Chapter 1

1. Advertisement issued by H C Sempill, 1828, quoted in full, Alexandra Hasluck, *Portrait With Background*, pp 19/21.
2. Public Record Office, Chancery Lane, London.
3. Information obtained by Father Laurence O'Donoghue from Genealogical Office, Dublin Castle.
4. Thomas Manners, Lord Roos, was created first Earl of Rutland in 1526. Belvoir Castle is the seat of the Dukes of Rutland. The original building was a fortress erected soon after the Norman conquest by Robert de Todein, the Conqueror's standard-bearer. The castle was several times destroyed but rebuilt on the same site—the summit of a hill overlooking the beautiful vale of Belvoir, which extends into the counties of Lincoln, Leicester and Nottingham.

Chapter 2

1. ES to W, 7/12/1829. WAA
2. Ibid.

3. Ibid.
4. Charles Fraser, NSW Government Botanist who had accompanied Captain Stirling to Swan River in the ship *Success* in 1827. He had reported enthusiastically on the climate, soil and plentiful water of this region.
5. ES to W, 10/3/1830. WAA.

Chapter 3
1. ES to W, 10/3/1830. WAA.
2. Ibid.

Chapter 4
1. No 620, 22/3/1830. Lands Department.
2. SDUR, S1 45, March 1830. WAA.
3. The *Eagle* was privately owned by the wealthy Captain Charles Pratt who migrated with his family to the Swan River in 1829. He engaged James McLean Dempster, then aged nineteen, to skipper the vessel which arrived in January 1830. Dempster married Pratt's daughter Ann who died in 1880 leaving him with seven children. He then married Frances (Fanny), youngest daughter of Will and Eliza Shaw.
4. The Rev R Davis left WA a few weeks later for Tasmania. He became first Archdeacon of Launceston and later third Archdeacon of Hobart.
5. Anne Whatley's Diary, 1830. Acc No 326, WAA.
6. ES to W, 10/3/1830. WAA.
7. ES to W, 21/1/1832. WAA.
8. Ibid.

Chapter 5
1. ES to W, 21/1/1832. WAA.
2. Ibid.
3. Jane E Currie's Diary, 1830. WAA.
4. This site is now part of the University complex at Crawley. Title to the grant—Swan River location 87—was issued in August 1832 and sold a few years later to Henry Sutherland, who succeeded Currie to sundry official positions he held in the colony. Currie eventually returned to the navy and retired with the rank of Admiral. HSJ Vol IV, part 2, 1950.
5. ES to W, 3/2/1832. WAA.

Chapter 6
1. ES to W, 21/1/1832. WAA.

2. W Shaw to Waghorne, 19/6/1831. WAA.
3. This grant was the Henty's Stoke Farm which Brown re-named Bassendean after a family estate in Scotland. Brown was later forced to sell it to help cover his debts.
4. ES to W, 21/1/1832. WAA.
5. The family in Western Australia was later to revert to the original spelling of the name, by which their descendants are known in the State today.
6. ES to W, 21/1/1832. WAA.
7. E Shaw to Anne Dibben, undated, circa 1832.
8. ES to W, 21/1/1832. WAA.
9. PG 30/1/1836. WAA.
10. Lands Department, Book 1, No 642, 22/8/1831.
11. ES to W, 21/1/1832. WAA.
12. Queries Book, No 1, pp A and D, 31/12/1830 and 5/1/1831. WAA.
13. ES to W, 3/2/1832. WAA.
14. E W Landor, *The Bushman or Life in a New Colony*, London, 1847.

Chapter 7

1. ES to W, undated, probably early 1832. WAA.
2. Ibid.
3. Ibid.
4. GFM p 63.
5. ES to W, circa early 1832. WAA.
6. GFM, p 63.
7. ES to W, circa early 1832. WAA.
8. Ibid.
9. Ibid.
10. Ibid.
11. Ibid.

Chapter 8

1. ES to W, 21/1/1832. WAA.
2. GFM, p 104.
3. Ibid.
4. ES to W, 3/2/1832. WAA.
5. Ibid.
6. Ibid.
7. E Shaw to R Casson, 23/1/1833. WAA.
8. W Shaw to Sir F Fowke, 9/1/1832. 12 15A, WAA.
9. Ibid.

10. ES to W, 3/2/1832. WAA.
11. Ibid.
12. Ibid.
13. SWP/10/80.
14. ES to W, 3/2/1832. WAA.
15. ES to W, 12/7/1832. WAA.
16. Ibid.
17. ES to W, 3/2/1832. WAA.

Chapter 9

1. Captain F C Irwin, *The State and Position of Western Australia*, London, 1835.
2. GFM, p 35.
3. GFM, p 164
4. GFM, p 120.
5. SWP 10/107.
6. *The Works of Ossian* [a legendary bard of the third century] by English author James MacPherson appeared in 1765 and triggered off a heated controversy as to their authenticity.
7. SWP 10/107.
8. SWP 10/120.
9. SWP 10/125.
10. SWP 10/88–99.
11. Ibid.
12. SWP 16/34.

Chapter 10

1. SWP 10/120–121.
2. SWP 10/128.
3. PG 4/5/1833.
4. GFM, pp 190–192.
5. Ibid.
6. PG 13/7/1833.
7. GFM, p 206

Chapter 11

1. A. C. Staples, *The First Ten Years in Swan River Colony.* HSJ, Vol V, part 7, p 83.
2. W Shaw to R Casson, 21/1/1833. WAA
3. Lands Department, Book 1. No 52, p 13, 4/7/1832.
4. Shaw had instructed Casson to pay £20 from the £200 legacy

to Captain Lilburn for freight on goods and stock purchased
at the Cape.

5. ES to W, 21/1/1833. WAA.
6. ES to W, 21/1/1833 and 17/3/1833 and E Shaw to R
   Casson, 23 and 24 January, 1833.
7. Will Shaw to R Casson, 21/1/1833, WAA.
8. W L Brockman to T Du Boulay of Shaftesbury, Dorset,
   30/1/1833, WAA.
9. ES to W, 17/3/1833. WAA.
10. GFM, p 197.
11. GFM, p 93.
12. B Maund and Rev J S Henslow, *The Botanist*, series of
    illustrated papers, London 1837–1842. (Made available to
    author by Mr D W Hennessy.)
13. See *Portrait With Background*, the story of Georgiana
    Molloy, by Alexandra Hasluck.
14. GFM, p 126.
15. CSO, 25/11/1841.
16. GFM, pp 218, 219.
17. Hugh Edwards, *Islands of Angry Ghosts*, Hodder & Stough-
    ton Ltd, 1966.

Chapter 12
1. CSO, 20/12/1834.
2. CSO, 24/10/1837.
3. GFM, p 215.
4. PG 18/10/1834.
5. GFM, pp 236–239.
6. GFM, p 253.
7. GFM, *Descriptive Vocabulary of the Language of the
   Aborigines*, included in his Diary and also published separately.

Chapter 13
1. Lands Department, Book 1, No 225, 7/8/1834.
2. PG 25/7/1835.
3. HSJ Vol II, part 18, 1935, pp 25–30.
4. HSJ Vol I, part 5, p 3.
5. HSJ Vol I, part 5.
6. HSJ Vol II, part 18, 1935, pp 25–30.
7. PG 30/1/1836.

Chapter 14

1. PG 30/1/1836.
2. CSO 25/2/1841.
3. Ibid.
4. CSO 23/10/1837.
5. CSO 24/10/1837.
6. Letter Book 525, Letter No 455, 4/11/1837, pp 308 (b), 309 (a) WAA.
7. Letter Book 525, Letter No 455, 4/11/1837, pp 307 (b), 308 (a) WAA.
8. GFM April 1833, p 179.
9. PG Nov 1839.
10. CSO 24/9/1839.
11. Lands Department, Book 1, No 391, 23/2/1836.
12. Lands Department, Book 1, No 392, 2/3/1836.

Chapter 15

1. GFM, p 272.
2. GFM, p 372.
3. Memorial to Governor by Settlers and Owners of Sheep and Stock in WA, March 1842. WAA.
4. An account of the Clifton Johnston and other families who came out under this scheme is given by F M Johnston in his *Knights and Theodolites*, published by Edwards & Shaw, Sydney, 1962.
5. CSO 18/1/1841.
6. CSO 25/2/1841.
7. CSO 22/4/1841.
8. CSO 7/11/1839.
9. CSO 14/10/1840.
10. CSO 22/4/1841.

Chapter 16

1. Edward Hamersley's brother Hugh was married to Mary Anne Phillips, daughter of John Phillips of Culham, Oxon, presumably the sister of Samuel Pole Phillips. The estate of Culham is close to Pyrton, the Hamersley family seat in the same county.
2. Edward Hamersley returned from England in 1850 with his wife, five sons and one daughter. The Culham property was thereafter divided, Phillips keeping the south-west portion including the original homestead.
3. PG 19/6/1841, 26 June 1841, 3 July 1841.

4. PG 19/6/1841.
5. CSO 19/7/1841.
6. CSO 7/8/1841.
7. Ibid.
8. Ibid.

Chapter 17

1. Lands Department, Book 1, No 1170, 13/8/1840.
2. Lands Department, Book 1, No 458, 14/2/1843.
3. Letter from Isaac Wood to his father, Isaac Wood, of Bradford Tannery, Manchester. The property of Miss Edna Read of Perth, Western Australia.
4. E W Landor, *The Bushman or Life in a New Colony*, London, 1847.
5. Ibid.
6. Frances Tree Mitchell, Diary, December 1839. WAA.
7. Dr S W Viveash, Diary, HS472, WAA.
8. E W Landor, *The Bushman or Life in a New Colony*, London, 1847.
9. The *Western Mail*, Centenary Number, 1929.

Chapter 18

1. CSO 5/3/1844.
2. CSO 4/5/1842.
   CSO 20/5/1842.
   CSO 28/5/1842.
3. CSO 4/5/1842.
4. Ibid.
5. It was not until 1904 that the export of wheat from Western Australia became of any importance. In that year the exportable surplus of a yield of 2,013,237 bushels was valued at £1,580. [The *Western Mail*, Centenary Number, July 1929.] Wheat exported 1972–73 was 82,671,000 bushels valued at $111,744,000. [Australian Bureau of Statistics.]

   In 1852 a very small sample amount (85 gals to the value of £12 15s od) was exported but apparently led to no immediate increase in the demand for West Australian wine. In 1859 211 gals of WA wine, worth £105 10s od, was exported. This was probably the first authentic commercial export of WA-grown wine. The year 1972–73 saw the export of 313,538 litres, valued at $297,000 [Australian Bureau of Statistics.]
6. CSO 20/5/1842.

7. Ibid.
8. James Backhouse, *A Narrative of a Visit to the Australian Colonies*, London 1843.
9. A few of the early landholders and merchants, including Mr Sam Moore of Oakover, did bring in a small number of Indian and Chinese servants who integrated over the years into the European community. In the 1880s there was another move to introduce Asiatic labour, and a number of Chinese and Indians immigrated in this decade.
10. John Galvin, employed by Mr Pollard of Dandalup, confessed to murdering an eighteen-year-old boy by battering his skull with an adze while he was asleep. He pleaded being overcome by an uncontrollable homicidal impulse. A mask taken of his head showed his skull to have been of abnormal proportions.
11. Grey's 'Report on the best means of promoting the civilization of the Aboriginal Inhabitants of Australia' (London, 1840) was circulated to colonial governors by the Colonial Office. He became Governor of South Australia in 1840, of New Zealand in 1845, of the Cape Colony in 1854 and of New Zealand for a second time in 1861. He was knighted in 1848 and died in England in 1898. [*Sir George Grey*, by J Rutherford, London 1961.]
12. Rica Erickson, *The Drummonds of Hawthornden*, Perth, 1969.
13. Gerald de Courcy Lefroy, Diary, 22/7/1845. 648A WAA.

Chapter 19
1. Frances Tree Mitchell, Diary, December 1839. WAA.
2. Rev J R Wollaston, *Picton Journal*, 1841–1844 WAA.

Chapter 20
1. According to the report of Colonel Henderson in 1858 the asylum was required for sixteen 'Imperial Lunatics' (convicts) and sixteen 'Colonial Lunatics' male and female. *Historical Notes*—R McK Campbell, RN 633, WAA.
2. 'The Late Mrs John Drummond', Colonist, The *Geraldton Guardian*, 29/10/1918.
3. Miss Charlotte Chauncey to Miss Mary Shaw, Shaw papers, WAA.
4. ES to W, 21/1/1833.
5. E Shaw to E Whitfield, 12/8/1857. SWP. WAA.
6. Rev J R Wollaston, *Albany Journal*, 1853. WAA.

Chapter 21

1. Lands Department, Book 5, No 764, 31/1/1856.
2. Col J Bruce was Military Commandant of Western Australia from 1854 to 1870. He acquired land not only in Fremantle but around James Gallop's home in Dalkeith. He made this land over to his son Ned, and spoke of it always as 'Ned's lands'. Ned Bruce followed a military career abroad and took little interest in this inheritance but his name is perpetuated in the flourishing suburb of Nedlands and its important thoroughfare Bruce Street. T Joll, *The West Australian*, 1 March 1975.
3. Lands Department, Book 6, No 334, 1/10/1857.
4. E Shaw to M Drummond, 17/6/1862. Shaw papers, WAA.
5. E Shaw to M Drummond, 9/3/1864. Shaw papers. WAA.
6. This was part of a 10,000-acre block leased by J B Ridley in January 1851. Ridley obtained freehold of Victoria location 171 in 1858. It was transferred to J H Monger of York in 1862, to W Hatch in 1863 and to W Bayliss in 1870. Information from Mr W de Burgh, Gingin.
7. Robert Brockman was a brother of William Brockman of Herne Hill. He took up land in the Northam district and moved north to properties named Mimmegarra and Nambung in 1855.
8. CSO 43. 1861.
9. E Shaw to Mary Drummond, May 1862. Shaw papers, WAA.

Chapter 22

1. Lease Book No 2, Nos 2691, 2692, 2693, ACC 660/127. WAA.
2. E Shaw to E Whitfield, 29/9/1865. Shaw papers, WAA.
3. Ibid.
4. Ibid.
5. E Shaw to E Whitfield, 8/7/1869. Shaw papers, WAA.
6. Ibid.
7. E Shaw to E Whitfield, 22/4/1870. Shaw papers, WAA.
8. E Shaw to E Whitfield, 23/4/1869. Shaw papers, WAA.
9. E Shaw to M Drummond, 9/3/1864. Shaw papers, WAA.
10. CSO 1860. CSR 460. 24/9/1860.
11. Page from memorandum of Captain N Cooper. 1794. Shaw papers, WAA.
12. Alexandra Hasluck, *Thomas Peel of Swan River*, Melbourne, 1865.

Chapter 23

1. This residence was soon to become the home of John Forrest and his bride, Margaret Hamersley.
2. Eliza Shaw's last journal, 25/12/1875. (In possession of Mrs H Hamersley.)
3. Ibid.
4. Eliza Shaw's last journal, 29/12/1875. (In possession of Mrs H Hamersley.)
5. Eliza Shaw's last journal, 29/1/1876. (In possession of Mrs H Hamersley.)
6. Eliza Shaw's last journal, 10/3/1876. (In possession of Mrs H Hamersley.)

Chapter 24

1. Eliza Shaw's last journal, 21/2/1876. (In possession of Mrs H Hamersley.)
2. Eliza Shaw's last journal, 31/3/1876. (In possession of Mrs H Hamersley.)
3. James Morrison had married Clara de Burgh in 1870. The Robert de Burgh's other two daughters were also married into well-known families around Guildford, one to Charles Harper of Woodridge and the other to Henry Brockman, youngest son of the William Brockmans of Herne Hill.
4. Eliza Shaw's last journal, 27/3/1876. (In possession of Mrs H Hamersley.)
5. Eliza Shaw's last journal, 7/4/1876. (In possession of Mrs H Hamersley.)
6. Ibid.
7. Eliza Shaw's last journal, 18/5/1876. (In possession of Mrs H Hamersley.)
8. Ibid.
9. The *Georgette* completed its scheduled trip to Geraldton but was soon afterwards wrecked near the mouth of the Margaret river on the south-west coast. The passengers were rescued by Grace Bussell and a half-caste stockman named Sam Isaacs who rode to and fro through the surf until all were safely ashore. Miss Bussell, 'Australia's Grace Darling', soon afterwards married Frederick Slade Drake Brockman, grandson of William Brockman, late of Herne Hill.
10. Eliza Shaw's last journal, 27/5/1876. (In possession of Mrs H Hamersley.)
11. Eliza Shaw to granddaughter Mary Green, 10/10/1876, Shaw papers, WAA.

12. A story persists that his end was somehow faked by relatives in official positions and that he was spirited away to the United States in a whaling vessel. It is said that his daughter whom the Drummonds had adopted visited him in America soon after her marriage to a member of a wealthy Murchison family.

13. Fanny was not after all left destitute, as Eliza made provision in her will for her 'unmarried daughter and companion in trouble and out of trouble, Hester Frances Shaw'. She bequeathed all her personal property for her 'exclusive use, benefit and disposal, strictly free of all control of interference of any husband or husbands, person or persons whatsoever'. She also asked that £1,000 of her estate be invested in her name to bring in a yearly interest.

14. A letter from Captain Dempster's son Edward to his brother Andrew, written on 26 April 1881, tells something of the family's reaction to this latter-day romance. 'I have no doubt you are much taken aback by the Dad's marriage with Fanny Shaw so soon after poor Mama's death. Janie is very irate about it and the Sweetings declare it disgraceful and infamous ... I like Fanny. She has failings no doubt but she's a kind-hearted, unselfish little thing and is very fond of the Dad and he would not I think have lived long without someone to comfort and take care of him. She was independent in means and did not marry with a view of benefitting herself. For my part I think she has got the worst of the bargain for the poor old fellow allows his old propensity to still prevail.' Further family letters indicate that Fanny tended to share this 'propensity' but that things improved when both decided to 'sign the red card'—ie, 'the Pledge'.

15. G J Gooch, *The Lure of the North*, Perth 1952.

Bibliography

Australian Dictionary of Biography, General Editor Douglas Pike.

BACKHOUSE, I, *Narrative of a Visit to the Australian Colonies*, London, 1843.

BASSETT MARNIE, *The Hentys*, Oxford University Press, London, 1954.

BATTYE, J S, *Cyclopaedia of Western Australia*, Perth, 1912.

BOLTON, G C, *Alexander Forrest, His Life and Times*, Melbourne University Press, 1958.

BURTON, REV CANON A, *The Story of the Swan District*, Perth

CLARKE, C M H, *A History of Australia*, Melbourne University Press, 1973.

CROWLEY, F K, *Australia's Western Third*, Macmillan and Co, London, 1960.

CROWLEY, F K, *Forrest*, University of Queensland Press, 1971.

ERICKSON, RICA, *The Drummonds of Hawthornden*, Lamb Paterson Pty, Ltd, Perth, 1969.

ERICKSON, RICA, *The Victoria Plains*, Lamb Paterson Pty, Ltd, Perth, 1971.

ERICKSON, RICA, *Old Toodyay and Newcastle*, Toodyay Shire Council, 1974.

GOOCH, G J, *The Lure of the North*, Perth, 1852.

HASLUCK, ALEXANDRA, *Thomas Peel of Swan River*, Oxford University Press, Melbourne, 1965.

HASLUCK, ALEXANDRA, *Portrait with Background*, Oxford University Press, Melbourne, 1955.

HISTORIC PRESS *1829–1929, Western Australia's Centenary.*

IRWIN, F C, *The State and Position of Western Australia*, London, 1835.

KIMBERLY, W B, *History of West Australia: A Narrative of her Past, with Biographies of her Leading Men*, Ballarat, 1897.

KNIGHT, W H, *Western Australia: Its History, Progress, Condition and Prospects*, Perth, 1870.

LANDOR, E W, *The Bushman: or, Life in a New Colony*, London, 1847.

MILLETT, MRS EDWARD, *An Australian Parsonage, or the Settler and the Savage in Western Australia*, London, 1872.

MOORE, G F, *Diary of a Settler Ten Years in Western Australia*, London, 1884.

OGLE, N, *The Colony of Western Australia*, London, 1846.

ROBERTS, JANE, *Two Years at Sea*, London, 1837.

WOLLASTON, I R, *Picton Journal 1841–1845*, and *Albany Journal 1848–1856*, Perth, 1948 and 1955.

OFFICIAL DOCUMENTS

Colonial Secretary's Office Records. (Inward and outward correspondence.)
Survey Department documents.
Lands Department documents.
Toodyay, Resident Magistrate's correspondence.
Government Gazettes.
Australian Bureau of Statistics.
Lease Book. WAA.

PERSONAL MANUSCRIPTS

Letters of Eliza Shaw to Waghornes, 1829–1833.
Letters of William Shaw to Waghornes, 1829–1833.
Letters of William Shaw to R Casson, 1829–1833.
Letters of William Shaw to Sir F Fowke. WAA.

Shaw Papers:
Material relating to W & E Shaw and descendants. Acc No 1062A.
Letters from Eliza Shaw to daughter Elizabeth Whitfield.
Letters from Eliza Shaw to daughter Mary Drummond.
Letters from Eliza Shaw to granddaughter Mary Green.
Last Journal of Eliza Shaw, 1875–1877. (Property of Mrs H Hamersley.)
Diary of Ann Whatley, 1830–1831.
Diary of Jane Currie, 1829–1832.
Diary of Frances Tree Mitchell, 1838–1840.
Diary of Dr S W Viveash, WAA, 1220A.

Reminiscences of William Wade. WAA. 1026A.
Canon P U Henn, The Shaw Family, Feb, 1948. WAA.

OTHER SOURCES

Journal and Proceedings of The Royal Western Australian
    Historical Society (Inc)
Maund, B, and Henslow, J S, *The Botanist* (illustrated papers),
    London, 1837–1842.
The Western Mail, Centenary Number, 1929.
Perth Gazette and *West Australian Journal.*
Inquirer and Commercial News.
Swan River Guardian.

Index

Landor, Edward W.: his comments on the local situation, 73, 162–4; and friendship with Shaws, 162; describes a local Swan River family, 165–6; negotiates withdrawal of Belvoir from sale, 226–7

Lautour, Col Peter, 42–3, 59

lead mining, 198, 213

Leake, George, 42, 67, 78, 88, 160; Will Shaw takes out mortgage with, 141; appointed member of Legislative Council, 145; Will Shaw sued by 161; prosperity of, 186

Leake, Miss (George's daughter), 78, 81

Legislative and Executive Council, 73, 114, 180; Gov Hutt appoints four non-officials to, 145

Leicestershire: Shaws' home at Thrussington, 23–6; and leave for Swan River from (1829), 29–31

Leicestershire Militia: Will Shaw joins (1806), 22

Leichhardt party, disappearance of, 217

Leitch, Sewell and Meagher (solicitors), 229

Lennard, Edward Barrett, 59, 70

Lilburn, Captain (of the *Egyptian*), 30, 43, 61; character, 30, 34, 35; shark incident, 33; dines out with Shaws at Cape Town, 35; at Fremantle, 36, 43; brings mails and parcels for Shaws, 84–5; and visits Shaws at Belvoir, 87

Little, Mr (horse-breeder), 191

Logue, Joseph Keyes, 197

Logue, Lucy Ellen (*née* Shaw), 201 232, 236; birth (1832), 85, 87 sister Mary takes charge of, 129; schooling, 167; marries Major Logue, 197–8; and settles at Ellendale in Champion Bay, 198; Mary's visits to, 199, 200; death of father, 205; Eliza writes about Belvoir troubles to, 228; later years of, 235

Logue, Major, 199, 201, 208, 231–232; Lucy Ellen Shaw's marriage to, 197–8; settles at Ellendale, 198; Bob Shaw acquires property near, 210, 211; Eliza writes about Belvoir to, 228; arrives at Belvoir, 229; and suggests Eliza should come to Champion Bay, 229; completes sale of Belvoir for Eliza, 233; later years, 235

Loton, William Thornley, 230; buys Belvoir estate, 233

Lotus, 182

Lukin, George, 32

Lukin, Lionel, 32, 46

Lyon, Robert Menli, 109; offers Shaw land grant at Upper Swan, 53; and transfers his entire grant to Shaw, 54–5, 102–3, 139; defends Aborigines, 55, 95–96, 97–9, 102; and his views on emigration to W. Australia, 98–99; accompanies Aboriginal prisoners to Carnac Island, 99–100, 101; Brown's alleged hostility to, 102–3; advocates convict labour, 109, 139, 185; and advocates introduction of missionaries, 125; Shaw's boundary dispute and, 139–40; takes job as boatman, 139–40; characteristics, 139–40; leaves settlement and changes name to Milne, 140

Mackie, Judge, 131, 132, 133, 137, 156, 196

Mackintosh, Euphemia (*née* Drummond), 153; brother's opposition to her marriage, 188

Mackintosh, Ewan: marries Euphemia Drummond, 188; Will Shaw sells Toodyay block to, 197

Markram (farm labourer): accompanies Shaws to Swan River, 30, 33, 35, 40, 44–5, 52, 59–60; deserts Shaw, 64; works his passage back to England, 87–8

McDermott, Marshall, 111

Mangles, Capt James, 115; botanical specimens sent to, 115, 116

Marquis of Anglesea, 35–6, 64

Matilda Bay, 57

Mendie (Aboriginal), execution of, 157

Mermaid, 47, 115

Swan River Settlement—*cont.*
declining population of, 108;
and convict labour advocated,
109; Aborigines raid Shenton's
Mill, 116; and attack Upper
Swan barracks, 117; report of
shipwrecked survivors, 117–18;
Governor Stirling returns, 118,
119–20; unemployed, 121; settlers' debts to government, 121–
122; and settlers demand action
against Aborigines, 122–3; and
Battle of Pinjarra, 123–4; com-
parison of progress in other
colonies and, 142–3; Stirling re-
signs and succeeded by Governor Hutt, 143–5; and Hutt's
land reforms, 145–6; and
schemes to encourage labour immigration, 146–7, 172; Landor's
comments on local situation,
162–4; social activities, 164–5;
local family described by Landor, 165–7; and education, 167;
law prohibiting distillation of
spirits, 169–71; transportation
of delinquent juveniles to,
172; slump in 1840's, 172–3;
Hutt's Aboriginal policy, 173–4;
Hutt replaced by Governor
Clarke, 178; and Irwin succeeds
Clarke, 180; Moore becomes
Acting Colonial Secretary, 180;
and Brown's role in development of Perth, 180–1; Irwin
institutes State School system,
181; Governor Fitzgerald takes
over from Irwin; mining and
pastoral development in north-
west, 183–4, 198–9, 203; first
convict labourers arrive in, 183–
184; and effects and conditions
of, 185–7; floods and fires, 187;
first settlers move to Champion
Bay from 188–9; establishment
of Volunteer Force, 193; neglected properties and families
leaving, 194–5; growing economic prosperity, 194–5; building
works and road development,
195; Gov Kennedy succeeds
Fitzgerald, 196; and importation
of 'needle-women', 201; Governor Hampton succeeds Kennedy,
204; influx of lower-class immigrants, 207–8; Eliza Shaw becomes Post-Mistress, 211–12;
end of transportation, 213–14;
development of Perth, 215–16;
Forrest expedition into the interior, 217; diphtheria epidemic
(1875), 219; interdependence of
farming community, 221 2
Swan River Guardian, 143
'Swan River Mania', 27
Sydney, 110, 143

Tanner, William (and family), 67,
68, 70, 76, 82, 90, 95, 205, 224,
233; Baskerville leased to Shaw
by, 112–13, 128; takes over tenancy of Woodbridge, 112; sails
for England, 129; lends money
to Shaws, 129; appointed member of Legislative Council, 145;
supports Shaw in boundary dispute, 149–50; extends loan to
Will Shaw, 160; social activities,
164–5; returns to England, 194;
death of, 197
Tasmania, 184, 204
Thrussington, Leicestershire, 85;
Shaws' home in 23–6; and departure from, 29–31
timber industry, 179, 203, 213
Tomghin (Aboriginal), 118; employed as shepherd by Shaw,
124–5; and kills Coroor, 125
Toodyay, Shaws' property at: purchased by Will (1839), 151, 160;
Nat takes over running of, 151–
152; and is severely wounded
by Aborigines, 155–6; fire des-
troys pasture at, 187; Eliza
Shaw's visit to, 218
Toodyay valley, 167, 187, 204; personalities living in, 152–4;
Aborigines in, 154–5; convict
depot in, 183; and fires, 187
transportation, 24–5; of delinquent juveniles, 172, 180–1; of
convicts, 183, 184, 185–6; and
end of, 213–14

Upper Swan *see* Swan River settlement
Upper Swan Church: Will Shaw
buried at, 204

270